WELL, **HOLY GOD**

My Life as an Irish, Catholic, Agnostic Correspondent

PATSY McGARRY

MERRION
PRESS

First published in 2024 by
Merrion Press
10 George's Street
Newbridge
Co. Kildare
Ireland
www.merrionpress.ie

© Patsy McGarry, 2024

978 1 78537 496 8 (Paper)
978 1 78537 497 5 (Ebook)

A CIP catalogue record for this book is available from the British Library.

Typeset in Sabon LT Std 11.5/17pt

Cover design by riverdesignbooks.com

Merrion Press is a member of Publishing Ireland

WELL, **HOLY GOD**

Patsy McGarry was born in November 1952, and grew up in Mullen, Frenchpark, County Roscommon, moving to Ballaghaderreen 1962. He attended University College Galway and left with a BA in English, History and Geography, and a HDip in Education. Following a spell in teaching and then radio in Dublin, he became a freelance journalist and theatre critic for *The Irish Press*. In 1992 he won a national media award for political coverage in the *Sunday Independent* on the fall of Charles Haughey. In 1993 he began working for *The Irish Times* and in 1997 became Religious Affairs Correspondent. In 1998 he won the European Writer of the Year award. He has published a number of books, including *Christianity, While Justice Slept: The True Story of Nicky Kelly and the Sallins Train Robbery* and *First Citizen: Mary McAleese and the Irish Presidency*.

This book is dedicated to my far-flung family, whether in Ireland, Scotland, Brussels, Australia, the US or Canada, as well as 'the Galway Gang' (you know who you are!), great friends down all the decades.

Contents

Introduction

The Church into which I was born in mid-twentieth century Ireland was a cold house for Catholics, to borrow Eoghan Harris's evocative phrase from David Trimble's Nobel Peace Prize speech in December 1998. Trimble was referring to the position of Catholics in Northern Ireland. In both jurisdictions on the island conditions within the Church were frosty, owing to its deep distrust of the body as the greatest threat to eternal salvation.

It accepted, with regret as yet another Divine mystery, this temporary life of three score and ten wherein all Catholics were subject to constant temptation by that unHoly Trinity of the World, the Flesh and the Devil, succumbing to any or all of which meant Hell, forever and ever. Amen. The choice was stark: live out this short existence by Church diktats or be damned to that hotter place already full of Protestants, apostates, atheists, agnostics, followers of all the other religions and of none – all such 'pagans' as found in England.

Irish Catholics were encouraged to discipline the body through practices such as regular fasting (by an already hungry population) and the celebration of suffering as the best routes to be nearer my God to Thee. This was life in 'the Church that Paul built', an extraordinary institution created in the later nineteenth century by the remarkable Paul Cullen, unacknowledged father of twentieth-century Ireland and the country's first cardinal.

However cold, his Church did offer shelter of sorts but, above all, it provided a meaning for generally hopeless lives.

Though he died in 1878, Cullen created the Catholicism with which most of us remain familiar, and a worldwide spiritual empire whose influence is still felt. In 1849 he was appointed Archbishop of Armagh in a country still traumatised by the Famine, followed by Archbishop of Dublin in 1852. On his watch an astonishing building programme got underway, with grand cathedrals, churches and imposing presbyteries appearing across Ireland. By the later nineteenth century it was said there was a church/chapel within a three-mile walking distance of every Irish Catholic. Priest numbers grew accordingly – to 3,500 by 1900, or one priest for every 892 Catholics in Ireland.

Cullen also brought in religious orders from abroad to assist those at home in building convents, reformatories, industrial schools, orphanages and Magdalene laundries. What he put in place would mean that by 1922 the new cash-strapped Irish Free State found itself dependent upon an 'army' of 13,000 priests, nuns and brothers to provide education and healthcare. A Department of Health was not set up in Ireland until 1947, and even today the Church controls 88 per cent of primary schools in the Republic.

The slow undoing of this Church began just over 100 years after its beginning. In 1958 the First Programme for Economic Expansion was published by the Irish government, leading to the State's first real period of prosperity, which allowed it to introduce free education at second and third levels in 1967, the effects of which cannot be exaggerated. It was also in 1958 that Pope John XIII was elected pope, he who established the Second Vatican Council and threw open the Vatican's windows, thus setting the Church on a new path.

By 1961, when I was eight, there was one priest for every 558 Catholics in Ireland, where the population was at its lowest ever:

2.8 million. Such was their number then that between a third and a half served abroad. There was nothing for them to do at home. But the seeds of destruction in the Church were already at work, whether in residential institutions for women and children at home and abroad, or in dioceses around the world. This became all too evident in North America, Australia, New Zealand, Africa, the UK and in Ireland itself as the twentieth century came to a close – I, with others, would help expose and document what was going on.

In early 2002 I was asked by the late John Wilkins, editor of the UK Catholic weekly *The Tablet*, to write about the Church's clerical child sex abuse crisis. My article focused on the phenomenal number of Irish-named clergy among those convicted abroad in relation to the issue. Wilkins declined to publish it. In April 2002 he sent me an email suffused with apology. He would 'never be forgiven by my readers in Ireland or of Irish origin, who are a considerable number. They would misinterpret what you are saying and would take it as a *Tablet* attack on their culture.'

The article was instead published in *The Irish Times* on 2 May 2002, headed 'An Irish Disease?' I braced myself for yet another kicking by the usual would-be self-appointed defenders of the Catholic Church in Ireland. There was only silence.

The clerical child sexual abuse scandal was a tragic denouement to 'the Church that Paul built', that remarkable edifice now crumbling. For believing Irish Catholics this has been a deeply distressing experience. It will take from the 200th anniversary celebrations of Catholic Emancipation in 2029. Yet what is disappearing is a comparatively recent form of institutional Church in Ireland. History would indicate that in its ruins lies a new form of Catholic Church waiting to be born.

In this book I recall my own experience of growing up in the cold house that Paul built and where that led me to personally, while also concentrating on some of the bigger stories on which I reported, as well as the frequently bizarre background to how these emerged. And so much more.

That is religious affairs. All human life is there.

1

In the Beginning …

Hidden behind the men at the back of the kitchen, I was not sure whether it was the right thing to do. The old priest had a fearsome reputation for contrariness, which was evident in the demeanour of all the people around me. They were silent and stood stiffly as the Mass was coming to an end. The hand in which I held my farthing had become sweaty and I worried about that too. Would he notice the dampness when I gave it to him? Would he be angry about that as well? It was time to stop thinking and just do it. I ran forward with my hand outstretched and said, 'Here, Father.'

Confused at first, Father Donnellan took the farthing, my entire worldly possession, with its bird (woodcock) on one side and a harp on the other. He looked at me directly and smiled. It was the first time he had smiled that morning. 'What is your name?' he asked.

'Patsy McGarry,' I replied.

'Ah, like your grandfather,' he said. 'You're a good boy. Thank you.'

I retreated to the men at the back, including my father. A neighbour whispered to him, 'That child will go far.' To which my father replied, 'Sure where would he leave it!'

It was the only time we had the stations in our house at Mullen, a townland about a mile and a half from Frenchpark in north Roscommon. Our house had been transformed for the occasion: new wallpaper everywhere, with new curtains on freshly painted windows, and all the outside walls recently whitewashed. There was even talk of getting the roof thatched again, but it did not happen as it soon became clear that the job could not be completed on time.

Far and away the biggest change was in Grandad's room. He had a bedroom all to himself in what was a traditional Irish country cottage, with two rooms and a large kitchen between the two. One of the two rooms was divided by a wooden partition – my mother, father and then baby Mary were on one side; me, Seán and Pearse, killing one another in the one bed, were on the other.

Grandad's room was turned into a dining room for the priest's breakfast after the station Mass. His four-poster bed with its canopy on top was taken out altogether. A table covered by a white linen tablecloth was installed with all the Christmas delph on it. The room was transformed into a place of wonder to my eyes, with its new wallpaper, borrowed chairs and the centrepiece table covered in a starched white tablecloth, atop which the cutlery gleamed with attention-seeking sparkle as you walked by.

I did not dare touch any of it, following threats of immediate and terrible consequences. But my attention was soon focused on what looked like a big yellow orange cut in half and laid out in a bowl. I had never seen the like before and, inevitably, I had to taste it. I was an adult before I touched grapefruit again.

My grandfather was not at the station Mass that morning. Indeed, I never remember him going to Mass. Religion was never huge in our house. On Sundays I would sometimes go to early Mass in Frenchpark with my mother, on the back of her bicycle. I always preferred going to Mass with her. I had her to myself. We would sit, silently, in the body of the church as she prayed, the only time I remember my mother in the middle of people and not talking to someone. At the altar Father Donnellan spoke in Latin, a language that only God and he understood.

My mother's silent reverence impressed me, and I stayed quiet. She had a deep, private faith but was never pious. After Mass we would go up to Annie Cox's shop, not far from the church, where we would be brought into her kitchen for tea and sweet cake, before we left eventually with *The Sunday Press*. Only newspapers from the Fianna Fáil press stable were allowed in our house.

Going to Mass with my father was different. That was always for second Mass and involved sinking into the gloom of the deep back seat of his Morris Minor, so low you could not see anything out the windows except clouds. Then, in the church, we would go upstairs to the gallery at the back with all the other men chatting about politics or cattle until all went silent as Frankie Martin's oaken baritone soared through the familiar hymns, accompanying himself on the gallery's asthmatic organ.

Only then, and during the consecration, did they stop talking. During the consecration they would take out a handkerchief or lay down a cap, go down on one knee, head low and bless themselves as the bells rang three times to mark the moments when bread and wine became the body and blood of Christ, before rising to pick up again wherever they had left off in the conversation so inconveniently interrupted.

After Mass we would usually adjourn to Kelly's pub, where the minerals and Tayto crisps, in their opaque bags, could stave off the boredom only for so long while the men drank, laughed and chatted. Where my father and the other men were concerned, the highlight of those Sunday mornings was Frankie Martin's singing, which took them to a sacred place no religion could reach. And then there were the few pints together afterwards. It was how they kept holy the Sabbath day.

Many years before the stations in our house, there had been one in Toolan's, up the hill behind our house in Mullen, during one of those fraught general election campaigns in the early 1930s when the Irish State was still young. My grandfather was in his forties with a young family during the War of Independence period, but his sympathies were well known. One day at the crossroads near our house, Black and Tans in a Crossley tender tried to arrest him, but my Aunt 'Baby' (Winifred), then about six, kicked up such a fuss, roaring and screaming, that they left him alone.

He became a founder member of the local Fianna Fáil cumann in Mullen. Memories were still fresh and bitter over the defeat in 1923 of Fianna Fáil's predecessors in the Civil War by the state's founding party, which supported the 1922 Treaty with Britain and which, by the 1930s, had morphed into Fine Gael. It was well known at the time, particularly among Fianna Fáil supporters, that most Catholic bishops and priests supported the Treaty and, so, Fine Gael. This was the case with the then parish priest in Frenchpark, who said the station Mass in Toolan's that morning and who, in his sermon, made his political allegiance clear. He advised everyone present to vote Fine Gael in a forthcoming general election. This was too much for my grandfather, who did the unthinkable. He stood up and challenged the priest. 'Father, where does it say that in the gospel?' he asked.

There was consternation. The priest was apoplectic at the impertinence, while everyone else was astonished that my grandfather would challenge him at all, never mind publicly.

Matters settled down and Mass proceeded. As it came to an end people rose from their chairs to leave, all except my grandfather. He couldn't get up at first, leading to one of the great myths of the era that he had been stuck to the chair by the priest for challenging him. It was a tale well ventilated by my grandfather's friends, despite them being well aware of the truth – that during last-minute preparations the Toolans had painted the chair that morning and it had not dried before my grandfather sat on it.

This was not my grandfather's only run-in with that parish priest. He and his good friend Pat Breslin were accomplished concert flute players and in regular demand at country-house dances. One such dance was organised locally to raise money to buy an ass (donkey) for a local woman whose husband had died suddenly, leaving her with a young family to rear on her own. She could use the ass to cart out turf from a nearby bog to sell locally and in Frenchpark. The dance was in her house and was well under way when the parish priest arrived to clear the lot of them.

The clergy at the time took a dim view of this type of event, believing them to be 'occasions of sin'. They were also rivals to the new parish halls that priests were building in many places at the time, such as in Frenchpark. The clearance of that house did not sit well with my grandfather or the people in Mullen generally, particularly in the circumstances. There didn't appear to be anything Christian about it.

The only day of the week Grandad left our house was Friday, when he would cross the fields to where my aunt lived and she would go into Frenchpark to collect his pension for him. He would arrive back at our house later in the day with sweets for us. Once or twice he might be a bit merry, as occasionally my aunt would bring him a bottle of stout or two from Frenchpark, but he was not a drinking man.

On one such Friday evening he arrived back at our house, took out the tin whistle and played a tune which I would later recognise as 'The Blackbird of Avondale'. It was about Charles Stewart Parnell, born in Avondale in County Wicklow and known in the late nineteenth century as the 'Uncrowned King' of

Ireland. As an MP at Westminster and leader of the Irish Party, he and Michael Davitt of the Land League oversaw the greatest revolution in Irish history: the peaceful transfer of the land of Ireland from mainly absentee landlords to the people of Ireland. Parnell also began a campaign for an Irish parliament in Dublin to run Irish affairs, known as Home Rule. But he was brought down by a divorce case where he was cited as co-respondent with Katharine O'Shea, who had been married to another Irish MP. Hard-line evangelical Christian supporters of Britain's governing Liberal Party and, eventually, the Catholic Church in Ireland combined to oust Parnell, who died not very long afterwards in 1891 aged forty-five. My grandfather was then fourteen.

I did not take much notice of him playing the melancholy tune that Friday evening until I saw the tears running down his face. I began to cry too. I was very fond of my grandfather. He noticed me and, as if awoken from an old reverie, he stopped playing and told me, 'It's alright, Patsy. Don't worry, everything is alright.' I asked him, 'Why are you crying, Grandad?' and he said, 'Ah, it's a tune about Parnell. I'll tell you all about him when you grow up.' He never did. He died when I was twelve, still too young to understand the heartbreak of a country at the loss of Parnell in 1891, or to understand my grandfather's grief over sixty years later.

He was not religious, 'oul Patsy' as they called him, but he had his rituals. On 23 June every year, 'Bonfire Night', we'd have our own small fire at the crossroads near our house. We children were too young to go to the big one at Regan's crossroads, about a mile up the road at the back of our house. So we would have this small fire, the novelty alone of which was enough for us. Grandad would play a few tunes and, as the evening drew in, while sparks from the fire competed with stars overhead, he would lift an incandescent sod of turf from the fire with a tongs and carry it over to our field, where he would place it carefully, 'for luck'. It was probably an old fertility ritual.

✠ ✠ ✠

In later years, I would wonder whether my grandfather's indifference to the Church and religion was more personal than political. His wife, Beatrice, my grandmother, was dead long before I was born. She died in her fifties after a pain-ridden struggle with stomach cancer that continued for years throughout the 1930s. She was also deeply devout, particularly to St Philomena. Through her long illness she wore St Philomena scapulars around her neck. She would leave these to my father, her youngest child.

Beatrice was also, by all accounts, a formidable woman from an equally formidable family, the Regans of Eden near Fairymount, about four miles from Mullen – up there on good land, not at all like the swampy rushes that were our acres. The wonder was that she married my grandfather at all. Beatrice had spent many of her younger years in New York, where she made some money working as a domestic servant before returning home. Clearly, although my grandfather had no wealth, he had charm. He had a job at a local quarry near Frenchpark, played music, was a regular at country-house dances and Beatrice was in search of a husband. They married and had four children: two boys and two girls. He was, according to one of my aunts, 'a pure slave, working in the quarry all day before coming home in the evening to cut the meadow with a scythe while she was lady of the manor entertaining the local Royal Irish Constabulary [RIC] men's wives'.

My father would never acknowledge that his mother ever entertained RIC men's wives. It was beneath his republican dignity.

11

Worse, his mother's people, the Regans, were 'all Blueshirts', as he referred to Fine Gael supporters. When reminiscing about the past, he preferred the story of how the Black and Tans tried to arrest his father at the crossroads and failed.

Beatrice pushed her two sons, identifying education as their way ahead. In 1930 or 1931 she decided that her eldest son, my uncle Seán (christened John Joe, but he changed it to the Irish version), would be the first person in Mullen to get a secondary education. But you could say that education ran in the family.

The house I grew up in was built by my great-grandfather Patrick McGarry. He was born in 1843, right in the middle of the Famine. In 1849 William Murphy, a Catholic businessman based at Smithfield in Dublin, evicted over 270 people and levelled fifty-seven houses he owned on lands at Mullen, Rahella and Listrumneale. The evictees included many McGarry families, of which there were quite a few in the townland of Mullen right up to my own time there. I believe my ancestors were among those evicted, since in my great-grandfather's time we lived beside the Carricknabraher river, known locally as 'the Mullen river', on ungenerous land at the edge of the bog in a copse of trees shared with the Bruens and the Dohertys.

Then, in the later nineteenth century, a new road was created, connecting Castlerea to Frenchpark, which cut through my grandfather's field, creating a v-shaped area where it met the old road. With the money he got for selling the strip of his land through which the 'new line' road was built, my great-grandfather built the house I grew up in sometime in the 1860s or '70s. Having built the house, however, he did not move from the old homestead, but instead used the new building as a cowshed. Then he was approached by the authorities to see if he would agree to it being used as a school while the new Mullen school was constructed nearby. He agreed. One of the teachers in the new temporary school was Liza Dillon, my soon-to-be great-grandmother. They married, and when the new school was built, they moved into what I would know as 'our house'.

I have often wondered whether having a mother who was a teacher gave my grandfather the status to make him acceptable to the Regans as a worthy partner for their Beatrice, considering how little he brought to the table where land and wealth were concerned. Education was always prized by people in rural Ireland, eliciting respect for the priest and the teacher, while also giving them a unique authority.

My grandmother was determined that her two sons would also garner such respect. However, having had no more than a primary education herself, she did not know when the secondary school year began. It was a February in the early 1930s when she took Seán by ass and cart to St Nathy's College, Ballaghaderreen, about eight miles away. St Nathy's was the nearest secondary school to Mullen. Though Mullen was in Elphin diocese, St Nathy's was the diocesan college of Achonry and one of the oldest, tracing its history back to 1810. The education offered there was classical, with subjects including Greek and Latin, and had a two-fold intent – as with all Catholic diocesan colleges – to produce priests and a loyal Catholic middle-class who might act as a bulwark against possible future persecution, as had been suffered by Irish Catholics in the past.

The president at St Nathy's, Canon Ambrose Blaine, was so impressed by my grandmother's determination to have her son educated that he agreed to take him on as a day boy. Years later, Seán would remember how the Canon introduced him to his new class with the line, 'This blessed fellow has no Latin and less Greek, then neither had Shakespeare.' Seán cycled the sixteen-mile round trip to St Nathy's six days a week, including the half-day on Saturday, for five years. Sometimes, as he recalled it, he studied Shakespeare by candlelight in winter evenings at home. Like many of his generation, Seán went on to become a civil servant in various government departments, mainly Lands and Agriculture. He never forgot his debt to the Church for the education he received at St Nathy's, despite not being particularly devout. To compound that loyalty, he became convinced that, while he was a pupil there, the family could not even afford the small fees, yet the St Nathy's authorities never brought it up with him. He doubted it was even brought up with my grandparents either, as his mother spent most of the 1930s fighting cancer, and whatever means they had was spent on treatments for her.

His secondary education meant that in later years Seán could attend University College Dublin (UCD) in the evenings, where he took a degree in commerce and German. It also meant he was something of a fish out of water among his civil service colleagues, whose better-off parents had the means to send them to some of Ireland's more prestigious boarding schools run by Catholic religious orders. He remembered a conversation with these colleagues one day where they adjudged that 'all the best people were in Fine Gael'. They assumed that was his background too. He did not disabuse them, feeling it would be unwise, but it clarified for him that while Fianna Fáil was in government for much of his adult life, it was not always in power.

My father never went to St Nathy's, though he may have attended the newly opened vocational school in Ballaghaderreen. Part of his myth was that he had indeed attended St Nathy's but was expelled for bringing in contraband to the boarders. He liked to portray himself as a rebel and, in fairness, it could be true. For most of his life my father regarded the Catholic Church, as an institution, with suspicion, while at the same time being very friendly with individual priests. But any certainties of faith he had were shattered in 1961, though I was too young to realise it at the time, and he did something that was unthinkable in the rural Ireland of the day: he stopped going to Mass.

As mentioned, my grandmother had suffered greatly with stomach cancer through most of my father's teen years in the 1930s, when there was little by way of pain relief. His eldest sister May, by then a nurse in Liverpool, came home to look after their mother. My grandmother's protracted suffering left a deep mark on all four of her children, not least my father, who was the youngest. I remember my Uncle Seán, then in his eighties, weeping when he talked about what his mother had gone through in her later years.

In those years when she was dying, Beatrice wore scapulars of St Philomena, to whom she was devoted, around her neck. Scapulars were rectangular pieces of cloth worn as a reminder of the saint to which the bearer was devoted. Beatrice offered up her agony and prayed for her family, which would have included two of her children who never made it past infancy. One was Claire, who died of diphtheria at the age of two, and then there was Patrick, who was stillborn and, so, not baptised. Both were buried in a *cillín*, an informal graveyard for deceased unbaptised children down the Mullen road, one of the most perfect spaces in the area. Neither child, being unbaptised – and it is not known why Claire was still unbaptised at the age of two – could be buried in consecrated ground, nor could people who took their own lives. I can only guess at the distress the teaching that her innocent baby daughter and son were in Limbo ('closed down' by Pope Benedict XVI in 2007) and would never get to Heaven must have caused someone as devout as my grandmother. The children, my late aunt and uncle, were buried anonymously in a field and their graves have long since disappeared under the hooves of cattle.

In February 1961 the Vatican directed that St Philomena be removed from the calendar of saints due to serious doubt as to whether she ever existed. This had a profound effect on my father, who had inherited the St Philomena scapulars from his dying mother. As a result, he fell away entirely from regular religious practice and attended only Masses for weddings and funerals. It was quite a statement in the Ireland of the day.

✠ ✠ ✠

I remember 1961 for very different reasons. The first was the cover of the New Year edition of the *Dandy* comic, which delighted me because it was so clever. On it you had Korky the Cat with the numbers 1-9-6-1, and when you turned the cover upside down, the numbers remained 1-9-6-1.

Then, later that year, I got a bicycle for my sixth birthday. It had belonged to Patricia Kelly, a daughter of the pub family in Frenchpark. My father painted it blue – a colour he rarely favoured (it was associated with the Blueshirts), but he made exceptions. After this momentous event, every Friday after school I would do the messages for my mother in Frenchpark. I would set off for Kitty Murray's with the 'wet' radio battery hanging off the bike's right handlebar. I would leave it in to Kitty and pick up a charged one, then get the messages in Keenan's grocery shop and call into Ms Gannon's in the post office for that week's *Dandy* and *Beano* comics, before heading up to Frankie Martin's to collect more messages. He annoyed me every time, beginning our interactions with, 'And how are all the Mullen peasants today?' I'd try to ignore him.

I once told my father about this and he said, 'Take no heed of him. Sure, they're all Lord de Freyne's bastards in Frenchpark.' The Frenches/de Freynes were local landlords. I had no idea what a bastard was but understood it to be a bad thing. I even thought it might be a collective term for people from Frenchpark. One day

I asked my mother, 'Mammy, what's a bastard?' She was shocked, and responded, 'Where did you hear that language?' I told her Mack had said it (we called our father 'Mack'). 'Don't heed him and don't be using that sort of language around this house,' she said. So it was that bad! So bad it surprised me that my father would say that about Frankie Martin, seeing as he sang hymns at second Mass every Sunday.

Frankie was not married then, but he later wed Norah, with whom he would go on to have eleven children, each given a name beginning with a letter, in sequence, from 'Frank Martin'. When the eleventh child was born a neighbour asked him, 'Well Frankie, are ya finished now?' Frankie replied, 'No. We're going to start on the address: Ballaghaderreen Road, Frenchpark, County Roscommon.' But they didn't.

✠ ✠ ✠

Frenchpark had been named after the Frenches, a Norman family who came to Ireland in 1169 and arrived at what became Frenchpark in 1666, where they controlled 36,000 acres. The first de Freyne – Arthur French to give him his correct name – had been a Whig/Liberal MP for Roscommon until 1832, when he was made a baron and took the title 'de Freyne'. In 1846 starving local people burned Lord de Freyne's effigy outside the door of his eighteenth-century mansion, Frenchpark House. At that time, during the Famine, 30,000 people living in the 135 square miles around Frenchpark existed on one meal of boiled cabbage every two days. Famine ravaged the area and one old woman told the young Douglas Hyde (later Ireland's first president) as he was growing up there that it killed everything. 'Poetry, music and dancing stopped. Sport and pastimes disappeared. And when the times improved, these things never returned as they had been.'

One of the background noises to my childhood was the demise of Lord de Freyne's demesne and house near Frenchpark. In 1952 the Land Commission bought the de Freyne estate and for so long we went to school those mornings in the 1950s listening to the noise of chainsaws carried on the wind as they cut down the magnificent mature trees around the demesne, which was then divided among local farmers. The commission also removed the mansion roof, because you did not have to pay rates on a roofless building. It fell into disrepair. I remember visiting its ruins as a child with my father and feeling regret for the lingering grandeur of it all, a nostalgia for something I had never seen but suspected.

✠ ✠ ✠

While my father largely gave up on religion in 1961, I, on the other hand, went in the opposite direction. That, too, began with a death, in my case that of a kitten. On the flag floor inside our front door in Mullen there was a natural indent in the stone. It was smooth and hollow, and we would pour milk in there for the cat and her kittens. We would then lie around on the floor watching them as they lapped it up. It was a Sunday morning. Seán, eighteen months younger than me and the bane of my life, had been outside and barged in the front door, which caught one of the escaping kittens violently and it died on the spot. Witnesses were myself, him, my brother Pearse and our baby sister Mary, then about four – all of us at that point (three more would arrive in later years).

Trauma is a mild word to describe our reaction to the kitten's death and its manner that morning. Our mother was just as upset, but, to distract us, she suggested that we have a funeral and bury the kitten in the garden behind our house, which is what we did. We got a small cardboard box, filled it with cotton wool and placed the kitten inside before putting on the lid. The sad funeral party headed for the garden. I began to dig, but less than six inches down the would-be grave filled with water and Mary got very upset. 'You can't put him down there. He'll be all wet,' she said. As if it mattered. But she was right. None of us wanted to see our dead kitten in a watery grave.

I went to higher ground, near the stile at the back of the garden, which we used on our way to school. I dug into the dry clay and soon had a nice square hole cleared for the cardboard box. We placed the cardboard 'coffin' inside and I shovelled the clay back into it, leaving a small mound which we marked with a stone. Eventually, our disconsolate crew made its way back to the kitchen.

Shortly afterwards I went to the second Mass that day with our father. Seán, Pearse and Mary stayed at home and Mam had already been to early Mass. She was preparing the dinner, while Grandad sat by the open fire whistling dryly through his moustache as he did, his attention lost in the flaming coals. It was not until I saw the coffin before the altar that I realised it was a funeral Mass. It was my first time attending the funeral of a person I knew. This was our neighbour, Pat Beirne, or 'the Poet Beirne' as he was known, given his predilection for making up rhymes. He had died in the bog earlier that week while cutting turf, and the only thing they could find on which to carry Pat out of the bog was a door. I was told none of this but picked it up from the shocked adults talking around me in our kitchen. Death, to my knowledge, did not happen in Mullen and, as far as I was even aware of it, it was always hearsay.

I knew and had liked Pat Beirne, who was a regular visitor to our house. And here he was now in the coffin before the altar in our Church of St Asicus. I began to feel queasy at the thought of Pat inside it. Afterwards, my father and I followed the hearse in a line of cars to the graveyard in Cloonshanville, with its lonesome yew trees and ancient ivy-covered ruins. It is where generations of my own family are buried. Six men carried the coffin from the hearse to the grave and the priest led prayers. I was stunned and soon felt weak as Pat was lowered into the earth. These feelings only got worse when I heard the clay hitting his coffin: that hollow, meaningless sound announcing blithely, 'That's it!'

Looking at all the faces around the grave I realised all of them, every single one, and every single person I knew, was going to end up like that – my father, Mam, my grandfather, Seán, Pearse, Mary, myself, all of us – in a coffin deep underground. I wanted to go home. I wanted to go to bed or, better still, get under it, which I always did when terrified, whether by thunder, a steamroller passing outside, or a low-flying plane overhead.

We went home directly from the funeral. It was too late for Kelly's. I must have been very quiet on the way home because about halfway there my father asked me if I was alright. I said I was. 'He was a good man, Pat,' said my father, 'and maybe he's in a better place now.' It surprised me. My father never talked about the afterlife, but clearly he saw that I was in some distress. He must have said something to Mam too, because she was particularly solicitous, as was Grandad. I think it was around then, but I can't be sure, that Grandad said to me, 'Patsy, don't think too much.' It was the only advice he ever offered me. I have rarely heeded it.

Following my encounter with reality in the graveyard at Cloonshanville, I became very religious. We were already heading that way at school. Mrs Forde, our teacher, was a deeply devout woman who took the religious element of her teaching duties very seriously. I wanted to impress her, always. My earliest memory is of her and Mam talking at the stile at the back of the house. Mrs Forde cycled that way twice a day, to and from Mullen school. She lived in Frenchpark. It was clear she and Mam liked one another. I was not yet at school, but Mam was teaching me to count and read at home. On that particular afternoon, Mrs Forde was telling Mam about how one of her pupils had actually stood up on a desk that day, and she turned to me and said, 'Sure you won't do that when you come to school will you, Patsy?' I said I would not, and I meant it. I was always on my best behaviour with Mrs Forde, in school or not, and learned my catechism, everything, to please her.

She was a good teacher, if strict, and soon I could do no wrong in her eyes. I remember the precise moment when that was sealed. A priest, the diocesan examiner, came to the school to check on how well we knew our catechism and the Bible stories about Jesus. Everything was going well until he asked, 'And who was John the Baptist's father?' Silence. I could see Mrs Forde, sitting over on a window ledge beside a statue of the Virgin Mary, looking nervous. I put up my hand and when the priest gestured towards me, responded, 'Zachary.' Thereafter I walked on water as far as Mrs Forde was concerned.

Before he left the school that day, the priest gave each of us a card with a depiction of what I would come to know was Salvador Dalí's *Christ of St John of the Cross*, with its crucified Jesus, head bowed to the world below his nailed feet. It has remained one of my favourite religious paintings.

The fact of the matter was that religion made more and more sense to me, with its explanation of this brief life as but a temporary route to the eternal. It was soon obvious to me that I would be a priest when I grew up, bringing explanation, meaning and comfort to people with no answers. What better way to spend your life than helping people in this life on their journey to the next one? It made such sense, emotionally and symmetrically. I lived with that decision until late adolescence. Even later. It framed my young life.

I became very scrupulous about sin. I would count each one with the accuracy of a conscientious accountant and confess accordingly. I strove, continuously, to be in a state of sanctifying grace, which was not easy with a brother like Seán. He took every opportunity to provoke me. At one stage I became convinced he was the greatest threat to my eternal salvation as he brought out all sorts of rage in me, leaving me bereft at disappointing God once more. Worse still, I knew that should I die in one of those rages, my destiny was clear: Hell! This would be Seán's fault too, although it would hardly matter by then. Seán also taught me the futility of turning the other cheek. He'd just hit you on that cheek too.

One winter's evening I was saying Mass at a table in Grandad's room, with boxes stacked to make a tabernacle and a curtain draped from my shoulders like a priest. Seán's job was to ring the bell whenever I knelt before the 'altar'. The bell was a bottle with a spoon in it. He kept missing his cue. I'd kneel and nothing would happen. I'd hold up a cup and nothing would happen. I'd hold up a piece of cardboard and nothing would happen. I completely lost it and grabbed a shoe from the altar (we were in our socks and had put our shoes on the 'altar' beside the 'tabernacle') and threw it at him. It missed, flying to the kitchen where it knocked the Tilley lamp off the table and quenched all light except that from the open fire. We were terrified of the dark and there was panic as all of us roared crying. Grandad, who had been sitting by the fire, tried to calm us down. 'Scuth, scuth, scuth,' he said. I ran out of the house in my stockinged feet and up the road, roaring, to the field where my father was digging potatoes. The neighbours thought our house was on fire.

It was unusual for me to run to my father for support, but the thought of my mother saying, 'Patsy, I'm surprised at you' in a tone of serious disappointment would be worse. She was over the fields in the dark milking the cows and had left me in charge. Calm was restored eventually and, with it, relief when it was realised what had actually happened. Seán, the bane of my young life, had struck again.

One particular November in those years I decided to rescue from Purgatory everyone I knew who had died. These included my grandmother and Pat Beirne. It was believed then that only saints went straight to Heaven, while everyone else did a term in Purgatory first. My rescue attempt meant, first, being in a state of grace, having made a confession and received Communion, as well as making separate visits to the church in Frenchpark for each of the dead and saying the ritual prayers.

The hardest part was preparing for that rescue mission. It meant staying in a state of grace all week from confession the previous Saturday and Communion on Sunday until I did the messages for Mam on the Friday when I planned to effect the great escape from Purgatory. And it all had to be done despite Seán. He could ruin it by driving me into a temper and I'd have to go to confession and Communion again before rescuing all those people. Remarkably, I avoided his provocation – I don't know how – until the following Friday. But I have wondered many times since, what people in Frenchpark must have thought was going on, seeing this gossoon entering and leaving the church at regular intervals that winter's evening. Still, and single-handedly, I freed everyone I knew of who might be in Purgatory to enter eternal life in Heaven.

I developed a deep faith and felt very close to God at times. There was a tree in our garden with a stump in the middle, and at twilight I would sit there looking up at the infinity of stars and 'drive' through the universe for hours, the cries of a lone unseen curlew above for company. I would leave that tree stump with great reluctance. Going back into the so-called real world seemed to be wilfully leaving behind a deeper reality. But Mam had called, 'Patsy, come in for your tea.'

Similarly, when I'd be sent into the bog to keep an eye on our cattle as they grazed there in summertime, I would lie on the rough heather for entire afternoons exploring great seas and nations in the clouds while chewing on a sweet slip of long grass – just me and God and his creation. It was bliss. All was harmony, all made sense. At times like that I used to think I might become a monk. But then I felt an even deeper urge to help make the world a better place for people. It was what God would want. Jesus was about 'doing', not just 'being', I felt. And I experienced no hint of doubt, even as so much else fell away.

✠ ✠ ✠

Even though I doubted that I had been found under a head of cabbage or was left at the front door, I was sure there was a perfectly acceptable explanation for my birth, which I would find out in time. I was in no particular hurry. It did not interest me that much. Then, one day at school, my cousin Paddy Sharkey, who was a bit older than me, said, 'You know we come out of our mother's belly. Like cattle.' I was appalled. We all knew how cows had calves and why you brought a heifer or cow to a bull. We were surrounded by that reality. But they were animals. We were human, made in the image and likeness of God. Above all that.

After school that day I said to Mam, 'Paddy Sharkey said we come out of our mammies' bellies, just like cattle do.' From her reaction I knew immediately it was not true. Besides, I already knew babies did not come from their mother's bellies. Hadn't I seen this with my own eyes? Peg Martin, Frankie's mother, was a midwife. Not that I had any idea what that meant. Didn't I see her myself come through our room, where Seán and Pearse and I slept, on her way into our parents' room with a big bag in her hand and next morning there was our brand-new baby sister Mary. I wished I had thought of that in time when Paddy Sharkey was going on with his oul' nonsense. But I hadn't.

Mam was so angry with Paddy. 'That fella! Don't heed that fella. He doesn't know what he's talking about. Next thing he'll be telling you there's no Santy Claus.' He had, but some innate wisdom prevented me from saying so at the time. Some of the older classmates at school, whom I trusted, explained how they had helped 'do Santy' the previous Christmas. I found it very hard to accept. It would become a pattern, this resistance on my part to lose a treasured myth that gave such meaning, depth, comfort, consolation and colour to life.

But what Paddy Sharkey and the others said about Santy Claus troubled me, despite my resistance. I sought out reasons why they were wrong. All the adults I knew said there was a Santy Claus. Every Christmas morning in our house Santy's boot marks were there in the ashes beside the smouldering fire. There was the half-eaten slice of Christmas cake on a plate and the sherry glass with a sip taken out of it. And hadn't Seán heard Santy on our roof one Christmas night? It must have been a right thump too, for him to hear the sleigh through all that thatch.

Ignoring widening fissures of doubt, I wanted above all to continue to believe in that hearty man with the big white beard who even knew my mother personally. That time we met him in Castlerea he said, 'Well, and how are you, Teenie?' That's how well he knew her. He called her 'Teenie', and only people who knew Mam well ever called her Teenie. That was on our way into the cinema, where we watched a Three Stooges film with Larry and Curly soon hammering Moe (or was it Larry and Moe hammering Curly?) and then Seán started to roar and we all had to leave. Mam was mortified.

The Santy Claus mystery continued to obsess me until I decided one day to ask Mam straight out. By then, to my mind, she, Grandad and I ran the house. My father was the only health inspector in County Roscommon and was gone for the day most days. Increasingly, Mam would leave me in charge when she had to milk the cows, or call over to the shop across the road run by 'old Mrs Mitchell', or be up the road where Mrs Mitchell's son P.J. lived in a slated house with his wife, Beatrice, and their clean children, Pat and Margo. 'Look at the cut of ye,' Mam would say to us when we came in from the garden, pointing to the dirt on our hands and clothes. 'Why can't ye be as clean as Pat and Margo?' I felt like saying, 'Maybe if we had a slated roof we would be clean too.' But I didn't because I knew it would annoy her.

I thought a slate roof was the height of sophistication. Our cousins across the fields had one and I loved being there when it rained. You could hear it on the roof. And stairs. I used to dream of living in a house with stairs. What must that be like? There were steps up to a shed next door to my aunt's near Fairymount, and I was awestruck by how my view of everything changed so dramatically by just going up one or two steps.

Anyhow, Mam and I were going to the well, the 'far well', for drinking water one day, and I decided I'd ask her about Santy Claus. We'd normally go to 'Callaghan's well' because it was nearer. It was in a field belonging to Kate and Thady Callaghan, who lived in the bog. The path to their house went by the well, which was near the road.

We kids were afraid of Kate Callaghan. On Fridays she'd come up the road from Frenchpark roaring and shouting after collecting her pension and having a drink. We'd hear her when she got to the crossroads below our house and we'd run inside. She and Johnny Mullaney, who lived farther up again, in Fall

Mór bog, would have a drink on Fridays in Frenchpark and on their separate ways home took the opportunity to insult all and sundry they met, including when they passed our house. On this particular Friday the word had gone out that Kate had fallen into the well as she crossed the field to her house, so no one went near that well for water over the following couple of weeks.

As we struggled back to our house from the 'far well', I asked Mam the overwhelming question about Santy Claus. Laying down her two buckets, she began, 'Alright, and between the two of us ...' She let me in on the secret behind the sweetest myth of all, but whatever disappointment I may have felt was more than made up for by a belief that I had crossed into a world where I was respected and trusted as a grown-up. No longer a believer in that myth, my role now was to help sustain it.

2

A Grand Metropolis

If 1961 was a turning point in my father's life, 1962 was one for me and the rest of the family. That was the year we moved to Ballaghaderreen, leaving Mullen, where the family had been since before history, as well as the house my great-grandfather had built. It also meant leaving Grandad who, at eighty-five, decided to stay. My Aunt Baby (Winifred Sharkey) and her family moved in to take care of him.

With the arrival of our second sister, Sinéad, in June 1962, there were now six children in the family, which had meant nine altogether in that small house – my mother, father, Grandad and us six, who included the then two youngest: Declan and Sinéad. For my parents it was a case of either build or move, and a broader consideration had entered their thinking: our education. That was when Ballaghaderreen came into the picture. At the time, in our area of north Roscommon, the town was unique when it came to schools. It had a girls' national school and convent secondary school run by the Sisters of Charity, a boys' national school run by the De La Salle Brothers, a vocational school, and St Nathy's College for boys, run by the priests of the Achonry diocese. No other town in the county could compete when it came to educational options. It also had a secretarial school.

I do not know when my parents decided on the move to Ballaghaderreen, but I do remember that for two years before it my father was clearly saving. Among the more fortunate of men in our locality at the time, he had a good, well-paid, secure government job, while so many others struggled to make a living off poor land and many more emigrated, mostly to Britain, sending money home to their wives, who reared the family at home. The husbands would come home at Christmas, and in the summers to save the hay.

My father's good fortune was not accidental. It was due in no small part to Dan O'Rourke, a legendary figure in Roscommon. Based in Castlerea, he had been on the management team that masterminded Roscommon's senior footballers winning of the All-Ireland in 1943 and 1944, and went on to become president of the Gaelic Athletic Association (GAA) between 1946 and 1949. He was also a Fianna Fáil TD. As a young man, my father trained to be a psychiatric nurse at the psychiatric hospital, or 'mental' hospital as it was known locally, in Castlerea, but he was also very active in the local Fianna Fáil cumann there, and he soon became Dan O'Rourke's right-hand man. O'Rourke would have a significant influence over his later career.

In the late 1940s Castlerea's hospital was transformed into a tuberculosis (TB) sanatorium by the new Minister for Health, Noël Browne, in his ultimately successful war against that disease. The psychiatric patients were transferred elsewhere, and Castlerea became the main centre in the west for treating TB patients until 1952, when Merlin Park Hospital opened in Galway. My mother began work at the new sanatorium in December 1948, as a student nurse. Her parents and my Uncle Pat, her twin brother, were afraid she might catch TB and did everything they could to stop her, but to no avail. She wanted a job and independence, and Noël Browne gave her both. All her life she planned to write to him – particularly after she read his autobiography, *Against the Tide* – to thank him for what he had done for her and for all those hundreds of TB patients. 'He was the first man to give me a job,' she said, 'and we thought he was God.' But she never did.

'It was awful at the beginning,' she remembered. 'They [the patients] came in on stretchers and went out in coffins.' My father remembered the patients 'dying like flies'. Young men like him had enough to do just carrying in the patients on arrival, and the dead out. And the surgery at the time was primitive. Ribs would be removed, 'a couple at a time', over three separate operations to collapse the lungs, my mother said. Parts of lungs would be taken out. It was 'brutal, terrible'. My father had retrained to nurse the TB patients and most of his work in the early days was taken up with palliative care, relieving pain. At first patients were confined to bed after operations, then they were put on their feet the very next day to undergo physiotherapy, 'with the blood seeping through the stitches', he said.

Despite this, the atmosphere was very 'happy go lucky', which is perhaps not so surprising as most of the staff and patients were young. 'Very beautiful boys and girls,' my mother remembered. My father said the female ward was like something out of Hollywood: 'The finest-looking girls you'd see, and all dead in a week.' But even the high death rate didn't affect the place as might be expected. There was 'no moodiness, except for the odd oul' staff nurse', said my mother. One less pleasant memory was how they were always afraid of their lives bringing the bodies to the morgue at night, and bodies were removed to the morgue only at night. Finally, streptomycin, a cure, came on stream and soon people did not need the brutal surgery any more.

My father remembered the stigma associated with the disease, and with the nursing staff at the sanatorium, in the beginning. People in Castlerea 'were afraid of their lives' to have anything to do with the nurses in case they would pick up the disease. They did not want to serve them in shops, pubs or cafés, he said. But 'eventually they ended up marrying them'. The development of streptomycin helped remove the stigma. Many members of the great Roscommon All-Ireland (1943/44) football team ended up as patients in the sanatorium. One regular visitor was a member of that team, Jack McQuillan, who, on the potent platform of TB and football, was elected to the Dáil, with Noël Browne, in 1948. He remained one of Browne's most loyal supporters until 1965, when he lost his seat.

My parents never lost their reverence for Dr Noël Browne as long as they lived. I saw him in the flesh, so to speak, when I was a student in Galway. He was slight and soft-spoken, not at all the stuff of legend. He was barely audible. Then, gradually, his audience was drawn into his train of thought, and he grew in volume, hurtling to such rage as I have rarely witnessed. The subject was one of the myriad injustices with which he was preoccupied. The substance I forget, but the style of expression, the sincerity of his anger and its depth have always remained fresh in my memory.

The coalition government of which Dr Browne was a member fell in 1951, when he attempted to introduce a scheme to care for mothers and their children to the age of sixteen. It was opposed by the formidable and combined forces of the medical profession and the Catholic Church. That same coalition government decided to introduce more health inspectors to uphold and improve sanitary standards in Ireland. It was Dan O'Rourke who suggested to my father that he should apply. This would mean him attending a course at University College Cork. When my father was accepted, O'Rourke lent him the money so he could afford to go.

Once qualified, my father was posted to Dublin, which he hated, so O'Rourke arranged for him to be transferred to Longford and later to Roscommon – for his entire career my father was the only health inspector there. Our move to Ballaghaderreen was also influenced by this job. It was not a good look for the county's only health inspector to live in a small, traditional, thatched country cottage with eight others, six of them children, and no electricity, running water or bathroom.

✠ ✠ ✠

It was October 1962 when I found out we were moving to Ballaghaderreen. I was sworn to secrecy – which, of course, I loved. There is nothing quite like the satisfaction that goes with being selected to share in adult intimacies at that age. I think I was told because Mrs Forde had begun to train me to be an altar boy. That followed a crisis at Mass in Frenchpark a few weeks earlier, when no altar boys had turned up to serve. Father Donnellan was furious and did not hesitate to let that be known to the packed church. Worse, there were lads from Mullen school in the congregation who had been trained as altar boys, but they remained in their seats, too terrified of him to do otherwise. At school the next day Mrs Forde was so angry with them. That was when she began to train me, even though I was just nine, in the Latin responses, beginning: *Ad Deum qui laetificat juventutem meum* (to God who gives joy to my youth). This was a response to the priest's opening words at Mass: *Introibo ad altare Dei* (I will go to the altar of God), also used by Buck Mulligan in the opening lines of Joyce's *Ulysses* as he prepared to shave himself, holding a bowl of lather aloft in the mild morning air at the Martello tower in Dublin's Sandycove.

I never did serve Mass, being deemed too old when we moved to Ballaghaderreen a month later. But, however excited I may have been about our imminent move, that October it all soon seemed academic because the end of the world was nigh. Everyone said so. The Cuban Missile Crisis was destined to end in nuclear war and that was all our adults could talk about. I wondered what the end of the world would be like but just couldn't visualise being here one minute and gone the next. It was while attempting to do this one day that I passed a blackthorn bush at a turn in the road on the way home from school and plucked a sloe berry from it. I bit it and, as the dry bitterness seized my mouth, I spat it out. That, I decided, was what the end of the world would taste like.

My tenth birthday was the following month and, as a treat, my father brought my mother and me to Ballaghaderreen to show us the house on the square. I had been to the town once before, to get my First Communion suit at Flannery's big department store there. What fascinated me most about the shop were the little boxes speeding on wires overhead carrying money to and from the cash office. Then we went to Spellman's on Pound Street for our dinner. It was the first time I had had oxtail soup. A feature of growing up in Mullen was that everything was homemade, everything was organic. We kids put no value on that at all and believed anything that came from a shop was better. I hated our salty 'country' butter, made by our mother, preferring the 'shop butter' instead. The first tinned food I remember in our house was mackerel, bought by my father seemingly as an afterthought one Friday afternoon.

On that birthday visit in November 1962, my father borrowed an electric bulb on a long lead from Mrs O'Donnell next door (the tranquillity of whose life was to be powerfully disturbed weeks later!) as we entered this enormous three-storey house on the square in the very centre of town. It had been a pub, by then closed for seventeen years, with an archway underneath, which is why when we reopened the pub it was known as 'The Arch Bar'. Offices on the first floor had been closed more recently. Despite the electric light, we couldn't see half of the house, as it went back and back and back as well as up and up and up. It was huge. My father and a few men had already done some work on it, but there was a lot more to do before the move from Mullen on 7 December – a Friday, of course, for luck!

And what a miserable day moving day was, when heavy rain ensured that everything was wet as the Mullen neighbours called around with goodbye offerings and Tom Callaghan's lorry was packed with all our goods, and the house and Grandad were left behind as Aunt Baby, her husband, Brian, and their family moved in. 'Chaotic' is hardly an adequate word to describe it all.

Though Mullen was about eight miles from Ballaghaderreen, the journey traversed centuries as we left behind an old way of life for electricity, running water, stairs, a slated roof and space. We were on our way to a grand metropolis of 1,200 people, and it has remained the centre of our universe since.

✠ ✠ ✠

If priests, nuns and Brothers had been absent for much of our lives in Mullen, this was not the case in Ballaghaderreen. They were all over that small town and, unlike the God they represented, they were visible everywhere. There were the Sisters of Charity, who ran the convent national and secondary schools as well as an industrial school, which was to make an unflattering appearance in Mary Raftery's and Eoin O'Sullivan's 1999 book *Suffer the Little Children*, though we knew nothing of the children's conditions there then. There was the De La Salle Brothers' school for boys and St Nathy's secondary boarding school for boys, where all the teachers except for two laymen were priests. There was the presbytery of the Cathedral of the Assumption and St Nathy, where the administrator and his curates lived, and about three miles north of the town lived the Catholic Bishop of Achonry, James Fergus, in his 'Palace', or Edmondstown House, built in 1864 by the last of the Costello family, local landlords.

Deference was innate in the town. Men and boys meeting Brothers or priests on the street would salute them, or step aside on a footpath to let nuns pass. Apart from their superior standing as 'God's anointed', they were also a huge factor in the town's economic life, with their schools a major contributor both as employers and consumers, as was the lay, State-run vocational school. In the early 1960s the town was in serious decline, with some of its major businesses, Duffs and Flannerys for example, on a precipitous downward trajectory. There were also the creamery and Cunniffe's bacon factory, but no other major employer was there throughout the 1960s. So the contribution of schools to the town was very important.

The decline meant that the streets were so quiet we kids could play soccer on the square without interference from traffic, until the gardaí cleared us. It was so quiet in summertime that our dog Fóla, named by our father after one of the ancient names for Ireland, would sleep in the middle of the street opposite our house with little danger of disturbance by passing cars.

While education was the big business in Ballaghaderreen, there were constant rumours of a German film factory coming to the town. In St Nathy's College one of our teachers, Father Michael Giblin, in breaks from attempting to inculcate us with a love of Irish, would detail the journey of that factory, on the back of a truck, from the Ruhr in deepest Germany across the European continent to Calais, from there to Dover, then to Holyhead, Dublin and finally across Ireland until, eventually, it got stuck at the narrow bridge over the Lung river about four miles from the town. 'And it'll stay there until they widen the bridge,' he assured us in that wry way of his.

In those days to be in Ballaghaderreen was to live in hope. The focus was not on the past, or the present, but on an eternally beckoning future. Everything would be better then.

Priests were involved with every single organisation in the town, which, even as a youngster, I thought ludicrous. What had being a priest got to do with bridge or golf or whatever-you're-having-yourself? And they were on the committees, usually in the chair. I couldn't see what any of that had to do with faith.

Despite these misgivings, my own faith deepened in those years and I used to feel particularly close to God in the town's magnificent cathedral surrounded by age-old, impressive trees. The interior was dark, gloomy and comforting, as we imagine the womb, with an extraordinarily ornate high altar – built by James Pearse, father of 1916 leader Patrick – dominating all. As befits a cathedral, its liturgical ceremonies were theatrical in their flourish, particularly on Holy Saturday nights in a ceremony that went on for four hours with hundreds of candles in the darkness and a dramatic renunciation of the devil led by the bishop and many priests.

By the time we moved to Ballaghaderreen I was even more resolved on becoming a priest. My sincerity in the matter was beyond reproach as I punished my young soul scrupulously for frequently imagined sins, mostly of omission. I was young and holy and attending the Brothers' school, where penance was our daily lot whether we liked it or not. No one liked it.

Coming from a small mixed school in Mullen, where we had one female teacher for most of my time there, then two, and which was not without its severities at times, was no preparation for the De La Salle Boys' School in Ballaghaderreen. The regime was violent and brutal – and included sexual abuse, though I didn't know that at the time. Coming from where I had been, where I was, to quote Patrick Kavanagh, 'king of rock and stone and every blooming thing', to that was a deep shock. I was intimidated by it all and fell behind academically until I realised that one sure method of survival in those cruelty stakes was to do well at my studies.

Another revelation was how brutal my classmates could be to one another, though I escaped that myself. The atmosphere of all-round aggression was something I was not at all used to. Nor was sport. In Mullen school there was no sport. So I lacked the basic skills when it came to Gaelic football, for instance. I could not pick up the ball with my foot or solo, and I resisted playing the game to avoid making a fool of myself. It also meant I bled less. In those years I was cursed with seemingly endless nose bleeds, which could be set off by the mildest contact.

I also had a moral problem with aggression on the sports field. I could not reconcile my then deeply held beliefs with aggressively tackling someone to get the ball off them, not least as I couldn't care less if they held onto it. More difficult still, I could not understand these men of God, these Brothers, already brutal in class, shouting from the sidelines at us to 'get' someone or 'take the ball off him'. I used to ask myself how that could be Christian. So, I ended up in the backs. There, I was defending, and that suited my moral outlook. I was protecting. It helped that, for the most part, it didn't require as many skills.

Ballaghaderreen in those years was probably the most monocultural and least diverse place I have ever lived. In the entire town there was just one (white) Protestant family; all others were white Catholics. Mass attendance levels were stratospheric, clearly influenced by the hugely disproportionate number of clergy in the town and the Church's prime role in the local economy.

That Protestant (Church of Ireland) family were the Fitzgeralds and the father was our local GP. There was just one son and he, Steven, sat beside me in the Brothers' school. He was excused from morning prayers, the Angelus, preparations for Confirmation and all school attendances at Masses. Steven was the most polite, mild-mannered boy in the school. It was bad enough that his parents insisted he wear braces on his teeth, but the idea that, including the worst ruffians in our class, it was he alone and none of the rest who was destined for Hell seemed outrageously unjust to me even then. I could not accept it and the sky didn't fall. You might say this was the beginning of a process of questioning that led me to a place where even Protestants would not go.

No sooner had I 'conquered' the Brothers and successfully accommodated myself to the sometimes brutal savagery of the atmosphere in the school, than it was time to leave and attend St Nathy's College as a day boy. Built from what had been a barracks set up following the French invasion of Killala in 1798, when General Humbert led his forces north of the town towards defeat by the British at Ballinamuck in County Longford, St Nathy's still retained much of the air of stern discipline you would find in a barracks. Conditions for boarders were spartan, a euphemism for sustenance just about sufficient to sustain human life, with punishment to match.

Few escaped that punishment, even day boys like myself, which consisted mainly of canings across the hands. That continued until fourth year, when we were aged fifteen or sixteen. Most priests were comparatively sparing of the rod, but some could lose control. I remember one priest losing his temper with a classmate of mine and kicking him physically, brutally out of the class after thrashing him with a cane. The same small man was regarded by all of us as someone to avoid since he had a reputation for 'interfering' with boys, not that any of us then were clear on what exactly that meant.

In the years since, I have heard allegations of sexual abuse against at least one priest from my time at the college but, for my own part, I never witnessed any such abuse while attending there. Indeed, I remember many of my priest-teachers with affection, both as educators and as people. Despite this, I never excelled at St Nathy's. As a day boy I always felt like something of an outlier there, outside the loop, but I never wanted to be a boarder either. Ironically, it was while I was there that my relationship with religion began to take a radical turn for the worse, but not because of anything I witnessed or experienced at the college.

I have often said that had I remained at Mullen school until I finished sixth class, Mrs Forde would have made me a priest. It is probable that, had I been a boarder at St Nathy's, the same might have happened. Whether I would have survived the subsequent seven-year formation at Maynooth or, worse, whether I would even have retained my faith after ordination are other matters. There can hardly be a more difficult situation than to be a priest who has lost faith.

In my early teen years my religion questions were mainly focused on the institutional Church. Why was there so much bullying and hectoring of people generally on the part of some priests and other religious figures when that was so clearly not Christian? How could men of the cloth be so physically cruel, even gratuitously so, in the classroom? How could all the comparative wealth and worldly power of the Church be justified?

I realised early on that my greatest difficulty in becoming a priest would be in taking a vow of obedience. I had seen enough to know I would do what was asked of me only if I believed it to be right. I had come to believe that many of the priests teaching at St Nathy's were there because they were told to be there, not out of vocation or choice.

The Second Vatican Council (commonly called Vatican II) had begun in 1962 and, every Sunday when he was back in Ballaghaderreen from Rome, Bishop James Fergus would celebrate the Sunday Children's Mass at 10 a.m. He would tell us 'boys and girls', in his gentle, reassuring way, about what was happening at that council and the changes it might bring. It meant that through my early teens I took a keen interest in goings-on at the council and was excited by the opening up of the Catholic Church to the world, a situation that the council ushered in, and, particularly, by the document *Gaudium et Spes* (Joy and Hope), the Pastoral Constitution on the Church in the Modern World, published in 1965. I read about it in pamphlets and in reports in *The Irish Press*.

While at St Nathy's I found that document and studied it in detail. It reshaped my Catholicism into something much more proactive. *Gaudium et Spes* educated me in ideas of social justice, to which I was strongly drawn. This was also probably down to the house I came from, which very much belonged to the social democratic wing of Fianna Fáil. I remember the great satisfaction my father got from that aspect of his job as health inspector, going around Roscommon condemning houses as uninhabitable or in need of refurbishment, so the people living in them could successfully apply for grants to rebuild. I remember being with him as he drove along the by-ways and boreens of our county, encouraging people living in run-down cottages – somewhere a thatched roof had caved in – to avail themselves of these grants.

My father was determined to change their living conditions. He was a peculiar political hybrid. Unusually for a devoted Fianna Fáil man, he had a painting of James Connolly, one of the founders of the Irish Labour Party, on one of the upstairs landings in our house. Then, some years later, when he became a county councillor, he wrote in a letter to the *Roscommon Herald* about how 'My Fianna Fáil colleagues don't know whether I'm for them or against them. Sometimes I'm both, which isn't easy, but for a man of my capabilities it is no bother.'

As a public servant, he was not allowed to stand for election for most of his career, despite being privately very active in Fianna Fáil locally. However, the Fine Gael-led coalition of the mid-1970s changed that law, allowing him to stand for election, which he did successfully for Fianna Fáil in the 1974 local elections for the first time. In a later election campaign, his slogan was 'Vote McGarry No. 1 – the man who put a roof over everyone who needed it in County Roscommon.' As always with my father, there was some truth lurking there.

Throughout my teens, Catholicism dominated my thinking, including on questions of sexual behaviour, and I was comfortable with that, particularly with its emphasis on respect for women and the dignity of every person. But our sex education classes at St Nathy's were, literally, comical. This was hardly surprising because it involved a celibate instructing the virginal in what was wholly hypothetical. We had to submit anonymous notes to the priest concerning our queries about matters sexual. I will always remember his response to one such note. He read it aloud, as he did all notes. 'How long does it [intercourse] last, Father?' To which he replied, 'I don't know, boy. I never experienced it.'

What we boys knew about sex we learned from one another.

More broadly, where the Church was concerned, I was very excited by the sort of future Vatican II indicated for my still-probable life as a priest. It also saw the gloom in our cathedral dispelled by bright colours, with the priest facing us at Mass and speaking in English or Irish instead of Latin. I was, myself, the first lay reader at a Mass in that cathedral and in the diocese of Achonry. I was relaxed with a Church that seemed to be losing so many of its edges, one that was easing into and becoming comfortable with the world in which we actually lived. I was excited about where this seemed to be headed, particularly when it came to social action by the Church on behalf of the poor and less well off, by then my chosen people.

But in July 1968, my Inter Cert year, we had the *Humanae Vitae* encyclical from Pope Paul VI upholding a ban on artificial means of contraception, despite the view of a great majority of a commission he had set up on the matter recommending change in that teaching. I followed that debate closely, and the fallout – the rejection of the encyclical by so many clergy I admired and by so many liberal lay Catholics. It seemed to draw a line under forward movement in the Church, bringing it back to its more familiar, authoritarian ways. That was the issue, more than contraception, and I knew where I stood. In conscience, I could not accept that encyclical.

This was just one significant event in a year that shaped so much of my thinking for life on so many matters: the assassination of Martin Luther King in April reinforced my deep conviction of the equality of all human beings, further reinforced by the sickening assassination of Bobby Kennedy that June. His murder was a reminder, as if that was necessary, of the tears and grief in our house in November 1963 when his brother John F. was assassinated in Dallas. The Soviet invasion of Prague in August 1968 deepened my belief in democracy and opposition to totalitarianism, whatever it might be called or call itself and wherever it might be found in politics or religion. And then there were the events of 5 October 1968 in Derry city, when peaceful civil rights marchers were ruthlessly hammered in the streets by an out-of-control Royal Ulster Constabulary (RUC). As with many in the Republic of Ireland from my background, the events of that day struck a deep, primal chord in me, with their resonances of centuries of oppression of Irish Catholics by ruthless British regimes. Yet, even then, I did not believe violence was the way forward in Ireland. I never have. I had every confidence that the civil rights movement in Northern Ireland and its inspired leadership would overcome some day.

Thrown into the mix of that pivotal year in my young life, Pope Paul VI's *Humanae Vitae* encyclical was like a depth charge where so many of my Catholic convictions were concerned. Fearful of change, that Hamlet of popes vacillated before coming down in favour of the status quo. The prospect of change, even dropping slow, seemed to stall.

Still, as my teens progressed and I fell in and out of love, the idea of priesthood was never far from my mind. Yet there I was, almost fifteen and rejecting a teaching of the pope on the basis of what seemed reasonable. Clearly, I was on a slippery slope. I began to drift further and further away from the institutional Church while retaining a belief in Jesus and his social teachings. However, even His divinity soon proved a problem. I began to have great difficulty with the entirety of redemption theology, the teaching that Jesus came to this earth to placate a God, his father, over a disobedient humanity by taking on his own head the burden of human sinfulness and purging it through his own death to win back the favour of his father. Seriously?

That theology soon seemed to me cumbersome and 'worked', constructed to fit a preconceived idea into which I could no longer buy. While I continued to pray and attend Mass, even as these doubts assailed me, soon my threadbare belief in the divinity of Jesus extended to include divinity itself. At Christian Doctrine class in St Nathy's one day, I asked the priest conducting it, 'Father, how do we know there is a God?' He looked at me as though I had asked him, 'Father, how do we know there is air?' It was clear he thought I had just set out to cause trouble and he became angry. I repeated the question in a milder manner, to emphasise that I was being genuine. He still didn't get it. Belief in God was so real for him.

It struck me that he probably had never stopped to ask whether or not there was a God. The question most likely seemed nonsensical to him as, self-evidently, God's reality was everywhere: 'Can't you see?' But I could no longer 'see'. Yet I struggled to hold on to God because I knew that along with Him would go deep and cherished meaning from my life. I would lose an entire dimension to my being. God had been so central to my life for so long, at the very core of my thinking self. I began to feel bereft as my doubts grew ever more solid. I had entered what became a prolonged process of bereavement.

In the meantime, not only did I keep up religious practice, but I was asked by two priests at St Nathy's whether I had considered becoming a priest. I attended a few charismatic movement gatherings in the town where some people spoke in tongues, but I was not convinced. Yet, even as my doubts grew, I became increasingly careful not to challenge other people's faith as I already had intimations of what that loss would mean for them too.

I have rarely ever challenged the faith of other people, whatever their religion. When I have done so, it has been because some begin to insist that the rest of us live by their beliefs, as individuals or as a society, whether we share their beliefs or not. In time I would come to see each faith, or indeed the lack of it, as a valid cultural expression of a people's understanding of this existence. On a Dublin street one day I realised I was walking on glass blocks over a basement. They let the light in at various angles, all of them true. It struck me that they represented a good metaphor for the various religions, with each block providing a unique perspective on the reality above and below.

Despite all this inner turmoil, the shreds of faith remaining – its social justice element in particular – spurred me to take a dramatic step when I was seventeen. I helped set up a youth club in Ballaghaderreen. There was nothing for the young people of the town to do that particular summer of 1970. The idea came to me and I felt it was what I should do, although I was mortified at what it would entail, calling a meeting of the young people of the town and speaking in public before them. But I did it anyway and we set up a committee, of which I was elected president. Soon we were rocking through what became one of the most exhilarating years of my life. We organised our own dances (hops), had charity walks, packed fruit to raise funds for a clubhouse, wrote and staged our own Christmas show, arranged bus trips to football matches and opened our own shop.

It was after our first 'hop', held in September that year as a farewell to colleagues returning to boarding schools, that I first came up against certain 'attitudes' in the town. Loads of buns, cakes, biscuits and sweets were left over afterwards and we decided to bring them to the Tinker (later 'Itinerant', later 'Traveller') children, then living in tents out the road beside the town dump. I was not prepared for the squalor and misery we met there. At our next youth club meeting I suggested we organise a survey of the camp and prepared a questionnaire to establish what income people lived on in those camps. I wrote up a report on what we found and sent it to the *Roscommon Herald* with an appeal to the people of the town for money or clothes or whatever they could offer, to help the Tinkers, and we would distribute what was donated. It was met with a grim silence, except from the lovely Mrs Burns, who lived across the street from our house. She offered clothes. There was no more.

It was not a good time in the town. Not long beforehand it had been announced that the much-talked-about German film factory was not coming after all, and our local football team had been knocked out of the county championship. One football-mad local stalwart was heard to say, 'The factory's gone, the football's gone, and McGarry [me!] brings the Tinkers.' I didn't, but my father ensured that houses were built for some of those desperate families in Ballaghaderreen.

A side-effect of that article in the *Roscommon Herald* was that the paper's editor, Micheál O'Callaghan, a friend of my father's, called to our house and asked whether I would like to be a journalist. I had already been thinking that way. When you're losing your convictions about most things, what's left?

My father said, 'No. He'll go to university first.'

Religion, of course, did not come into anything we did at the youth club. From the beginning I was determined that ours would be the one club or society in the town where there was no religious involvement, even though the Sisters of Charity were so good as to lend us their hall for meetings and to pack fruit to raise funds. I always got on with nuns. The youth club grew rapidly to involve a great many teenagers in the town but then hit a plateau. It became clear that some parents were worried about what we might be getting up to and I realised it was time for some realpolitik. We would have to have some clergy involvement to win over the confidence of those uncertain mothers and fathers. So we decided to ask a younger priest in St Nathy's and a younger nun at the convent to be patrons of the youth club. I assured both that all they would have to do was allow us to name them publicly as such, and they agreed.

It helped where our membership was concerned that the priest was Father Jimmy Colleran, who never subjected any of us, his pupils at St Nathy's, to corporal punishment. He was also hugely into sport and had introduced basketball at the college, as well as starting a magazine (*The Torch*). Remarkably, he also helped build a swimming pool at a turn in our local river, the Lung, for young people in the town. And we were all in love with Sister Immaculata, who was not much older than ourselves. Their being patrons worked, and soon there was hardly a young person over twelve in the town who wasn't a member of our club.

It was all such a tremendous experience, personally, and the satisfaction was immense. I remember, during Christmas week of that year, going up to the local hall one evening for a rehearsal of our show, *Christmas Frolics*, most of which I had written, cast and was directing. There was a stunning sunset over Bockagh Hill behind the town, with streaks of deep red across the sky's deepening blue on that crisp afternoon defined by a frosty air. I thought I would burst with happiness. I wanted to get on my knees right there on the street and thank the great God, who might yet be presiding over all of that munificence. I also began to understand another reason why humanity may have invented the divine, if it had: to have a focus for expressions of gratitude to the transcendent just for being. Staring at the descending sun I held fast and allowed a wave of emotion to wash over and through me. It felt great to be so alive.

As a representative of the youth club, I was allowed to attend meetings of the town's new parish pastoral council. At the time Ballaghaderreen was in uproar over plans by the bishop and priests to remove all the trees from around the cathedral, those stunningly beautiful mature oak and beech, which they planned to replace with a car park. It would leave the cathedral naked in the middle of a vast tarmacadamed space, a Neo-Gothic protrusion in a desert of black. I stood up at the meeting when it came up for discussion and, with all the nervous confidence of my years, denounced their plan a mite too forcefully and so, probably, distracted from the substance of what I was saying. I told them the people of the town were furious about it all and did not want it to go ahead, which was true. When I sat down, there was silence. Not one person on the council rose to agree with me, including many whom I knew to be deeply opposed to what the clergy planned. They had told me so. I could not understand their silence then and was deeply disappointed at what I saw as their lack of backbone. There was no further discussion on the topic and all those beautiful trees were destroyed. I was too young then to understand that many of my fellow council members were economically dependent on the clergy for employment or business or both.

I did have one opportunity for petty revenge and I took it. I had written a sketch for our *Christmas Frolics* concert in which there was a news bulletin with a final story that read 'And Ballaghaderreen's contribution to Conservation Year 1970 has been to knock down all the trees around its Cathedral.' It did not go down well with one woman in the audience. She walked out. But then, almost all her children were priests, Brothers or nuns.

✠ ✠ ✠

Spiritually I was now increasingly without form, if not void. I only had questions. No answers seemed adequate. I was, you might say, ready for university. During my undergraduate years in Galway, I read widely and devoured material in the hope of reconnecting with a God who, increasingly, was absent. In earlier years at St Nathy's I had been excited when I first came upon Thomas Aquinas's five proofs for the existence of God, until I discovered they were proofs only for the probability of such an existence. One stifling student summer in the backstairs of an apartment complex opposite the United Nations (UN) building in New York, where I was working as 'vacation relief', I waded through Pierre Teilhard de Chardin's *The Phenomenon of Man* and a Penguin edition of St Augustine's *The City of God*. I would wander into churches wherever I was in those years, hoping to find 'something'.

At university in Galway I studied philosophy but abandoned it after a year because it seemed no more than a supermarket of ideas, each begging 'Buy me. Believe in me.' An impoverished colleague on that philosophy course stole a book on ethics, which he couldn't afford. Later in the year I asked him whether, having read the book, he had returned it. He said no. I asked whether he needed further proof of the uselessness of philosophy. I was being 'lost' and I knew it. The most helpful book I came across in those years was by Catholic theologian and priest Hans Küng. I still have his *On Being a Christian*, even though it too failed to stem my ebbing faith. Years later I interviewed Küng himself and discovered that it was indeed true that you should not meet your heroes. He came across as a self-satisfied, arrogant man.

By second year at university I had stopped attending Mass altogether. I would go to meetings at suburban houses in Galway and at the university of groups such as the US-based evangelical Campus Crusade for Christ, the Charismatic Renewal Movement, the Bahá'í and the Moonies, followers of Sun Myung Moon. There were others too. All preached abandonment to faith. All were friendly and all offered that familiar welcome: 'Wipe your feet on the mat and leave your mind at the door.'

But I could never leave my mind at the door. This soon meant that I believed in just 70 per cent of the Ten Commandments. The first three, being centred on God, were now not relevant, although I could still believe that honouring parents, not killing, not being party to adultery, not stealing, not lying and not coveting my neighbour's things or his/her partner were necessary and good guidance for life. Add in the UN Declaration on Human Rights with its emphasis on the dignity of the individual, which I had been taught all along as part of my Catholic tradition, and that was me as I arrived at the foothills of adulthood: a priest without a Church, a believer without a god.

I missed, deeply, the intimacy with God I had once had. I missed above all the extraordinary extra dimension and depth He had added to my life, the solid assurance, the shape to this existence, the direction, the stimulus, the happiness. Without God my spirit felt so flat at times that it was like a wet newspaper stuck to a damp pavement unable to lift itself, whatever the effort. I lost God with deep reluctance. I moved on eventually, having no alternative and as one does after an irrevocably broken relationship.

I was a very active student at university in Galway, whether in politics, journalism, drama or debating – with a brief attempt at mountaineering. I loved my time there. I learned to live without answers to the big questions but with strong convictions about this life, about how we should relate to one another, against which I 'sin' regularly. I owe most of those convictions to the Catholicism that shaped me. It has left me with some of the things I most aspire to have: a clear conscience; a strong sense of social justice; respect for the person; compassion; an attachment to family, friends and community. And I have also learned to forgive myself, frequently, and to start again. And to forgive others too – most of the time!

This has made me into that peculiar hybrid, an Irish Catholic agnostic. Irish and Catholic through cultural background; agnostic through lack of conviction. When I went for the job as Religious Affairs Correspondent of *The Irish Times* in 1997, I told my interviewers I was an agnostic and asked, 'Would you appoint a member of a political party as the newspaper's political correspondent?'

I don't know whether the question proved important, but I got the job.

3

Mary's Bridge Too Far

It is a truth rarely acknowledged that people from deeply rooted communities can end up meeting relatives in the most unexpected circumstances. 'Surprise' hardly does justice to my reaction in January 1998 at the reception following a service in Dublin's St Patrick's Cathedral when Ireland's new president, Mary McAleese, walked towards me, hand outstretched, and said, 'Hello, Patsy McGarry, I'm related to you.' I had never met her before. I had not even voted for her. Her Roscommon roots and mine intersected with my maternal great-grandmother's Flanagan family, a member of which, Father Michael Flanagan, was chaplain to the First Dáil. He opened its proceedings with a prayer at Dublin's Mansion House in January 1919.

My delight in discovering I was related to Ireland's eighth president was soon tempered as I quickly discovered that a substantial cohort of the population of County Roscommon, where her father, Paddy Leneghan, came from, were making similar claims. Her Roscommon ancestors took seriously the biblical injunction to 'increase and multiply', while she herself was the eldest of nine children.

I may not have met Mary McAleese before that, but she had already provided me with my first scoop as Religious Affairs

Correspondent of *The Irish Times*. Just over a month earlier, on that routine Sunday morning of 7 December 1997 in the old *Irish Times* newsroom off Fleet Street in Dublin, there was no great promise of anything about to happen. Then my phone rang. It was a Church of Ireland contact. She was very excited. 'Patsy, Patsy, the new president, Mary McAleese, will be attending the Eucharist service in Christ Church this morning. Herself and her husband, and we don't know what she is going to do.'

McAleese had been inaugurated as Ireland's newest president less than a month beforehand and had announced that the theme of her term in office would be 'building bridges'. I asked my source, by then barely able to contain herself, whether it was known if the president planned on taking Communion at the service, something Catholics were forbidden to do in Protestant churches. 'I don't know,' was the reply, 'but in her time as president, Mary Robinson never attended a Eucharist in Christ Church, even though her husband [Nick] is Church of Ireland.'

It seemed clear that Mary McAleese, a Catholic from Belfast, was planning to take Communion in Christ Church Cathedral, seat of the Church of Ireland united dioceses of Dublin and Glendalough. All hell would break loose, and I had to be there.

I told colleagues on the news desk and then crossed to the picture desk, where photographer Frank Miller was on duty. He loaded up with gear and the two of us crossed the city on foot through Temple Bar to Christ Church, picking our way through the detritus of the night before – where many, obviously, had celebrated not wisely but too well.

We arrived in the cathedral before the 11 o'clock service was to begin. We went up a side aisle of that wonderful building, so redolent of histories past and now about to witness history present. Or so we hoped. It would be a great story, on so many levels, but not least against the background of ongoing peace talks in Belfast. The cathedral was filling up but there was no sign of President McAleese.

Arriving near the top, Frank poised his camera on a tripod, discreetly and to one side. As is customary prior to such services in Christ Church and elsewhere in the Church of Ireland, a clergyman, in this case Canon John Bartlett, told the assembling congregation that those present from other Christian traditions who regularly took Communion were welcome to do so at the service. It was then McAleese arrived with her husband, Martin, and their children. The family group was accompanied by the dean of Christ Church, John Paterson. They sat in a pew towards the front. Also in attendance were British Ambassador Veronica Sutherland, Lord Mayor of Dublin John Stafford, Mayor of Warrington Roy Humphreys and the MP for Tatton, former BBC correspondent Martin Bell.

Yes, there was definitely something going on.

Frank and I waited, out of sight and to one side, as the service got under way. There is no experience in journalism quite like the scent of being on a big story about to happen. It has been said that the practice of art is about living more intensely; so is being a reporter/photographer present at a moment in history. There we two were, concentrating wonderfully.

President McAleese, her husband and their children meanwhile were clearly appreciating the splendid cathedral choir as it sang the 'Credo' in Latin from Schubert's Mass in G major. After that, Church of Ireland Archbishop of Dublin Walton Empey spoke of the importance of the president's theme of bridge-building. It was 'hugely important in this land at this time, especially when another sectarian murder has taken place'. This was a reference to the death of Gerry Devlin (36) at St Enda's GAA club in Glengormley, Belfast, the previous Friday. The Loyalist Volunteer Force had been blamed. Archbishop Empey told McAleese that she and her family were prayed for every Sunday in every Church of Ireland church in the State.

In his homily, former Beirut hostage Terry Waite, patron of the Warrington Male Voice Choir, which also sang at the service, spoke of how a resolve to build bridges of understanding and friendship with Ireland developed after the IRA bombings there. On 20 March 1993 two young boys, Johnathan Ball and Tim Parry, had been killed in the explosion at Warrington in north-west England. The second reading was by Dr Kenneth Milne, Church of Ireland representative on an inter-Church study on sectarianism chaired by the president.

Clearly, all this was prelude. The context was acute. Almost five months earlier, on Friday 18 July, Gerry Adams and Martin McGuinness had called on the IRA to renew its ceasefire. A ceasefire announced in 1994 had ended in February 1996, when a huge IRA bomb was exploded at Canary Wharf in London, killing two people and doing enormous damage to property. In June that year Provisional IRA members murdered Garda Jerry McCabe at Adare, County Limerick, during a robbery of a post office truck on its cash delivery. The following week a bomb was set off in Manchester, injuring 212 people and destroying huge areas of the city centre.

However, the election of a new Labour government in May 1997 in the UK, led by Tony Blair, followed by the election of a new Fianna Fáil-led coalition in the Republic, led by Bertie Ahern, seemed to offer new hope. On Saturday, 20 July 1997, the IRA responded to the call from Adams and McGuinness, and announced that it was renewing its ceasefire. Then, on 9 September 1997 Sinn Féin joined the multi-party peace talks under way at Stormont. Almost a month before the service at Dublin's Christ Church attended by President McAleese, in a radio interview on the tenth anniversary of the IRA Enniskillen cenotaph bombing, which killed eleven people (on 8 November 1987), Adams said he was 'deeply sorry about what happened'.

This was the context in which Frank and I lay poised, waiting. What President McAleese seemed about to do would have great political as well as religious significance. During an at-times brutal campaign before her election the previous month, she had been portrayed, bitterly and inaccurately, as a right-wing Catholic. That she – the first Northern Ireland-born, Belfast-born President of Ireland – should take Communion at a Church of Ireland Eucharist as one of her first acts in the role would be momentous in its implications, if it happened.

And then it did.

We couldn't possibly have anticipated the fallout.

✠ ✠ ✠

My motivation for applying to be Religious Affairs Correspondent of *The Irish Times* earlier that year was political, not religious. My experience in print journalism to that point had been writing about politics, and I was determined to hold religious leaders to account in the same way as their political counterparts were: respectfully but without deference. That religion and politics should come together so significantly in a single event was not something I had expected to occur less than nine months into the role. That it happened in Christ Church might have seemed like destiny to someone of a more supernatural cast of mind.

Coming from such a monocultural society as I did in Roscommon, I had a particular interest in Protestants – the only minority I knew. They were few and interesting where I came from. Among them was Douglas Hyde, first president of Ireland, who was buried about six miles from Ballaghaderreen in the old Church of Ireland graveyard at Portahard. He grew up nearby, where his father had been pastor. Hyde was home-educated and learned his Irish from the local people in that area of north-west Roscommon, which was still Irish-speaking towards the end of the nineteenth century.

In our house Hyde's name was writ large. In 1893 he was co-founder in Dublin of the Gaelic League, or Conradh na Gaeilge as it was known in Irish. My father was a member and spoke Irish on every occasion he could until he died in 1999. He wore the old gold fáinne all his life, an indicator that he spoke Irish.

Such was Hyde's standing in our house that when the last of my six siblings arrived in 1965, I suggested to my parents that they should call him Douglas, and they did. I was twelve then and knew everything. It probably helped that they were running out of ideas for names anyhow. Calling my new brother this would not be without difficulty. When it came to his baptism in Ballaghaderreen, the priest, a contrary, belligerent man of the cloth, almost exploded. 'We can't call him that, it's a Protestant name,' he pronounced. My blessed and quick-witted mother rescued the situation. 'We'll call him Peter Douglas then, after the first pope and the first president.' Father McVann calmed down and it was done, but we only ever knew our baby brother as Douglas.

In 1968 it was decided locally to mark the seventy-fifth anniversary of the Gaelic League that summer with a ceremony at Hyde's grave. My father and Father Michael Giblin, who taught Irish at St Nathy's, recruited a gang of us kids to clean up the graveyard in advance. It was overrun with weeds and briars, and Hyde's own grave was sunken, its headstone covered in moss and lichens. I remember being outraged that a man who had done so much to create the identity which led to the creation of the Irish State should have been so neglected in death. I was also keenly aware of the pivotal role Protestants, particularly members of the Church of Ireland, had played in Irish history. Parnell had been key to the success of the Land League and the Home Rule movement of the later nineteenth century. There was also the Anglo-Irish Literary Revival of that period and afterwards, involving Protestants W.B. Yeats, Lady Gregory, John M. Synge, Sean O'Casey, and later George Bernard Shaw and Samuel Beckett – all from a Church of Ireland background.

No petty people indeed. 'We are one of the great stocks of Europe; we are the people of Burke; we are the people of Grattan; we are the people of Swift, the people of Emmet, the people of Parnell. We have created most of the modern literature of this country. We have created the best of its political intelligence,' as Yeats told the Seanad of the new Free State in 1925 when he opposed plans to outlaw divorce, which until then had been allowed under the new State's constitution. Divorce was banned in the Catholic Church, which by 1925 was beginning to see its teachings reflected in the laws of the new Ireland, whatever the beliefs of the country's minorities. It seemed so unjust, particularly to those Protestants without whom there might not have been any Irish identity.

As a teenager, with a pronounced tendency to spontaneous combustion at perceived injustice, this reached a new intensity when I discovered that at Hyde's funeral in 1949 the entire government of the day sat in their State cars outside St Patrick's Cathedral in Dublin rather than risk their Catholic souls by going inside. Just two Catholics ventured into the church for the service: the then French ambassador and the poet Austin Clarke, who wrote, caustically, in his poem 'Burial of an Irish President' about John Costello and the Irish Cabinet 'hiding around the corner ... dreading Our Father in English'.

It was then a reserved sin in most Catholic dioceses, pardonable only by a bishop, for a Catholic to attend a Protestant service.

Fianna Fáil was represented at Douglas Hyde's funeral by Erskine H. Childers, a member of the Church of Ireland who later became Ireland's fourth president. His then party leader, Éamon de Valera, attended the burial at Portahard with the then President of Ireland and Hyde's successor, Seán T. Ó Ceallaigh. Neither entered the church but stayed in the graveyard 'right to the end of the service', as *The Irish Times* noted at the time.

The same religious apartheid had operated at Hyde's inauguration in 1938. It was preceded by separate religious services: one at the (Catholic) Pro-Cathedral in Dublin, attended by Taoiseach de Valera, his government, the opposition, the diplomatic corps and other State representatives; the other at St Patrick's Cathedral, attended by President Hyde and some fellow Church of Ireland members. All later attended a reception in Dublin Castle, which was hailed as a great advance in ecumenical relations.

In 1968 Éamon de Valera was president and expected to attend the ceremony in Portahard at Hyde's grave to mark the seventy-fifth anniversary of the Gaelic League. However, owing to some glitch in his schedule he didn't make it on the day, although he made a private visit some days later. My father and some others were told in advance, so most of our household were there when he arrived in this enormous black Rolls-Royce, the likes of which I had never seen before. By then de Valera was a very old man to my eyes and had to be guided by an aide-de-camp to Hyde's graveside, where he paused for a few moments, tall, stiff, pale and seemingly absent even as he exchanged mild pleasantries with people. He was not distracted by my bored three-year-old baby brother Douglas, who mortified my mother as he disturbed the solemnity of the event by roaring throughout. In my life I had never seen my father as silent, or for so long. To him de Valera was as near divine as any man could become.

The visit was brief and de Valera was soon gone. It was the only time I saw him in person.

This awareness of how the new Irish State treated minorities, particularly its Protestant minority, remained with me as I grew older. In the later 1980s, as an annual Douglas Hyde Conference was being planned by Roscommon County Council for Ballaghaderreen, I wrote an article about Hyde, his neglect and contribution to Ireland, for *Magill* magazine. It was greatly facilitated by details and photographs given to me by Hyde's grandson, the late Douglas Sealy, then living in Howth, County Dublin.

That spurred me on to research and write another article for *Magill*, looking at the experience of the Church of Ireland minority in this State from 1922 to 1988. Members of the Church of Ireland have always been the largest Protestant minority in this State, usually numbering around 125,000. The Church had reached an accommodation with the Irish State in the decades since it was established in 1922. In May of that year, then Church of Ireland Archbishop of Dublin John Gregg went to see Michael Collins following the murders of thirteen Protestants in west Cork's Bandon valley to ask whether the Protestant minority should stay on in the new Ireland. Collins assured him that the new Free State government would maintain civil and religious liberty for all. Those Protestants who remained settled into a comfortable (in the main), if separate, existence, where, under the radar of the less-than-sympathetic ethos of a dominant Catholic Church, they avoided the limelight assiduously while the State helped sustain their schools and hospitals.

My article was published in February 1989 under the title 'Pressure on Protestants', with the subheading: 'How the Protestant population in the south has been reduced by two-thirds in 60 years and how again and again the Protestant ethos has been assaulted.' One event stood out in this rapid decline among Irish Protestants in the new State during the twentieth century – the introduction by the Catholic Church in 1907 of its 'Ne Temere' decree, which insisted that before a Catholic could marry a Protestant, both partners had to give an undertaking in writing that all resulting children would be raised Catholic. Even with that done, the marriage ceremony was to take place in a side chapel in a Catholic church. Up to that time in Ireland, it had been the custom in mixed marriages that the boys would be raised in their father's denomination and the girls in their mother's. But not in twentieth-century Ireland, at least until 1970 (from then, only the Catholic partner was required to give a commitment to raise the children as Catholics).

The effect of 'Ne Temere' on the Church of Ireland population in the new Irish State was dramatic. A statistic provided by the Church of Ireland Dean of Cashel, the late David Woodworth, in 1989 was indicative. He told me about four Church of Ireland families in the south-west, each of which had thirteen children in the 1930s, and how by the 1980s not one of their descendants was Church of Ireland. I described this in the article as 'bloodless genocide'. It seemed accurate.

This lesser position of Protestants in the new Irish State due to the 'Ne Temere' decree was underlined in the infamous 'Tilson case' of 1950. Then President of the High Court Justice Gavan Duffy held that Article 44 of the 1937 Constitution, recognising the 'special position' of the Catholic Church in Ireland, elevated Catholic claims on children over those of a Protestant partner in a 'mixed marriage'. Ernest Tilson was Protestant, while his wife, Mary Barnes, was Catholic. They had four children, some of whom Tilson insisted be educated as Protestant, though, as required by the 'Ne Temere' decree, both parents had signed an undertaking on their marriage in 1941 that any children they had would be raised Catholic. Tilson challenged this legally, right up to the Supreme Court, but lost on the grounds that the right to provide education for their children was the responsibility of both parents, not just the father, and that one parent could not unilaterally decide to ignore a pre-nuptial agreement.

Shortly after that *Magill* article appeared, I was contacted by then Church of Ireland Archbishop of Dublin Donald Caird, an Irish-language enthusiast who conducted services in Portahard church at the start of what became annual Douglas Hyde conferences there; he also gave lectures himself at these conferences. Archbishop Caird was nervous that the article might convey an impression that members of his Church were unhappy with how they were being treated in Ireland and this was not so, he insisted. To allay his concerns, I wrote an article for *The Irish Press* conveying his positive views, but what he was really saying to me was 'do not disturb'. Protestants in southern Ireland had worked out a comfortable modus vivendi in the new State and did not want to be a focus of any attention.

This 'do not disturb' position of its small Protestant minority was not unique to Ireland. On a visit to predominantly Muslim Iran in 2000, I came across the same mentality when interviewing an Armenian priest there. Father Jacob Arakelian was a charming, wily old fox. He was seventy-seven and parish priest of the Armenian St Bethlehem Church of New Julfa in beautiful Isfahan, central Iran. He hadn't a word of English but proved an excellent communicator. Of Iran's estimated 67 million people then, 0.5 per cent were Christian, and of those about 40,000 were Armenian – Iran's largest Christian denomination. Another Armenian to whom I had spoken, on being assured he would not be named, said the Muslims looked down on them. Armenians could not get government jobs and tended to stay among themselves and employ one another. Since the 1979

Iranian Revolution more and more Armenians were emigrating, he said, just like the Protestant minority in Ireland in the early decades after independence in 1922. Generally, however, religious minorities in Iran experienced no real violence, he said. It was just the attitude. However, as far as Father Jacob was concerned, all was for the best in what was the best of all possible worlds for Armenians in Isfahan.

Similar sentiments of gratitude, for public consumption, were expressed by a group of Irish Dominican priests I interviewed in predominantly Muslim Istanbul some years later. Small minorities like to keep their heads down. In 1999, when I was reporting on the influx of Muslim Albanian Kosovar refugees into an unwelcoming and mainly Christian Orthodox North Macedonia, I interviewed the then head of North Atlantic Treaty Organization (NATO) forces there, Sir Mike Jackson. He was based in North Macedonia's capital, Skopje. I wanted to talk to him about his role as a junior officer in Derry on Bloody Sunday 1972, when fourteen innocent people were shot dead by the British Army. He did not want to speak about that, but as we discussed Kosovo, he made the interesting observation that 'wherever minorities are in double figures there is trouble'.

Minorities in single figures rarely cause problems. Protestants in the Irish Republic have remained at about 3 per cent of the population. Throughout the twentieth century they kept well below the radar in Irish public life. Yes, there were Presidents Hyde and Childers, both Church of Ireland, but they were very much the exception in Ireland's public life – particularly when compared with that much smaller minority in Ireland, the Jewish community, whose number never went over 6,000 in the twentieth century. Yet Jewish people have played a disproportionate role in Irish life, in politics, the law and the arts. In the 1980s and 1990s, when Fine Gael's Ivan Yates was the only Protestant (Church of

Ireland) TD in Dáil Éireann, there were three Jewish TDs, one in each of the major political parties: Mervyn Taylor, a Labour Minister for Equality and Law Reform from 1993 to 1997; Alan Shatter, a TD from 1981 and a Fine Gael Minister for Justice and Defence from 2011 to 2014; and Fianna Fáil's Ben Briscoe, a TD for thirty-seven years. Briscoe succeeded his father, Bob, who had been involved in the War of Independence and was a Fianna Fáil TD for thirty-eight years. Both Briscoes were lord mayors in Dublin, as was Gerald Goldberg in Cork. In law you had Justice Hubert Wine, while David Marcus was a major figure in Irish literary life and his brother Louis Marcus held similar status as a documentary filmmaker. Louis Lentin was a theatre director, as well as working in film and television production, and his 1996 *Dear Daughter* documentary with Christine Buckley, about her abuse as a child in Dublin's Goldenbridge Orphanage, was the first major breakthrough in disclosing the institutional mistreatment of children in twentieth-century Ireland. Then you had painter Gerald Davis, who was a significant figure in the art world. The contribution of this tiny community to Irish life has been extraordinary and it highlights the degree to which the much larger Protestant community in the Republic, generally, felt cowed for most of the twentieth century by its own history on the island.

In Christ Church that December morning I wondered whether that unease was about to change.

✠ ✠ ✠

As Frank Millar and I watched from our chosen spot, all indications were that the Republic's first Northern Irish Catholic president was about to endorse, in a most public way, a key Church of Ireland belief, its understanding of the Eucharist, simultaneously expressing an ecumenical religious and political conviction.

It was a radical and bold move for the new president, who was also among the most theologically literate ever to hold that office.

Frank and I were poised like hounds awaiting the moment. It happened. The photograph and report were on the front page the following morning.

Reaction was swift. Former Senator John Robb from Ballymoney, County Antrim, a Presbyterian, was impressed. Described as 'a liberal Protestant', in 1982 he had founded the New Ireland Group, which was dedicated to shaping a cross-community vision of Ireland. That same year he was appointed to the Seanad by Taoiseach Charles Haughey and served there for seven years. He had learned and spoke Irish. In a letter to *The Irish Times*, Robb said he saw the event in Christ Church as 'heralding the coming of a truly new Ireland. A transcendent moment of reconciliation on the metaphysical journey of a sadly separated people, a symbol of hope.' He continued, 'Thoughts came of Austin Clarke's confusion and sadness when he attended the obsequies of Douglas Hyde in the old Ireland of almost sixty years ago and of how, on Sunday, had he been alive, he would surely have been rejoicing.'

Not everyone saw it that way.

The standing committee of the (Catholic) Irish Bishops Conference met, discussed the matter, and repeated Church teaching that it was 'not permissible for Roman Catholics to receive Communion in Protestant churches or at Protestant services'. They said that, in the New Year, they hoped to publish a document further clarifying issues surrounding the Eucharist and inter-Church Communion. (That would bring its own discomforts.) A spokesman said the bishops did not wish 'to censure or embarrass' the president, but 'it is hoped the issue will not arise again'. Mary McAleese's action 'took everyone by surprise,' he added.

The language of other senior Church figures was less measured. Father James McEvoy, Professor of Philosophy at St Patrick's College, Maynooth, citadel of the Catholic Church in Ireland, said of McAleese that he would find it 'repugnant if she should ever again abuse the august office which she occupies in a way which would once more embarrass the Catholic Church, by giving scandal to its members'. The then Catholic Archbishop of Dublin, Desmond Connell, not yet a cardinal, really put the cat among the pigeons through his use of one word. He said that differences between the Churches meant that for Catholics 'partaking of the Eucharist in a Protestant church is a sham'. With that word 'sham' he successfully offended all Protestants, as well as more liberal Catholics.

Mary McAleese's visit to Christ Church that morning was part of her wider plan to visit all faith communities in those early weeks of her presidency and to participate in their services where possible. As she said at the time, as president she would 'represent every single person, irrespective of their faith systems or, indeed, if they have no faith system. There will be no favourites.' She knew exactly what she was doing, theologically, but there was also a political dimension involved, which was not as well-known at the time.

Before deciding to run for the presidency, McAleese had been party to the difficult negotiations which would eventually lead to the Good Friday Agreement of April 1998. She personally knew many of the key personnel taking part in those negotiations and had been involved with the Redemptorist Peace Ministry at the Clonard monastery in Belfast that facilitated the talks between John Hume and Gerry Adams, which began the process leading to the Good Friday Agreement. A key figure there was Redemptorist priest Father Alec Reid, who was among the first to suggest that McAleese should stand for the office of president. He and others said she should run because she was a Northerner who had strong connections to the Republic from childhood. Her father came from Roscommon and she had spent many years in Dublin. Her election, should it happen, would be a tremendous boost to the confidence of Northern Ireland nationalists and would, most likely, have a positive effect on the peace process, they said. As the first president of Ireland from the province of Ulster, she would also be in a unique position to bridge the ever-growing gap between the two parts of the island.

Mary McAleese also knew a key figure on the unionist side of the negotiations. David Trimble was leader of the Ulster Unionist Party (UUP), then the main unionist party. In 1988 McAleese had been appointed director of the Institute for Professional Legal Studies at Queen's University Belfast (QUB). Another contender for the post was Trimble, who had also been acting director of the institute until her appointment. She was the first Catholic and first woman to be appointed to the position. Neither distinction pleased some in certain quarters and the issue ended up being aired in the House of Commons. Four Unionist MPs – Cecil Walker, Roy Beggs, Clifford Forsythe and John Taylor – colleagues and friends of Trimble's, put down a motion challenging McAleese's appointment. QUB then issued a statement saying that she was appointed because she was the best candidate for the job. The motion never made it to the floor of the House of Commons.

When I asked him later about his role in this, John Taylor, deputy leader of the UUP at the time of the Good Friday Agreement, couldn't recall why he did so but said, 'Someone must have put me up to it.' For his part, Trimble said he became aware of that House of Commons motion only after the event.

In 1994 Mary McAleese was appointed pro-vice chancellor of QUB, the first woman to hold that post too, and, perhaps ironically, it was a role in which she won particular favour with John Taylor. She established an outreach campus of the university in Armagh, Taylor's constituency. He complimented her on the wonderful job she had done in founding such an institution in his city. 'I was very, very impressed by her dedication to that cause. She had worked hard on Armagh,' he said. 'I could relate to her as a Protestant [he is Church of Ireland] and a unionist. She is a very strong nationalist and a very good Catholic, not a nominal one like so many these days. We worked well together,' he said. The QUB outreach centre in Armagh was officially opened in February 1997, nine months before McAleese's election as president of Ireland.

✠ ✠ ✠

The controversy around President McAleese taking Protestant Communion just grew and grew. It would be fair to say that, in advance, few would have expected the bellicose furore that followed from the more traditional elements in the Catholic Church, while, instinctively, Church of Ireland members were deeply uncomfortable at finding themselves the focus of such public attention. As well as being a minority, they already lived with the burden of a history which, for so long, had seen their Church, the established religion of the British State in Ireland, reviled for being supported by enforced tithes paid by the almost 90 per cent Catholic majority on the island as a whole, as well as the system of 'penal laws' enforced in the seventeenth and eighteenth centuries not just on Catholics but also on Presbyterians, and described by Irish-born parliamentarian and, as some would have it, father of Britain's Conservative Party, Edmund Burke, as 'a machine of wise and elaborate contrivance, as well fitted for the oppression, impoverishment and degradation of a people, and the debasement in them of human nature itself, as ever proceeded from the perverted ingenuity of man'.

It was clear that Church of Ireland poise was shaken by Mary McAleese taking Communion in Christ Church. It was also the case that Archbishop Empey, then also in the eye of the storm, was a hugely popular, warm, good-humoured, compassionate man and wonderful pastor. Following the furore that greeted Mary McAleese's actions in his church, and driven by no more than instinct, I decided to attend the Eucharist service there again on the following Sunday. It was my intuition that some more liberal Catholics would be there to take Communion as an act of solidarity with President McAleese and in support of Archbishop Empey.

When I arrived in the cathedral, there, in a pew on her own, was US Ambassador to Ireland Jean Kennedy Smith, a member of the most famous Irish-American Catholic family and another key figure in the ongoing peace talks. When it came to the moment, she rose from her pew, proceeded up the centre aisle and took Communion. After the service, and with some uncertainty, I approached her for a comment. She was delighted to talk. She had attended Christ Church the previous Christmas Day with her son Stephen and had also taken Communion then. She intended to do so again on the coming Christmas Day, she said. In the US she had been attending Protestant churches and taking Communion for years before her appointment to Ireland. In New York she frequently attended the Presbyterian church on Fifth Avenue, near her apartment, she said. She had decided, in conscience, as a Catholic, that it was a good thing to do. She also felt it was very important as a sign of respect for other people's beliefs and a way of drawing all together. 'Religion, after all, is about bringing people together,' she said. 'We all have our own way of going to God.' She also regarded Archbishop Empey as a friend.

Meanwhile, Archbishop Connell had established a source which he blamed for the strongly negative reaction to his use of the word 'sham' in describing a Catholic taking Communion in a Protestant church: *The Irish Times*! Interviewed by myself, he said, 'I'm very sorry for the offence [caused].' He continued, 'If it will help, you can put that in. I blame that offence very much on the way *The Irish Times* put its headline: "Taking Church of Ireland Communion a sham, says archbishop". That was very bad.' He continued, 'It was very unfortunate that I used the word "sham",' adding, 'It came out, and I certainly didn't intend it in any way that would be offensive.'

The archbishop went on to explain that the Eucharist was 'the very life of the Church. The Second Vatican Council says that it contains the entire spiritual wealth of the Church: it is the foundation of our Catholic identity. Taking Communion is an expression of faith; isn't it a pretence [to partake] if you're not buying into what you're doing and if you do not share the faith?' He had attended 'the consecration of the Church of Ireland Bishop of Meath, and I think I am the first archbishop ever to attend a [Church of Ireland] consecration. We celebrated the Eucharist there, and I was present in the community, but I stopped short of taking Communion for the good reason that the taking of Communion was an identifying of myself. What I would say of myself, I would say of every Catholic. That is the meaning of our faith,' he said. As always, there was no doubting his sincerity or how troubled he felt at having caused offence.

Of course, the Archbishop was not alone in blaming *The Irish Times* for the negative reaction. As the 'Communion row' rumbled on, discomfort levels among some in the Church of Ireland grew and grew and soon needed a safe outlet too. There was no question of criticising the Catholic Church or President McAleese, but there remained that most popular scapegoat in times of difficulty, the media – in this instance *The Irish Times* again and, more particularly, photographer Frank Miller and myself. Word soon began to reach my ears from Church of Ireland sources that some senior figures now felt Frank's photograph and my report had been an invasion of Mary McAleese's privacy. That it had taken place during an act of public worship in a public building was being swept aside. The whole thing would come to a head over a year later, in 1999.

In the meantime, the Catholic bishops of these islands decided to publish a document on inter-Church Communion. Or, rather, why it must not happen. Against the background of the peace process in Northern Ireland, it seemed an act of gross irresponsibility, as it would amplify what divided, while politicians on all sides were striving to bring separated peoples towards a historic agreement that might usher in a peace, however uneasy. The 'One Bread One Body' document prepared by the Catholic bishops of Ireland, Scotland, England and Wales was scheduled to be published in April 1998 but, since the Good Friday Agreement was concluded in that very month, the bishops postponed publication 'for technical reasons'. No one was buying that. The document was published the following September instead.

The press conference at which this postponement was announced took place on 23 April 1998, just thirteen days after the Good Friday Agreement was signed in Belfast, and was one of those occasions when it might be argued that I crossed the line between being a reporter and a participant. I was so angry at what the Catholic bishops of this archipelago had decided to do at such a sensitive time, I made no secret of how I felt through the trenchant nature of my questions. The bishops present, of course, defended the document. However, while the late Auxiliary Bishop of Down and Connor (including Belfast) Anthony Farquhar, I felt, was simply going through the motions without conviction,

Archbishop Connell defended the document forcefully, although he wrote to me privately later that day saying he regretted being so strong in his response to my questions. 'I apologise for treating you roughly this morning. But I could not conceal my annoyance at your Easter Monday article in which you attacked the pastoral letter planned by the Conferences of Great Britain and Ireland even before it had appeared.'

The content of 'One Bread One Body' was widely anticipated and I had not held back in an article published on 13 April, Easter Monday of that year, about ten days before the Catholic Church document was published. As with any correspondent, I always felt my duty in reporting was to record fairly and accurately whatever I was covering, while in analysis or comment pieces, based on those facts, I would freely express my own opinions. I very much agree with the old maxim that in journalism facts are sacred while opinion is free. And, just as I think reports should be fair and accurate, I also believe it is more honest for readers to know where a correspondent stands, based on those facts.

The article to which Archbishop Connell had taken such exception was published in *The Irish Times* just three days after the Good Friday Agreement was signed in Belfast. It was headed 'Clinton's Communion adds to Catholic bishops' difficulties' and followed then US President Bill Clinton and his wife Hillary taking Communion at a Catholic Church in South Africa's Soweto on 29 March that year. This sparked a furore with Catholic Church authorities, which fed into the row over President Mary McAleese taking Communion at Christ Church four months previously.

The article read:

> So far it has been a tale of two presidents, one prime minister, one ambassador, and one Holy, Roman, Catholic and Apostolic Church. The issue is Holy Communion, the

problem the Catholic Church's unyielding stance on the matter. What brings it centre stage once more is the apparent conflict between the Southern African Conference of (Catholic) Bishops and the White House over the context in which President Clinton received Communion at a Catholic church in Soweto on March 29th, two weeks ago yesterday. The bishops say they didn't know in advance that President Clinton, a Baptist, and his wife Hillary, a Methodist, were going to receive Communion in the church.

The article recalled how the Archbishop of New York, Cardinal John O'Connor, said, 'the action taken by the priest in South Africa, however well-intentioned, was legally and doctrinally wrong in the eyes of the Church'. It continued:

> President Clinton has no regrets about receiving Communion in South Africa, according to Mr McCurry [his spokesman]. Here at home, the President, Mrs McAleese, has indicated that not only does she not regret taking Communion at Christ Church cathedral in Dublin on December 7th last, but that she intends doing so again.
>
> Another Catholic who took Communion at Christ Church, the American ambassador, Mrs Jean Kennedy Smith, has said she has been taking Communion in Protestant churches 'for years'. She too intends continuing to do so. Those two Catholic public figures are but the tip of an iceberg headed the way of authority in the Catholic Church, whereas Mr Clinton and his wife might well be said to be representative of impatient mainstream Protestantism on the issue.

I pointed out how this impatience had led 'British Prime Minister, Mr Tony Blair, an Anglican, to take Communion at Mass with his Catholic wife, Cherie, until written to by Cardinal Hume, Archbishop of Westminster, who suggested it was best that people respected each other's traditions'.

It was in this broader context that I referred to the planned 'joint document on inter-church Communion being prepared by the Catholic Bishops of Ireland, Scotland, England and Wales', which was expected 'to restate that it is not permissible for a Catholic to take Communion in a Protestant/Anglican Church, or for a Protestant/Anglican to do so in a Catholic Church, except in extraordinary circumstances'. Such strictures, I wrote, 'sustain division overtly, even while a substantial body of authoritative opinion exists within the Catholic Church itself that this need not be so'. I continued:

> We in Ireland are particularly affected by this. The divisions in western Christendom are probably more central to our problems than any other single factor. This being so, we have a moral right to demand that all Churches work tirelessly to resolve rather than sustain their differences. In fairness, the Church of Ireland and the Presbyterian Churches in particular have been investigating the sectarian beam in their own eyes of late.
>
> This has not been a noticeable feature of Catholic Church consciousness on the island. It has tended to hold to the role of oppressed rather than oppressor, and seems blind to a view that it might itself be contributing to the bitter sectarian hatred on our island by sustaining the divisiveness within which that hatred flourishes.

It was no surprise that this article did not please Catholic Church authorities in Ireland, but I appreciated Archbishop Connell writing me that note, which was typical of him. He was a man of deep convictions, who frequently became frustrated at this stubborn world's inability to see what was so very clear to him. There was also a certain naiveté about him when it came to this world, probably born of being a metaphysician at UCD for thirty-five years before his appointment as Archbishop of Dublin in 1988.

This 'innocence' was frequently underlined – as, infamously, when he was made a cardinal in 2001. A dinner was held in his honour that February day at the Irish College in Rome. No media was invited to the dinner, which was attended by then Taoiseach Bertie Ahern and then High Court judges Peter Kelly and Dermot Kinlen, as well as Ireland's retired Catholic Primate Cardinal Cahal Daly, Cardinal Thomas Winning from Scotland, Vatican-based Cardinal Edward Cassidy and a number of Irish archbishops and bishops. Lots of VIPs. We media languished outside the dining hall with the tempting but untouched desserts and limoncello laid out on table after table, each covered in pristine white tablecloths. The 'we' included colleagues Marese McDonagh of the *Irish Independent*, Joe Little of RTÉ, Emily O'Reilly of the *Sunday Tribune* (now European Ombudsman) and me.

We were waiting for a press conference that was to take place later. Very quickly we realised that, as speeches began inside, we could hear everything. Cardinal Connell did not know this and, in an unscripted address, he told the assembled gathering about what Ireland owed the Catholic Church and how this was not getting the recognition it deserved. 'Ireland is not Ireland without the Church,' he said, while at home 'the Church is to be forgotten as though it never existed'. He added trenchantly, 'Ireland is European because of Rome. Because of the Church, Ireland is a worldwide community.' No longer distracted by the limoncello or annoyed at being designated as the hungry beggar, Lazarus kept

74

outside that particular 'rich man's' table, we media, with our ears to the thin partition, knew we had abundant reward in this story, which would dominate the headlines at home. When the dinner ended, this was realised quickly by Cardinal Connell's entourage. Consternation ensued and the planned press conference was cancelled. Nevertheless, the new cardinal dominated all front pages and news broadcasts in Ireland the following day.

A hapless man, you could say Dr Connell became Archbishop of Dublin by default. His name was among the last to surface publicly during the nine months that elapsed between the death in April 1997 of his predecessor, Archbishop Kevin McNamara, and the announcement of his appointment in January 1988. Comparatively unknown, he was sixty-two and Dean of the Faculty of Philosophy and Sociology at UCD. He had been a close friend of both previous archbishops of Dublin, McNamara and Dermot Ryan. On 21 January 1988 he was announced as archbishop-designate. One unnamed parish priest thought the news 'dreadful'. He said Dr Connell's theology was 'an extreme right-wing kind learned before Vatican II'. Another thought it 'unbelievable', saying Connell 'had not a clue about life at the coalface and lived in a world of Kant and the older philosophers'. For his part, Dr Connell met the criticisms with good humour, commenting that he had lived 'not exactly in a teapot' and that 'the advantage of starting as a conservative is that you can only improve'. He would discover otherwise.

No one anticipated what lay ahead or the abject moments that awaited him particularly – as indicated when he reacted to criticisms of his handling of clerical child sex abuse cases at Maynooth in 2002, with 'I am as human as any of you ... it is the issue which has devastated my period of office.' Up to his appointment as archbishop, he had served just six months in pastoral ministry – as a chaplain to the Mater Hospital in

Dublin between his ordination in 1951 and going for further study to Louvain University in Belgium. He secured a doctorate in philosophy there and joined the philosophy department at UCD in 1953. His doctorate, on seventeenth-century French philosopher Nicolas Malebranche, dealt with the nature of the unknown intelligence of angels. It was this which prompted gay rights activist Senator David Norris to quip, after the archbishop condemned homosexuality, that Dr Connell 'may know everything there is to know about angels, but you can take it from me that he knows sweet f—k all about fairies'.

Essentially a private man, Dr Connell could be charming, kind, gentle and humorous, and he ran his university department without acrimony. Former students spoke of him with affection, while having mixed views about his beliefs. One described him as 'a quiet, long-suffering man' who was 'trying to live a theology of obedience, poverty and chastity in a time of frantic change'. However, his unequivocally orthodox stances on divorce, abortion, homosexuality, women priests and reproductive technology began to attract attention, often in instances where his brother bishops maintained more discreet, even though similar, positions. His 1999 statement that children whose parents planned their births through reproductive technology were less loved than those more conventionally conceived was greeted with incredulity. 'A profound alteration in the relationship between parent and child may result when the child is no longer welcomed as a gift, but produced, as it were, to order,' he said. At a State reception held in his honour that May 2001, hosted by Taoiseach Bertie Ahern and his then partner, Celia Larkin, the new cardinal spoke of the primacy of the family as an institution. It was hardly adroit but, in so doing, he could attend the reception while not allowing it to be interpreted as an endorsement of the taoiseach and Ms Larkin's personal arrangements.

Without doubt 2002 was Dr Connell's *annus horribilis*. It was the year when his handling of clerical child sex abuse cases was exposed most mercilessly. In April it emerged that he had not told gardaí that Father Paul McGennis, who had abused Marie Collins as a child in 1960, had admitted the crime. In October 2002 Mary Raftery's *Cardinal Secrets* programme, broadcast on RTÉ television, gave a damning account of Dr Connell's handling of cases involving eight priests of the diocese who had been involved in child sex abuse. As a result, he seemed to finally admit his own personal responsibility for much that had gone wrong in the archdiocese as far as the handling of clerical child sex abuse during his term was concerned. 'We failed them, I failed them, and there are no excuses for this failure,' he said on 19 October.

Dr Connell's relationship with the media could never be described as comfortable. Seven years into his episcopal ministry in 1995 he commented, 'No ferret of the old society could begin to match some elements in the media once they have scented a story.' In April 2001, at a fraught press conference in Maynooth, he commented as he was leaving, 'You people, I'm very sorry, I shouldn't say "you people", but you come along and treat us as if we are utterly indifferent to what was going on. And I have gone through agonies over this thing.'

When Dr Connell retired as archbishop in April 2004 there was a press event at Archbishop's House in Drumcondra to mark the occasion, at which he spoke respectfully about the role we had to play as media and the difficulties to which this could lead for people in positions such as he held. He was very fair. I responded how, through it all, we had admired his unfailing courtesy to us on a personal level no matter how fraught the situation. He sent me a note later that afternoon saying, simply, 'Your gracious words today affected me deeply and I thank you from my heart.'

I was moved by that. It was typical of his old-world courtesy and good manners. Dr Connell died in 2017, aged ninety.

✠ ✠ ✠

In that 1998 Easter Monday opinion piece to which he took such exception, I criticised the bishops' 'One Bread One Body' document forcefully because of the recklessness of its timing and a seeming indifference on the part of the Catholic bishops of these islands to its impact on the wider community in the context of the peace process and the Good Friday Agreement of that same month. It appalled me. Their document simply reiterated that Catholics should never take Communion in a Protestant church, and Protestants (including Anglicans) should never receive Communion in a Catholic church except in cases of death or of 'grave and pressing need'. As if to highlight the lengths to which the Catholic bishops of these islands were prepared to go to preserve this divisive teaching, there was a statement at the document launch in London by Cardinal Basil Hume, president of the Bishops Conferences of England and Wales. He said British Prime Minister Tony Blair, then technically still a member of the Church of England and an architect of the Good Friday Agreement, could receive Communion at a Catholic church while on holiday in Italy because there was no Anglican church nearby, but that he remained banned from doing so in Britain when attending Mass with his Catholic wife, Cherie, and their children. Cardinal Hume had already written to Blair instructing him not to receive Communion when attending Mass in Britain. The unacceptable irony in all this was that these same churchmen had been urging politicians for years to get around a table and work out an agreement which could bring peace to Catholics and Protestants in Northern Ireland.

Meantime, the 'privacy of Communion' debate in the Church of Ireland continued. It came to a head where I was concerned following the consecration of Canon Paul Colton as Church of Ireland Bishop of Cork, Cloyne and Ross in March 1999 at Dublin's Christ Church. This was six months after the Catholic bishops published 'One Bread One Body', leaving no room for manoeuvre when it came to Catholics receiving Communion in Protestant churches. They shouldn't.

I was aware that some leading Catholic figures would be in attendance at Canon Colton's installation. Among them were Cork politicians Micheál Martin and Simon Coveney. Also there were Joan Burton of the Labour Party, then deputy Lord Mayor of Cork Frank Wallace, and Cork Assistant City Manager Dan Buggy. All were Catholic, or from a Catholic background, and all received Communion from the new Church of Ireland bishop. I named them all in my report later. Micheál Martin told me it was not the first time he had taken Communion at a Reformed Church service. 'It's nothing new to us in Cork,' he said.

My only problem with reporting on that event concerned those Catholic public representatives present who did not receive Communion. I felt uneasy about reporting that they did not do so. Each might have had their own reason. However, I decided, eventually, and in the context of the wider political and theological debate, that people had a right to know that 'Mr Austin Currie TD, Mr Michael Moynihan TD and Mr P.J. Sheehan TD were also present.'

Cue, fire and brimstone from the Dean of Christ Church, John Paterson. In a letter to *The Irish Times* he accused me of 'gross intrusion' and 'questionable journalism', and asked whether *The Irish Times* was setting up 'a type of ecclesiastical thought police'. He wrote:

For Mr McGarry to 'play' one Church against another I find ecumenically unhelpful. For him to comment on the personal choices people make – even public people – on occasions such as the consecration of Bishop Colton I still find intrusive and distasteful. It is not being facetious if one says it smacks of nineteenth-century 'felon setting', 1950s 'McCarthyism', or 1990s 'outings'. Judging by the correspondence I have privately received, so too, it would seem, do many of your own readers.

Hell hath no fury like a dean in high dudgeon!

A regular in our pub at home in Ballaghaderreen once got involved in a deep conversation about life after death and was asked, 'John Pake, where will you go when you die, Heaven or Hell?' He replied, 'I don't mind, I have friends in both places.' Barely two years in the job and, already, I had enemies in both major Churches in Ireland.

4

A Painful Case

Darren McGavin is now a middle-aged man in his fifties. Our first meeting, in Dublin's St Stephen's Green shopping centre many years ago, was one of the few occasions in my life when I wept in public. I belong, very much, to the 'weep alone' brigade when it comes to emotional issues. But I couldn't help it then, even though Darren and I, drinking our coffee, were surrounded by so many people at tables nearby. I kept seeing the small boy, not the man before me, being brutalised. His recollection of incidents of sexual abuse by Father Tony Walsh were vivid, detailed and told with the calm delivery of a man who had been over the ground many times. By then, having talked to many other abuse survivors, I was somewhat familiar with the consequences such abuse would have had for Darren in his life as a young adult. I recognised the destructive pattern already: the addictions to drink and drugs, the utter turmoil, the confusions, broken relationships, accidental (if loved) children, the low self-esteem, the suicide attempts. Even so, I remain amazed at the resilience of survivors – women and men – who survive all that to live calm, ordinary, fulfilling lives. Wounded, but unbowed.

I cannot remember how Darren and I first met, but suspect it must have been through that sainted woman, the late Angela

Copley, whose gentle ministrations saved the lives of so many young men in Ballyfermot who had been sexually abused as children by priests locally. She lost some too. They could no longer cope. Angela, whose warm embrace was as big as her heart, was the 'go-to person' for many of us in the media reporting on the abuse of children in Ballyfermot parish and beyond. She and I spoke frequently, and through her I met Darren and others who had been abused as children by priests. Many did not want to discuss what they had been through publicly and that was always respected. Trust was crucial and losing that trust in just one case would be enough to end it where all others were concerned. And Angela was key to that trust. If she trusted you, then these people would too. She was like a great mother hen, fiercely protective of her damaged 'charges', with a typical no nonsense, down-to-earth Dublin sense of humour. Some agreed to speak to me about what had happened to them as background for articles I was writing. Darren, on the other hand, agreed to be interviewed by me for *The Irish Times*. So we arranged to meet in the Stephen's Green Centre, which he knew and was not too far from the paper's offices. His story remains one of the worst I've heard.

In June 2018 Darren spoke eloquently at Angela's funeral in Ballyfermot's St Matthew's Church. I was impressed by his composure as he spoke from the altar and remembered how he was panicking the first time he went to see her. 'She came out to the door to me and, the little nod – "Howya." I says, "Can I have a talk with you?", and she said, "We'll have a cup of tea and we'll go somewhere private." And we just started talking. That was twenty-one years ago. To say I was humbled and honoured to have her in my life would be an understatement.' There were 'many people like me in the Ballyfermot area,' he said.

Angela's son Derek then spoke of how, in setting up a support group for clerical child sex abuse survivors in Ballyfermot, she 'mothered' so many in the area. 'Myself and Gary are her sons, but there's a lot of sons and daughters out there my ma helped, that she mothered through the years.' He remembered one Christmas morning when the doorbell rang and a stranger asked, 'Is Angela there?' and she said, 'Bring him in, bring him in.' Said Derek, 'I thought it was just another visitor till he sat down and Ma starts bringing out the dinner. There was an extra plate there and I said, "I suppose I'd better get to know ya."' It was, he recalled, 'very typical. It was kind of funny in a way, the seriousness of what she dealt with. After a while it became normalised in our house.'

So extreme had been Darren's abuse by Tony Walsh that the former priest was sentenced in December 2010 to a total of 123 years' imprisonment. Five of the thirteen counts, for buggery, attracted sentences of ten, twelve, fourteen, sixteen and sixteen years each. The remaining counts, for indecent assault, brought sentences ranging from four to nine years each. As Walsh was to serve his sentences concurrently, sixteen years was the maximum time he would spend in jail for those crimes. Four years of that were suspended when a psychologist's report said it was unlikely that he would offend again. It was the most severe sentence imposed on a clerical child sex abuser in Ireland. Walsh remains in jail and is likely to be there for many years to come because he has since been sentenced in connection with the abuse of other children. In more recent cases he has begun to plead guilty.

At the trial for his abuse of Darren McGavin, Walsh pleaded not guilty. Sitting in that courtroom, one of the most remarkable things I observed throughout the hearing was the ex-priest's demeanour of complete indifference; there was not a hint of remorse. He was also tried in connection with the abuse of a second Ballyfermot man as a child. This man had asked us in the media not to name him in our reports because he had just told his two sons days beforehand about what had happened to him as a child and one son was unable to handle it.

What Walsh did to Darren McGavin as a small boy is unbearable to recall, never mind what it must have been like to endure. As he told me himself at that first meeting, and as relayed in his victim impact statement presented at the trial, prepared with psychiatrist Professor Ivor Browne (who attended the trial also), in one instance Walsh raped him with his wrists tied to his ankles as he was made to lie across a coffee table at the presbytery in Ballyfermot, which Walsh then shared with the famed Father Michael Cleary and his housekeeper, Phyllis Hamilton, with whom, it emerged later, Cleary had two sons. Darren was 'crying loudly' and 'hysterical'. Walsh, who had turned up the music to drown out the child's cries, took 'about an hour to calm me down. I then went home,' Darren said. This assault led to one of the sixteen-year sentences.

Another incident took place at Enniscrone, County Sligo. About fifty children from Ballyfermot were taken there for a break by Walsh and three other priests, including Father Cleary. Walsh took Darren to the sand dunes where he raped him. Sand caused the child to bleed, so Walsh brought him to the sea where he washed off the blood, but the salt water stung the child's wounds, adding to his pain and distress.

This was the incident which drove me over the emotional edge when Darren and I first met for that interview in the Stephen's Green Centre. The callous indifference of Walsh to the suffering of a small boy of six or seven, already bleeding because of the rape, was bad enough, but then to add further injury by dipping the child in salt water to help cover up the crime seemed monstrous.

Darren was also raped by Walsh in Dublin's Phoenix Park. Afterwards, Walsh wiped him with 'a purple sash [stole] he had with him'. He brought Darren back to the presbytery in Ballyfermot, 'put on Elvis records ... and gave me a glass of Coke'. He then showed me 'a Bible with pictures of Hell and said if I told anyone I would burn in Hell and never go to Heaven. Then he let me go home.'

One evening Darren told his mother a watered-down version of what was happening. They had been watching a BBC programme about child sexual abuse. Outraged, she went to the presbytery in Ballyfermot and knocked, accompanied by Darren's aunt. The door was answered by Phyllis Hamilton, who denied that Walsh was inside. Darren's mother insisted he must be in because his car was there. They thought they had seen him through a window. Hamilton went inside and Walsh came to the door. He denied everything. As Professor Browne put it in the victim impact report: 'then, knowing the game was up, Walsh stopped abusing Darren altogether and terminated their relationship'.

As well as Angela Copley, Professor Browne is a major reason Darren is still with us today. A pioneering psychiatrist, who helped remove the stigma from mental illness in Ireland and who was central in moving psychiatric care away from huge, forbidding institutions, this extraordinary man helped Darren stabilise a life that was out of control owing to substance abuse and turbulent, unstable relationships. A tall, elegant, reserved figure, his calm presence in the courtroom during the Tony Walsh trial made a deep impression on all. His presence in the courtroom, as well as that of Angela, was the support that enabled Darren to give evidence with confidence. Over the following years, until Professor Browne's death, he and Darren became like father and son, an addition to the psychiatrist's already large family; they were so close that Darren was one of those at his bedside when he died at the age of ninety-four on 24 January 2024.

Tony Walsh spent eight years trying to stop his trial from going ahead, exhausting the judicial review process en route. He had failed similarly in another case in 1997. That time, after another round-the-houses judicial review process funded by free legal aid, he eventually pleaded guilty and served time. But he forced the December 2010 trial involving Darren McGavin by denying all charges. The jury found him guilty, unanimously, on all thirteen counts after just ninety-four minutes.

All these years later Darren is still in recovery. He believes he always will be. He suffers bouts of depression but takes his medication and attends counselling. Darren's abuse by Walsh ended when he was eleven, but it took ten years before he felt he could do anything about it. The intervening years were marked by much drug abuse and as many as 'five or six' suicide attempts. Then he decided enough was enough and went to the gardaí, who were sympathetic and supportive from the beginning. That was in 1993. It would take seventeen years to successfully prosecute the case against Walsh, but Darren and the gardaí persisted. Detective Garda Brendan Walsh, now retired, was prosecuting garda in the case. Darren recalled, 'When I first met Brendan in Ballyfermot Garda station to give the statement, I'd never seen a guard step out of a room so much in temper and anger. Before we left the station that day he said to me, "This case is going to see me into retirement," and it did. It took that long to get the still "Father" Tony Walsh at the time [he was laicised later], locked up.'

Darren has three children from a series of relationships, two, both now adults, with one long-term partner, and a third with a more recent partner. He trained as a counsellor to help other people and has been in a good place for many years now.

✠ ✠ ✠

The Murphy Commission confirmed in its November 2009 report what I and other journalists, print and broadcast, had established through talking to Walsh's victims, men such as Darren, where the Dublin archdiocese's handling of the Tony Walsh case and that of other abuser priests was concerned. It had covered up such cases, redeployed abuser priests to avoid their exposure and to protect itself, and in all instances ignored the welfare of victims. Where legal action was taken, the archdiocese fought all the way to the steps of the Four Courts before then settling to avoid what might emerge in open court.

An example of how the archdiocese met these cases can be gleaned from a case concluded in 2003. It was January of that year and involved a then twenty-eight-year-old man who, with his family, spent eighteen years trying to get the Dublin archdiocese to acknowledge his abuse by Father Thomas Naughton at a parish on Dublin's northside in 1985–86. In 1998 Father Naughton received a three-year jail sentence, later reduced on appeal to two and a half years, in connection with the boy's abuse. This followed a garda investigation, which began in 1995 when the boy's family reported his abuse. Father Naughton sexually abused children throughout the 1980s across three parishes in Dublin and, in each case, this was made known to the Church authorities. In 1995 the abused boy's family also initiated a civil action against the archdiocese. The settlement of over €300,000, agreed in January 2003, followed protracted and difficult negotiations, and led counsel for the abused young man to seek a court order for the disclosure of documents that the archdiocese had said it was having problems locating and some of which it had said no longer existed. All were produced.

I interviewed the man at the heart of this settlement on the steps of the Four Courts that January day as the settlement – then the largest ever agreed in Ireland – was announced. He said that from then on he just wanted 'to live my life and be normal like everyone else'. He was 'delighted the Catholic Church has at last acknowledged the pain it caused a frightened young boy for so long. I am not sure how long it will take me to forgive them for taking eighteen years and numerous court appearances to do so.' He said, 'It was eighteen years ago that my father took me by the hand to the bishop's palace in Dublin. That is when this nightmare got worse.' He recalled how at that meeting with church officials Monsignor Alex Stenson, then chancellor of the archdiocese, 'told me I was lying and said I better tell the truth very quickly'. He remembered the monsignor said, '"Stop your lies, stop telling your lies." It was really fierce, really savage. I was terrified. But I said, "I'm not telling lies." And I wasn't. And that's what today means. It means that, finally, they have to admit that I was never telling lies, that all I ever told was the truth, just me, a ten-year-old child against all those big priests.' He continued, 'They fought us every inch of the way. It ends here today.'

The Murphy Commission investigated the handling of clerical child sexual abuse allegations in Dublin's Catholic archdiocese between 1975 and 2004, and its 2009 report described Tony Walsh as 'the most notorious child sexual abuser' to have come to its attention: 'It is likely that he has abused hundreds of children.' It also found that the archdiocese did not report child sex abuse allegations against Walsh to the gardaí for seventeen years after it first received complaints implicating him in such behaviour. Few cases better illustrate the Catholic Church's callous indifference to clerical child sexual abuse survivors in Ireland or elsewhere at that time as Darren's McGavin's does. And few cases better illustrate the lengths to which it would go to protect an abuser priest and itself from the scandal that would ensue if that abuse and its cover-up were ever made public.

Born in 1954, Tony Walsh was ordained in 1978. Even as a seminarian at Dublin's Clonliffe College, as emerged years later, he abused children and did so at the home of another abuser, Father Noel Reynolds, to whose house he had a key. In July 1978, two days after Walsh took up his first appointment as a curate in Ballyfermot, a complaint was received at Archbishop's House that he had sexually abused an eight-year-old boy. That was alleged to have taken place in June 1978 at Father Reynolds's house.

The next complaint came in 1979, when a mother went to the parish priest of Ballyfermot, the late Canon Val Rogers. He dispatched Father Michael Cleary to educate the woman's son on male sexuality. In 1985 Canon Rogers admitted this case had been 'hushed up'. Some time between 1980 and 1982 there were complaints to Archbishop's House about Walsh's abuse of young girls at a summer camp. In June 1985 he began attending a psychiatrist, but even after he was moved in February 1986 to Westland Row parish, in Dublin's south inner city, complaints kept coming. A housekeeper at his house in Ballyfermot said there were always children there and on one occasion she saw two boys coming from his bedroom. In January 1987 the housekeeper at Westland Row claimed to have found some of her underwear in Walsh's room. She also found condoms and syringes and said, 'a number of boys had slept overnight in his bed and a boy from Ballyfermot had been visiting'. Walsh denied this and protested that he did not know what condoms looked like. In April 1988 a woman alleged that her son was in Westland Row with Walsh. The following month, parents claimed Walsh had interfered with their daughter.

In May 1988 Walsh admitted to Monsignor Alex Stenson how, over the eight years he had been in Ballyfermot, 'he was involved with boys about once a fortnight'. That was ten years after the first complaint about him had been made to the archdiocese. Even then, he was not reported to the gardaí or to any civil authority. Instead, Walsh was sent to a centre in Stroud in England that treated priests with addiction issues and paedophile tendencies.

In November 1988 Walsh returned to Dublin and was appointed chaplain at a hospital for older people. In 1989 it was suggested at Archbishop's House in Drumcondra that the priest, then an admitted (to the archdiocese) child sex abuser, be appointed to the regional marriage tribunal, which dealt mainly with annulments, although in the end this did not happen. Two other child-abusing priests were already on that tribunal. After one of them, Father Ivan Payne, was convicted in 1998 of sexually abusing eight boys aged from eleven to fourteen between 1968 and 1987, I spoke to a female acquaintance whose brief marriage Payne had helped to annul. A practising Catholic, she was appalled that someone like him had taken part in the annulment process and, in retrospect, felt very disturbed at Payne's intrusive questioning during that process. She wondered about its intent.

In 1988 Tony Walsh signed a contract of good behaviour with the Dublin archdiocese, which nominated Father Michael Cleary as his spiritual director. Then, in August 1989 there were complaints about his dealings with a boy at Dublin's All Hallows College. Walsh was returned to Stroud for further treatment.

In March 1991 there were further reports of Walsh's contacts with children, so in April Archbishop of Dublin Desmond Connell (he became a cardinal in 2001) and Monsignor Stenson gave him a stark ultimatum: choose either dismissal from the priesthood or voluntary laicisation. Walsh ignored them. Archbishop Connell removed Walsh from public ministry, but he remained a priest. In August 1991, for the first time, a parent complained to gardaí about Walsh's attempt to pick up her son. The following month Archbishop Connell ordered him to go to the St John of God

Psychiatric Hospital in Stillorgan. The night before he did so, he attempted to pick up another boy and gardaí were alerted.

Walsh returned to Stroud in January 1992, where he posed in nearby streets as a priest counsellor at the clinic and agreed to babysit for a family. Luckily, the father of the family found out by chance who he was and he was not allowed near the family. Back in Dublin again by July 1992, he befriended a fifteen-year-old boy. One of the boy's parents went to the gardaí, who in turn contacted the archdiocese. More parents complained about Walsh's activities in December 1992 and May 1993.

In August 1993 a Church tribunal in Dublin decided that Walsh should be defrocked. A member of that tribunal was canon lawyer Father John McAreavey, then based at St Patrick's College, Maynooth, and later Bishop of Dromore diocese in Northern Ireland. In 2018 Bishop McAreavey resigned following controversy over his decision to officiate more than fifteen years earlier at the funeral Mass of known child abuser Father Malachy Finnegan, a priest of Dromore diocese.

In October 1993 Walsh appealed the Church tribunal's decision to Rome. While the appeal was in train, he abused a boy at the child's grandfather's funeral in west Dublin. The boy's mother contacted gardaí, alleging that Walsh had also abused her son a year earlier. In late 1994 there were media reports about this case. Early in 1995 Walsh admitted to gardaí that he had abused two boys in the 1980s. He was charged in connection with his abuse of the boy at the funeral in 1994 and sentenced to twelve months' imprisonment. It was the first of many such sentences. In May 1995 the archdiocese provided gardaí with other complaints about Walsh. Meanwhile, and inexplicably to all of sound mind, Rome rejected Walsh's laicisation as recommended by the Dublin tribunal and decided that he should remain a priest but spend ten years in a monastery.

In November 1995 a by now desperate Archbishop Connell petitioned Pope John Paul II to dismiss Walsh from the priesthood. In January 1996 Cardinal Joseph Ratzinger issued a decree confirming Walsh's dismissal. He refused to accept this and continued to believe himself a priest.

In December 1997 Walsh was sentenced to consecutive terms of six years and four years for assaults on six boys. On appeal, this was reduced to six years. He was in prison until 2001 on that occasion. In December 2010 he was sentenced to sixteen years in the case involving Darren McGavin. In 2013 Walsh pleaded guilty to two more abuse cases and in 2015 was convicted by a jury in relation to the sexual abuse of a girl. In July 2016 he was jailed for seven and a half years for raping a boy three times, once with a crucifix. There have been other cases, the most recent in July 2022, when he was sentenced to another four years for indecent assaults on three schoolboys in the 1980s.

Commentary is hardly necessary on the Church's handling of the Tony Walsh case. It encapsulates that institution's gross irresponsibility in addressing clerical child sex abuse, its callous indifference to the children abused and their families, and its primary concern for the abuser priest and the protection of itself, its reputation and its assets above all. The great damage it has incurred following the emergence of all of this into the public domain is the least it deserved. Some would suggest that justice demands more.

✠ ✠ ✠

Darren McGavin is one of the few abuse survivors whose story of abuse I have heard face to face. I rarely ask people who have been abused to tell me what happened to them. Over the years I have reported on hundreds of people who experienced such abuse by priests and Brothers as children. I have always felt that to ask them what happened is an invitation to relive the experience, and guilt prevents me from doing that unless they want to talk about it or it is absolutely necessary – which it rarely is. Most of the abused people I know have had their allegations tested at State inquiries or in the courts. Besides, studies in the US have shown that false allegations of clerical child sexual abuse, or of such child abuse generally, are very rare and in the low single percentages.

There is another reason why I have asked few abuse survivors to repeat their experiences to me face to face: my own mental health. Towards the end of 2022 I interviewed many men who had been abused as young boys at fee-paying boarding schools run by religious congregations. In all those cases, except one, I conducted the interviews over the phone or by email. The remove means I can better maintain control over my own emotions than when faced directly with a person still marked by the trauma of what happened to them as a child.

In that one exceptional case I had some prior acquaintance with the man concerned, and he asked that I meet him personally in Dublin for an interview about his horrendous experiences as a child at Dublin's Blackrock College/Willow Park School. Through extraordinary personal resilience, family support, and after 800 therapy sessions, he has healed significantly and has trained as a psychotherapist himself, in which role he helps others who have had similar experiences as children. Still, it cannot have been easy for him to speak so frankly to me.

In later correspondence, and addressing the matter from a professional perspective, the man said to me, 'I do think some psychotherapeutic debriefing could be useful in the heavy terrain some of you journalists enter regularly. Vicarious traumatisation and all that …' To date I have not felt that to be necessary. When people have commented down the years along the lines of 'I don't know how you stick it', I have replied sincerely, 'It's the anger, the rage that keeps me going. And, though it is one of the deadly sins, there is great energy in anger.' And there is.

This anxiety I have always felt about retraumatising survivors through having them repeat their experience of abuse as children was why I began to have concerns about leading advocacy groups dealing with the Mother and Baby Homes Commission, which published its report in January 2021. Thirty such groups appeared before that commission's investigation committee, almost one for every two of the sixty-four former residents who also gave evidence. The investigation committee was really at the hard core of that commission's work, where allegations were tested and challenged by lawyers, as opposed to its confidential committee, where hundreds of Mother and Baby Homes' survivors relayed their stories without challenge.

One advocacy group demanded that it be heard by the commission in a public hearing, but this did not happen and no one else made such a request. As the commission's report put it about that request, 'When asked for reasons why, no reply was received.' You do have to wonder what startling and original evidence the advocacy group had to offer the commission that it alone deserved to be heard in public with lawyers, lawyers everywhere and at public expense?

This advocacy group went so far as to conduct its own parallel quasi-inquiry into Mother and Baby Homes, expecting its findings to be accepted by the commission, a statutory body with strict terms of reference, none of which applied to their ad hoc inquiry with its self-appointed investigators and self-selected terms of reference. They had a firm of solicitors take statements from sixty-one survivors of the Mother and Baby Homes, in the process making those people relive experiences they could have relayed directly and just once to the commission itself. Their statements were then submitted to the commission, which found that fifty-five came within its terms of reference. To give the statements legal authority, the commission asked the advocacy group to have these sworn as affidavits. Just thirty-two of the relevant survivors agreed to go through it all again a second time in order to have their affidavits submitted to the commission. What purpose did it serve to have those people, the original sixty-one and those thirty-two repeats, go through all that when they could have just gone to the commission itself?

It was not dissimilar where the interdepartmental inquiry into the Magdalene laundries was concerned. It published its report in 2013. That inquiry was presented with a lengthy submission from an advocacy group, which expected it to be accepted as evidence. It was not, in that instance, due to concerns about its quality. In both cases the relevant advocacy groups subsequently lambasted the published reports of the Magdalene Inquiry and the Mother and Baby Homes Commission because their findings did not align with the groups' assumptions. Where the latter report was concerned, these advocacy groups were particularly severe in their criticisms, damning its entire 2,865 pages almost immediately on its publication. They were supported by some vociferous TDs in the Dáil, two of whom conveniently ignored the commission report's judgement on their own local authorities and their morally derelict management of Mother and Baby Homes in those areas.

For myself, nothing has spoken as loudly about those Mother and Baby Homes advocacy groups, some also active where the Magdalene Inquiry was concerned, as their complete silence since the end of 2022, from which time stream after stream of shocking abuse stories have emerged from men who were badly abused as boys at private fee-paying boarding schools in Ireland. It may be argued that those advocacy groups' primary concern is with the abuse of girls and women in relevant institutions, but little boys bleed too, whether in the sand dunes of Enniscrone after being raped by a priest or at Willow Park School in south County Dublin, where, after he was raped, one boy went home and tried 'to wash the blood off my underpants in our upstairs bathroom with a nail brush and Imperial Leather soap'. It didn't work. He put his wet underpants into a plastic bag and hid them. That night he dumped them in a neighbour's bin.

5

The Fugitive Bishop
and His Son

There was a light on in the church, but its door was locked that dark Saturday evening of September 1997 in San Miguel de Los Bancos. A poor, humid place with a gravel pathway down its street and wooden buildings along its sides, it looked like a 'Wild West' town from a John Ford western. The journey there by bus from Ecuador's capital, Quito, would challenge anyone, even those with nerves of steel, unfamiliar with such terrain and the occasional sheer drop at the sides of a bockety road. It was a steady two-and-a-half-hour descent from the western lowlands of the Andes, through mountain forests. Quito, at over 9,000 feet above sea level, is the world's second-highest capital city. (Bolivia's La Paz is the highest, at around 12,000 feet.) Swirling corkscrew roads, with drops of hundreds of feet alongside, lead to San Miguel de Los Bancos, which is at about 5,000 feet.

Arriving there and having found a bed at what was probably the only boarding house on its one street, which offered facilities worthy of the $5 a night charged, I went in search of the bishop known locally as 'Padre Eduardo'. Earlier, the Reverend at the door of its only presbytery had responded, 'Ah, Padre Eduardo', when I asked about Father Casey and whether he might be there. The village had one church and an ancient, battered evangelical hall. The Reverend at the presbytery next door to the church was a deacon from Spain's Basque country. He said Padre Eduardo had left and would not be back for about two hours. He agreed to pass on an envelope I gave him containing a letter of introduction and its attached request for an interview.

Two hours in a damp San Miguel de Los Bancos is a long time. Sad-looking chickens picked at the red dirt while soaked dogs slept in the middle of the street and some children on a balcony played with a balloon. At the boarding house, sleep was welcome. Three hours later it was dark.

A few months before this trip I had decided to go to Ecuador to see whether Bishop Eamonn Casey would agree to an interview. There was no point asking in advance. I knew the answer would be 'no', but I felt that were I to go there personally and meet him, I might be successful.

En route to the presbytery later I saw the white-haired figure, wearing glasses, emerge from a side door to the church. At sixty-six, he was taller and thinner than expected, wearing dark casual clothes and carrying an empty glass jug. The rapid gait, with its short step, the shuffle and slight stoop forward were unmistakable. 'Dr Casey,' I called out, and walked towards him. I identified myself. He was shocked, cool, civil, courteous. A child was dying in the church and he was going to the presbytery to get water to baptise it. Water in the village had been cut off some time before in a row between rival political factions, but it had just been turned on again.

I followed him to the presbytery. It was bare and frugal. We agreed that I would wait. He filled the jug with water from a kitchen tap and returned to his duties in the church. The presbytery sitting-room, off an open-plan kitchen, was sparsely furnished. A large empty fireplace dominated. It was chilly, though not too cold. The height and humidity meant that San Miguel was damp and cool. Beside the presbytery fireplace were bits of wood – some chopped, others with nails sticking out – piled into a large box in the corner.

There were two armchairs, a couch, a table with a Spanish-language newspaper spread on it, a television set and a wooden spiral staircase leading to bedrooms. Open shelves marked the division between the sitting-room and kitchen and were populated with a few paperback books. Three men lived at the presbytery along with Bishop Casey: a young Czech priest and a middle-aged Ecuadorian priest, neither of whom spoke English, and the Spanish deacon, who had moderate English. Later it would become noticeable that he spoke to Bishop Casey, whose Spanish was poor, in English only. This lack of Spanish was a problem in a house and village where only one other person spoke any English, and that poorly. It compounded the loneliness.

Most of the then approximately 5,000 population of San Miguel de Los Bancos, with its mucky red dirt tracks leading towards the mountains all around, lived in wooden shacks along those tracks, rather than in the village itself. They were poor *mestizos*, descendants of mixed Indian and European blood, who were paid less-than-subsistence wages by wealthy landowners who lived in Quito, about seventy miles to the east. Most earned a living by taming the perpetual growth of the region with machetes. They were employed to do so by generally absentee landowners. The poor pay was one reason why nearly every building along the street in San Miguel then was a business.

In the ten minutes it took to walk the length of the village, I had passed basic grocery shops, butcher's shops with raw red meat hanging in the open air, barbers, dressmakers, cafés and one electrical shop with two television screens on which small boys were playing computer games. Few shops had any windows.

There was also the boarding house where I had bunked down. Until 1995 the part of the road to Quito nearest Los Bancos had been a dirt track. But by the time of my visit, three years later, it was the only paved road connecting Quito to the Pacific coast.

Almost fifteen minutes after he left to perform the baptism, Bishop Casey returned to the presbytery. He was tense but adamant. He was clear. He had made a rule some years ago not to do any more interviews, and he would not breach it. It was best that way, not to drag everything up again. He regretted what this meant for me coming so far, but there was nothing he could do. He was very sorry, but that was the way it was. I soon realised there was no point in arguing. I accepted the situation, that my journey of almost 6,000 miles had been wasted and was for nothing. It was agreed that everything thereafter would be off the record. And so it has remained.

This was not entirely a surprise, but I still felt it was worth the effort. I had taken the trip during my holidays, on the off-chance. And it *was* worth it. We connected. Eamonn Casey was marvellous company and desperately lonely. He could not get enough news about what was happening in Ireland. His animation when talking about home was intense and moving. We talked of little else. He talked too about Los Bancos: his affection for its suffering people and their many dead infants; his anger at the wealthy landowners who did so little to help them. Bronchial infections were a common cause of death among children and of some adults too in that humid region. It was why the child, whom he had baptised earlier, was dying.

I had admired Bishop Casey since I saw an RTÉ *Radharc* programme in the late 1960s on the work he did in London for the emigrant Irish and in setting up the housing agency Shelter for homeless people there. He was what I believed a priest should be. At the time I had hoped to be a priest like him.

I had brought along a bottle of whiskey, which I intended leaving him as a gift, not knowing then his preference was for wine. That, and my colleague Nuala O'Faolain's book *Are You Somebody?* Everyone in Ireland, it seemed, was reading it then and I felt he would know most of the people mentioned in it. We opened the whiskey, a bottle of Bushmills Black Bush that I had picked for its quality. The hours passed.

When I left the presbytery later that Saturday night, enthused by his humour and the whiskey, I had already decided I would be at his 7.30 Mass the next morning, come hell or high water. Though stung by a bad hangover, I made it in time – and there he was before the Mass, walking up and down the centre aisle greeting everyone in his makeshift Spanish, towering above them all. Extending his hand to me, he said, 'Buenos días', then laughed. 'Habit!' he said.

It was a bright and cheery church, with lots of light and colour. Very different to the usual grimly dark, highly ornate, gloomy style favoured by the Spanish and South Americans in their churches. Since he had transformed it through painting its walls with simple bright colours following his arrival there in 1993, attendances had soared, he said. The large congregation was mixed between young and old, men and women. They sang hymns to the tunes of 'The Sound of Silence' and 'John Brown's Body'. Without prompting, individuals spontaneously recited prayers of the faithful from the body of the church.

His homily in Spanish, relayed with great enthusiasm and dramatic gestures, was about the victory of the Cross. 'The Cross is hope, the Cross is love, the Cross is victory,' he told them. He read from notes. He told me that it took him from Monday to Sunday to get the Spanish right. During the sign of peace handshake, he walked down the aisle shaking hands with everyone, including his Irish visitor.

Later, he invited me for breakfast in the presbytery. It included bread, hard-boiled eggs, tea and a local blackberry-flavoured yoghurt-like drink. He said he missed marmalade. Two other priests and a deacon who shared the presbytery with him were also at the table. Libia, a local girl, and a tiny, elderly woman, Cecilia, served the tea and eggs. Cecilia was very welcoming to this Irish visitor. She enthused in Spanish; the word 'gusto' featured a lot. Casey translated that she was very pleased for him that he had a guest. From her reaction, it was clear he had few visitors.

The priests and deacon left to say Mass in outlying parishes. Eamonn Casey had to say Mass again in the church next door. We walked to a low wall at the front of the church as he relayed some other Irish story. We shook hands. I said I hoped I would see him again. His voice cracked, and tears appeared in his eyes. 'Thank you … for the respect,' he said, and turned quickly towards the presbytery. He wasn't alone in being moved. He and I remained in contact down the years after that.

Bishop Casey's five years in Ecuador were due to end the following year, in 1998. He had been there with Boston's Missionary Society of St James the Apostle. Their Irish-American archbishop was Cardinal Bernard Law, who would be forced to resign in 2002 over his handling of clerical child sex abuse allegations in Boston. Despite this Rome stepped in, and Cardinal Law was appointed to a plum clerical post as archpriest at one of the four great basilicas in Rome, St Mary Major, which came with an apartment, a chauffeur-driven car and $10,000 a month in salary. It also meant that he was entitled to say one of the nine Masses that follows the death of a pope, as he did in 2005 when Pope John Paul II died. The people of Boston were outraged; not that Rome seemed bothered.

This was the same Cardinal Law who, on her State visit to the US in 1998, told President Mary McAleese, following her taking

Communion in Dublin's Christ Church Cathedral in December 1997, that she was 'a very poor Catholic president'. She corrected him brusquely, pointing out that she was 'not a Catholic president. I'm President of Ireland' where 'there were all sorts of people. I'm their President. I happen to be Catholic.'

No such favoured treatment would be extended by the Church to Bishop Eamonn Casey. On my return to Ireland after that visit to Ecuador, I began to write about his coming home to Ireland, but it soon became clear there was no appetite at senior level in the Irish Catholic Church, or in the English Catholic Church either, for his return.

Casey's resignation as Bishop of Galway on a May morning in 1992 had a seismic effect on the Catholic Church in Ireland. On Thursday 7 May *The Irish Times* had run a front-page story headed 'Dr Casey resigns as Bishop of Galway'. It had emerged that the bishop had a seventeen-year-old son, Peter, with Annie Murphy, then resident in Connecticut. It referred to payments from Galway's diocesan accounts, amounting to $115,000, made to her and a lawyer in New York in 1990, along with other regular payments to Annie over a period of fifteen years since the mid-1970s. This money was paid back into the Galway accounts almost as soon as these payments were revealed. Within days Annie Murphy was telling her story to the Irish media. A second cousin once removed of Bishop Casey's and twenty-five years old, she had been sent to him in Ireland by her devout doctor father as she recovered from divorce and a miscarriage.

The idea of an Irish Catholic bishop having sex, never mind a seventeen-year-old son, was deeply shocking to many of the Irish Catholic faithful. That such a bishop should also take money from diocesan accounts was a double whammy but, compared with what would emerge in following years, the morning of 7 May 1992 was a pale dawn indeed.

It was the beginning of the end for nineteenth-/twentieth-century Catholic Ireland. Fianna Fáil leader Albert Reynolds was taoiseach in 'a temporary little arrangement' coalition government with the Progressive Democrat Party, which has since disappeared. Minister for Health Dr John O'Connell was preparing a bill to allow contraceptives to be sold in public, and there were nervous whispers of a second referendum to allow divorce in Ireland. The first one, in 1986, failed to pass. Although abortion was banned, homosexuality was illegal and, according to a poll that year by Adelaide Market Research, weekly Mass attendance was the highest in the Catholic world at 78 per cent. This was all about to change, change utterly.

By the time of his downfall, Bishop Casey had been operating at a senior level in Irish Church governance for twenty-three years, from the time of his appointment as Bishop of Kerry in 1969. His exposure led to great embarrassment to the Church, which felt deeply damaged by what emerged. Great institutions, even religious ones, are merciless when it comes to individuals deemed to be a threat, and so it was where Eamonn Casey was concerned. The Church leadership was determined to keep him out of Ireland after his time in Ecuador, and as Cardinal Basil Hume, his successor as president of Shelter in London, made clear, Eamonn Casey would not be going back to the archdiocese of Westminster in London either, where he had served before becoming Bishop of Kerry. What was to become of him then, when he ended his time in Ecuador? That was the question.

In January 1998, en route to Cuba to report on Pope John Paul II's visit there, I interviewed Cardinal Basil Hume, then Archbishop of Westminster, at his offices in London. I had expected a saintly figure with a somewhat otherworldly demeanour, going by the cardinal's writings and reputation. The reality was quite different. What I met was a tall, thin Geordie, not unlike the late

Ireland international football manager Jack Charlton. Courteous, but steely, he said there were 'many reasons why it would be inappropriate for Bishop Casey to be in London'. I was taken aback by the vehement tone. It soon became clear that Cardinal Hume's primary concern was with protecting the Church's reputation. In that he was being consistent.

A 2018 investigation by the Independent Inquiry into Child Sexual Abuse (IICSA) in England and Wales found that 'safeguarding children was less important than the reputation of the church and the well-being of the abusive monks' at the leading Catholic and Benedictine Ampleforth and Downside schools in England during the 1960s and over the decades since then. Cardinal Hume, a Benedictine, had been abbot at Ampleforth from 1963 to 1976, during which time the authorities there, according to the IICSA report, hid allegations of 'appalling sexual abuse' against pupils as young as seven to protect the Church's reputation. No surprise then, that he would not indulge a return to London by Eamonn Casey.

Eventually a post was found for Bishop Casey in the southern English diocese of Arundel and Brighton, where Cormac Murphy O'Connor was bishop – a man with strong Cork connections who later succeeded Basil Hume as archbishop of Westminster, himself becoming a cardinal in 2001. It emerged that he too had covered up for an abuser priest in the diocese of Arundel and Brighton, transferring him to a chapel at Gatwick Airport, where the priest abused again. The priest concerned was jailed twice for abusing nine children in one case and three in the other.

To digress a little, none of that seemed to dismay Pope Benedict XVI, who, towards the end of 2010, made Cardinal Murphy O'Connor part of the apostolic delegation sent to investigate the Irish Catholic Church, including its child safeguarding standards, following publication in 2009 of the Ryan and Murphy reports, with their scarifying findings on sexual abuse by clergy in residential institutions for children as well as in Dublin parishes, and the cover-up of this by Church authorities.

A focus for that visitation was the four Catholic archdioceses in Ireland – Armagh, Cashel & Emly, Dublin and Tuam – with each visitation team led by a cardinal. Cardinal Murphy O'Connor led the visitation to Armagh archdiocese, seat of the Primate of All Ireland, then Cardinal Seán Brady. Rome did not appreciate the irony of, or was indifferent to, a perception that might arise from sending a cardinal with Archbishop Murphy O'Connor's record on child protection to investigate Armagh on such matters. Nor did Rome or Pope Benedict seem overly concerned that earlier in 2010 it had been revealed that, as a canon lawyer in the 1970s, Cardinal Brady himself had sworn to secrecy children abused by prolific child abuser Father Brendan Smyth while conducting a Church inquiry into that abuse. The cases were never reported to police and Smyth continued to abuse children for another twenty years, until 1993, when he was jailed for the first time.

But then Pope Benedict himself had form in the cover-up stakes. In the 2022 findings of an investigation in Germany, commissioned by the Church itself, it was found that when he was archbishop of Munich between 1977 and 1982, Benedict failed to act in four child abuse cases and the accused priests remained active in the Church. Initially he denied that he had failed to act in the four cases, but later he admitted that errors were made in his handling of them. He sought forgiveness for any 'grievous fault' involved, yet denied personal wrongdoing.

You might say the above are examples of black pots investigating black kettles.

Abuse allegations from the past were made against Bishop Casey himself in November 2005, while he was in Arundel and Brighton. The person making the allegations was his niece

Patricia Donovan, who said he had abused her in Ireland during the 1950s, from the age of five, when he was a curate in Limerick. He denied the allegations and, following a garda investigation, no charges were brought against him. In 2019 the case re-emerged in the media when it was reported that two other women had also made abuse allegations against the then Father Casey from his period as a curate in Limerick. One woman received compensation from the Residential Institutions Redress Board, but it is unclear whether this was linked to her allegation against Father Casey or arose from her experiences as a child in the relevant institution. In the other case a settlement was agreed after Bishop Casey's death in 2017 between the Church and the woman, who had initiated High Court action.

In 1998 strong opposition to Bishop Casey's return to Ireland from Ecuador was led by senior Irish bishops, particularly Archbishop of Dublin Desmond Connell, whose main concern was that Casey would be a constant source of media attention in Ireland. So Casey ended up working as a hospital chaplain in the Arundel and Brighton diocese. Still, as it became clear that his period in Ecuador was coming to an end, speculation continued in the media and elsewhere as to why he was not being allowed to return to Ireland. In 2004 this prompted his successor as Bishop of Galway, James McLoughlin, to say, 'The idea that the bishops are keeping Bishop Casey out of Ireland is the greatest rubbish because the man is coming and going.' He continued, 'Quite honestly, it is the press that are keeping him out, the media.' There may have been some truth in that, but it was far from being the full story.

Yes, Bishop Casey did visit Ireland occasionally while based in England, but, in reality, he was kept out of Ireland for fourteen years after the 1992 revelations, until 2006, when he was retired to the rural townland of Shanaglish, near Gort in east Galway, far away from the prying eyes of most media. He was also not allowed return to public ministry by Church authorities, so he could not say Masses in public. Why this should be so was raised frequently in the media, not least by myself. Considering what had been disclosed in the intervening years about the scale of child sexual abuse involving priests and its extensive cover-up by Church authorities, including bishops, this ongoing humiliation of Bishop Casey seemed more and more about revenge.

About two years after he returned to Galway, I was given an unexpected insight into the Church's concerns about him and why, probably, he was not being restored to full ministry. I was contacted by a woman who said she wished to talk to me about Casey, off the record. As it happened, I knew her. She was a very successful career woman, whom I admired as a person and had met a couple of times with a mutual friend. On this occasion we met in Dublin, and she told me how as a young woman in London she had had an affair with the then Father Casey. After his return to Ireland as a bishop, the relationship was not resumed, but they had remained in infrequent contact. What upset her most, then, was that when she met him in more recent years he didn't remember her.

By then it was clear that Eamonn Casey was in the early stages of Alzheimer's. He and I met at an event for Trócaire (the overseas development agency of the Irish Catholic Church) in Dublin not long before I had agreed to meet this woman, and even when I introduced myself to him it was clear he struggled to remember me or our phone calls. Even when he professed recognition eventually, I was not convinced. Previously, in May 2010, he had told me, 'My memory is gone badly for a long, long time. I got four mini strokes in my brain about eight years ago. They told me – they were very blunt – they said, "You've had four mini strokes." I said, "What does that mean?" "You're on your way to Alzheimer's or a stroke." And I said, "What can I do?" "Very little," they said.' That was while he was in the diocese of Arundel and Brighton.

His denial of recognising the woman who contacted me about him was very upsetting for her. The timing of her contacting me, as I and others in the media were querying why Casey was not being allowed return to public ministry, made me wonder. I asked her whether the then Bishop of Galway, Martin Drennan, was aware she was meeting me. She said he was. I realised then I was being told, through this woman, that the bishops could not restore Eamonn Casey to full ministry because they had no idea what else might be revealed from his past life to come back and haunt them should they do so.

Was I being manipulated by Bishop Drennan through this woman? Yes. Was he justified in trying do so? Probably. It was indeed believable that no one could know what else might be discovered from Bishop Casey's life.

For him, life in Shanaglish was congenial. By then in his eighties, he used drive into the town of Gort four or five times a week, buy a paper and go to the Lady Gregory restaurant for lunch. He became friendly with local man Robin Marcus, who had a garage on the Old Ennis Road. They drank together locally; Bishop Casey took wine, Robin pints. As Robin recalled it, 'We understood one another. He liked to banter a lot. We'd watch Vincent Browne [on TV3] in his house when we returned from the pub. Sometimes we'd go for a meal with my wife and she'd drive. We'd usually drink too much, it was part of the bargain. We enjoyed the craic. By God he could sing. Many's a time I was with him when people would come over and shake his hand. He was a great one to be with and said it like it is.'

Robin Marcus is a descendant of the Jewish Marcus family in Cork, a cousin of the late author and editor David Marcus and his brother filmmaker Louis. Robin's mother was Catholic and his father had to change religion to marry her. It meant he was estranged from his father's family. Through Bishop Casey and

Father Dermod McCarthy, former head of religious programmes at RTÉ, an arrangement was made for Robin to meet Louis in Dublin. 'We had a great chat, for hours,' he said.

As his Alzheimer's became more pronounced, Bishop Casey was admitted to the Carrigoran House nursing home in Newmarket-on-Fergus, County Clare. Among his visitors was Julian Filochowski who, in March 1980, had been with Casey when he risked his life to help people in San Salvador's cathedral at the funeral of Archbishop Óscar Romero, who had been assassinated by government forces. During Romero's funeral, more than fifty people died in a stampede near the cathedral. Filochowski recalled how 'the cathedral was packed with huge crowds outside. Soldiers felt the crowd was unruly and fired over their heads. It created panic. Most of the dead were crushed. Eamonn Casey went around among the injured and dead [regardless of his own safety] helping and supporting in any way he could.' That was primarily why Filochowski requested to see him. He wanted to meet Casey again while he was still alive. They went for a meal at Bunratty Castle. They talked about the Romero funeral, but Bishop Casey 'probably didn't remember it five minutes later' was his visitor's observation afterwards.

As a bishop, Casey felt strongly about what was happening in Central America and was very critical of US foreign policy there, not least in El Salvador. In 1984 he and Michael D. Higgins, then a lecturer at the university in Galway, organised a protest on the city's Eyre Square to coincide with the conferring of an honorary degree on US President Ronald Reagan at the university.

Bishop Casey died in May 2017, aged eighty-nine, after spending years in the County Clare nursing home. A total of eleven bishops and sixty-one priests took part in his funeral Mass at Galway's crowded Cathedral of Our Lady Assumed into Heaven and St Nicholas. The main celebrant was Bishop of Clonfert John Kirby, who succeeded Casey as chair of Trócaire, the Irish Catholic bishops' overseas development agency. Welcoming President Higgins before the Mass, Bishop Kirby remarked, 'ar chuid mhaith cúrsaí bheadh an intinn céanna ag an mbeirt acu, an tEasbag Eamonn agus Mícheál D.' (in a lot of things they were of the same mind, Bishop Eamonn and Michael D.).

In a carefully crafted homily, then Bishop of Achonry Brendan Kelly said Casey's funeral Mass was 'neither the time nor the place' to address events of twenty-five years previously concerning 'hidden realities in his life', including the fact that he had a son. These realities 'were nothing less than earth-shattering for the Church and for people in general,' he said. 'We are all sinners, but irresponsibility, infidelity and sin are particularly shocking in the lives of those who preach the Gospel.' Bishop Kelly recalled how there were also 'those of us who remember, with gratitude, his kindness and encouragement when personally we most needed it'. Afterwards Casey was interred in the cathedral crypt.

As Bishop of Achonry, Brendan Kelly had shared the platform with me many times at our annual St Patrick's Day parade in Ballaghaderreen, where his cathedral and residence were located. I was parade MC on many of those occasions. It was known that the priests of Galway diocese had wanted him, then parish priest in Spiddal, County Galway, as their bishop when James McLaughlin retired in 2005. Instead, a then Auxiliary Bishop of Dublin, Martin Drennan, was appointed to Galway. In July 2016 Bishop Drennan stood down as Bishop of Galway for health reasons, which meant that at the time of Bishop Casey's funeral Galway did not have a bishop. Speaking to Bishop Kelly in the cathedral after the Casey funeral, I asked whether it was likely he would now be 'translated' – a term used in Church circles when a bishop is moved from one diocese to another – to Galway. 'I'm too old,' he said. He was seventy and bishops retired at seventy-five. Nevertheless, the following December he was appointed Bishop of Galway.

✠ ✠ ✠

I never met Annie Murphy but always admired that feisty woman. There can be no doubt that her healthy self-esteem was a reflection of her being an American. Had she grown up in Ireland, there is little doubt that deference to the Church would have restrained her from going public about her sexual relationship with a bishop or in acknowledging the paternity of her son. That, and also how such an admission might have been seen in wider Irish society, where, most likely, 'blame' would have been placed at her door rather than the bishop's.

In particular, I admired her grace, composure and dignity as she was treated outrageously during an appearance on RTÉ's *The Late Late Show* in 1993, particularly her retort to the very biased host Gay Byrne on that occasion when he said, 'If your son is half as good a man as his father he won't be doing too bad.' She responded, in the face of such hostility, 'I'm not so bad either, Mr Byrne.' One of the questions Byrne asked her then was if Peter was Eamonn Casey's child. 'Yes, he is and you could put me in a firing squad and I'd say he is Eamonn's child,' she replied. Anyone who has met Peter Murphy would have no need to ask the question. He is cut out of his father, as they say.

Peter was thirty-eight when I interviewed him in 2013, and what was most striking was that this man has no idea of the implications of his very existence for so many Irish Catholics. It is not an exaggeration to say he represented, in the flesh, the beginning of the end of Catholic Church dominance in Ireland. Yes, the Church's decline was already under way before Peter's existence was disclosed in 1992, but its demise was greatly accelerated by his just being alive.

That he had no idea of this is hardly surprising, because his entire cultural background is American. He is a big guy. Relaxed, affable, with no chips on either shoulder. He is, he said, 'a fat single white guy, with a cat ... I'm basically any comedian's wet dream.' At the time he worked near Boston 'in consumer electronics. I sell televisions.' He spent three years at the University of Connecticut – 'I did more drinking than I did studying' – and was a 'typical jackass American of that age. I didn't know what I wanted to be, so I changed majors every three months and I majored in having fun. I loved UConn ... In what would have been my junior year I moved to Boston.' There, he went to Emerson College. 'It's an arts school. I never went to a lot of the classes. I hated structured academia.' His father got him his first job. 'To get [me] through school, to make a living, Eamonn, through the Irish Immigration Centre, got me a job at a hotel and I got a job in a bar called the Last Hurrah. It got me into the restaurant industry.'

He first became aware of his father as a small boy. 'I was five or six. My grandmother told me. I don't remember the instant when she told me. My mom always had this newspaper article with a picture of Eamonn blowing on some brass instrument, a trumpet.' One morning in 1983 or 1984, his mother, Annie, woke him, saying, '"Listen, wake up. Do you want to see your father?" And I said, "What do you mean? I've seen the photo." "No," she said, "do you want to see him?" Then she brought me downstairs ... I remember coming down the stairwell and [on the television screen] I could see [President Ronald] Reagan on the one side and I could tell there was another person on the other ... and I recognised him right away. It was, what do you call it? An epiphany. It was some Sunday-morning political show.'

He was fifteen years old before he met his father. It was 'in the law offices of the attorney Peter McKay, who represented the paternity suit my mom made … in New York. That was the first time I met Eamonn.' It did not go well. 'He didn't want to talk to me. In hindsight, I was the representation of the end of everything he worked for. Of course, I took it incredibly personally. I ran down. Got the elevator. Came downstairs. Tried to keep a stoic face. Saw my mom and burst into tears … You're fifteen, have questions. He didn't want to answer them. I felt slighted.'

The purpose of that meeting was 'to get something back for the years that my mom had to, basically, pay for me. For me the most important thing was meeting him. When you're fifteen, you don't understand. So, it was what it was.' They met again shortly after *The Irish Times* broke the story that revealed Peter Murphy's existence. 'I met him in 1992, a few months after, maybe June. I can't remember correctly. I met him quickly. He wanted to strike while the iron was hot. He met me right away. [At the first meeting] I was an angry little prick, but he was patient and calm, understanding. He said he wanted to do it again and I said, "Maybe." I agreed when I was up at UConn.'

Their second meeting was at the university. 'It was the fall of 1992 or spring 1993. I was still a little bit … I was not going to give in to him. He was entrancing. One of those figures. It was a heck of a lot more positive an interaction.' Their next meeting was in New York, 'and that was a great time, summer of 1993. He was so engaging. There was no agenda, no "Let's get into this." We just talked. He was very smart, the way he dealt with it. He really kept it open and airy and "Just let's have a good time and let's talk. You have a question for me, ask it. I may be able to answer it and I may not." That's just the way it worked. We talked about politics, anything, the day, the weather, I don't know, whatever came into my brain.'

They continued to meet regularly thereafter, 'at least two,

maybe three times a year. Somewhere around 2001 or 2002, it reduced down to one time a year. Because, I mean, at this [stage] he was seventy-five.' In the latter years they met in Boston. 'Always in Boston. The first few times in New York. I moved up to Boston in 1995. Once I moved up to Boston we always met there. He loved it ... I worked in the restaurant industry for a long time. I went to all the places either my friends managed or I worked at ... They loved to meet him.' These get-togethers 'were Olympic-like events of eating and drinking'.

It was about ten years before Peter and I met that he noticed for the first time that his father was losing his sharpness. 'I think it must've been 2002 or 2003. He got very flummoxed. At first I blamed it on the alcohol ... It was the following year that we needed to have lunches, not dinners. I don't know if that was the beginning of the deterioration or just ... he was seventy-six or seventy-seven years old.' Having seen his maternal grandmother deteriorate from Alzheimer's, Peter recognised the symptoms in his father. Then, following one of their phone conversations, 'I knew right away. About three years ago. I called him up and he didn't know who I was.'

Recounting the conversation, Peter said, in a mimicked Kerry accent, '"Who are you?" "It's Peter." "I don't know you." "Are you okay?" "I can't talk to you ... I ... I ... I'm sorry and I'm sorry, I can't talk to you." He could hear my voice. He knew he should know who I was.' It was the last time they spoke. 'I tried calling the number many times after that, and it just went, "This voicemail is full," and I just said to myself, "You know what, they've got their hands full."'

As to how they got on as father and son, Peter anticipates the question: 'Did I form a relationship? Did I get to love the man? Sure. But in the end we were never father and son. We were two people who got to know each other. Him, very much in the twilight of his life. Me, as a young adult. We became very good friends. That's all I ever wanted from him.'

Where the Catholic Church's treatment of his father was concerned, Peter was not impressed: 'It was ridiculous. I mean, all those years' penance in a foreign country and then the years he spent in England made it even more egregious and more painful because of how close he was to his goal and all he wanted to do was go home and say Mass. Was that so terrible? So, no, especially with what has come across our eyes in the last seventeen, twenty years ... all the paedophile scandals. To tell you the truth, I felt this way from the get-go. What did the guy do? He had an affair.'

Being forbidden to say Mass in public was something Bishop Casey found particularly hard, according to Peter: 'The last two or three times that we met, that was it. That's all he wanted to be able to do. He felt if he could do that he could really be at peace with everything that had happened. That was one thing that gnawed at him that he wasn't able to take part in or to do. His faith was paramount to who he was. No matter what he believed, that was a massive part of him. And the Church? He loved the Church. No matter what it did to him, he still loved it.'

As for Peter's mother, Annie, he said she didn't dwell on the past. She moved on. What happened was 'part of her life. She's got her art. She draws, writes stories and that.' Nor had he himself any sense of anger: 'I've no time for that shit, to be blunt. There's enough stresses in my life. I've to pay bills. I'm getting fat. I've got to lose weight. You know what I mean? I don't want to waste my time being angry about something neither I nor anyone else has any control over. That's the kind of stuff that gives you ulcers and cancer. Don't get me wrong. I'm far from perfect. I've got my own idiosyncrasies and asinine things, but [I'm not] angry about things [that happened] over a long period, about stuff I can't control.'

6

Heraclitus

For the first ten years of my period as Religious Affairs Correspondent of *The Irish Times*, Thomas Flynn was the Bishop of
Achonry, my local diocese in the West of Ireland and one of the
smallest on the island. I had known him since I was twelve, when
I started attending St Nathy's College in Ballaghaderreen. He
taught classical Greek, a subject for which I had no affection. The
college's last teacher of Greek, he introduced us to that strange
language, all the way from alpha to omega. Through him we met
Thucydides, Xenophon, the seemingly endless Peloponnesian
War, Euripides, Homer, Sophocles, Socrates, Herodotus, Xerxes,
Darius, Alexander, Plato, Aristotle, Athens, Sparta, all that awful
grammar, and Heraclitus.

One day he came into our classroom, animated about
Heraclitus. 'Lads,' he began, 'the philosopher Heraclitus said,
"No man steps in the same river twice", but ...', he paused to
allow this to sink in, then continued, 'but, no one steps in the
same river *even once*.' He pronounced 'even once' with emphasis
and waited for our astonished reaction. It didn't happen. We were
just bewildered. To us this was in defiance of common sense. We
had all stepped into the same river. Many times.

Father Flynn's habit was to pace up the centre of the classroom,

117

his soutane swishing at a steady rhythm. He'd genuflect the right knee slightly when he reached the back of the room, before turning to journey back again. It was also the case that his head shook involuntarily, which is why, with the typical sensitivity shown by teenage boys, he had been nicknamed 'Tommy Ding Dong'. When he cracked a joke or made a clever observation, as then, he literally pressed his tongue hard into his cheek as he waited for the penny to drop. It frequently didn't.

And so it was, as he and Heraclitus puzzled us, and he waited for a spark of enlightenment to fire in even one head before him. He repeated the phrase. 'No one steps in the same river once ...', he said again, pausing once more for dramatic effect, 'because, lads, it is never the same river.'

Our collective response was on the lines of a polite, 'Ah Jaysus, Father.'

Father Flynn delighted in such cleverness. You might say that he had a preference for the abstract over lived reality, a priest of his times. A generous teacher of a difficult subject, which many of us met with deep emotional resistance and couldn't see the point of, he was patient and kind and arranged extra tuition in his own free time for those of us who found Greek a bridge too far. He later became president at St Nathy's and then Catholic bishop of Achonry. Very few, in any walk of life, reach such heights as he did without leaving their home parish.

He was also helpful to me in a difficult situation. When I studied for the HDip in Education at University College Galway (UCG), Father Flynn was president at St Nathy's and gave me generous hours for teaching practice. He was supportive when I ran into problems with the Education Department at the university. By then I had a fairly high profile owing to activity in student politics and as auditor of the Literary and Debating Society, where I was responsible for organising and chairing weekly debates. I had

decided to 'do the Dip' more as a safety net, than because of any
ambition to teach.

I was immediately on the wrong foot with the Education
Department. One of its most senior personnel, Father James
Mitchell, then being talked about as a future Bishop of Galway,
took me aside and advised me to give up all my activities and
concentrate on 'the Dip'. I expect he didn't approve of my politics,
not least where the Church was concerned. I also felt that my
extra-curricular activities were none of his business, though I
didn't say it to him. Besides, 'the Dip' was not regarded as the
most onerous course at the university.

At one of our early lectures on teaching practice, another of
the Education Department's senior academics, who favoured the
old tried and trusted method of terrorising pupils on your first
arrival in the classroom, illustrated how we might do this, with
much sound and fury directed at the imaginary teenagers before
him. This was in the mid-1970s, when corporal punishment in
schools was still legal in Ireland. When I challenged him, saying
it was hardly necessary as I knew it was possible to maintain
control over hundreds of unruly students [at debates] on a
weekly basis without resorting to such methods, he was not
pleased.

Then I found out Father Mitchell was to be my teaching
practice supervisor. He arrived at St Mary's College in Galway,
where I was doing my practice then, for first class one morning to
find I wasn't there. I was at home (genuinely) sick with the flu and
had informed the St Mary's authorities that morning. However,
Father Mitchell hadn't been informed. He sent me a sharp letter
expressing his great annoyance. By then, and feeling put upon, I
replied in a way I shouldn't have. I told him that the reason I had
not informed him in advance was that I hadn't anticipated being
sick that morning or him being at St Mary's.

After that I knew my goose was cooked, having done my bit in ensuring that. I passed the written exam, but he failed me in teaching practice. It meant either repeating the teaching practice element to get the Diploma or leaving it all behind. Having to spend another year in Galway was not exactly a sentence, so I approached Father Flynn about getting teaching hours in St Nathy's for the repeat. I apprised him of the situation. He was sympathetic. Then I was told my teaching practice supervisor this time would be the senior lecturer whose methods I had challenged. He visited me at St Nathy's and failed me too.

Colleagues at UCG were outraged on my behalf and wanted to organise a campaign. Father Flynn was as unhappy. I did not want a campaign. I just wanted it all over with. The then Dean of the Arts Faculty at UCG, Professor Mairéád Ní Éimhigh (or 'Ma Heavy', as we students referred to her), got involved and was also sympathetic. Along with a junior lecturer in the Education Department, she appealed to me to do another stint of teaching practice at St Nathy's. I knew then that this was to get them off the hook and felt seriously tempted to refuse but, for once, common sense prevailed.

Father Flynn was only too happy to help. On this occasion my teaching practice supervisor was the junior lecturer in the Education Department. I passed. Inevitably this experience coloured my view of Father Flynn and, though he had a reputation for being slippery, I liked the man.

He was Bishop of Achonry for thirty-one years, from 1976 until 2007, and spokesman for the Catholic bishops until 1997, the same year I became Religious Affairs Correspondent at *The Irish Times*. When I was appointed to the job, he invited me to meet him at 'The Bishop's Palace', where he lived near Ballaghaderreen. He presented me with two books – *The Catechism of the Catholic Church* and *The New Dictionary of Theology* – as gifts. I still have them.

He was very traditional and old school when it came to Church teaching. Famously, it is said his fellow bishops blamed him for losing the November 1995 divorce referendum. Just before that referendum he told Joe Little of RTÉ that Catholics who divorced and lived with a new partner as husband and wife would be refused the sacraments. It annoyed a lot of people, on both sides of the debate. The 'Yes' (to divorce) side won by just over 9,000 votes. Many on the 'No' side blamed Bishop Flynn's trenchant RTÉ interview and, of course, RTÉ for their loss.

Our paths crossed regularly in Ballaghaderreen, mainly at St Patrick's Day parades, where I was usually MC. Even during the torrid years of emerging scandals and statutory reports, Bishop Flynn was never uneasy or unpleasant with me, despite the fact that he didn't like the media and despite some torrid commentary by myself on the Church's handling of clerical child sexual abuse. We did have one terse, difficult conversation arising from that issue. That was when I questioned him on his handling of a clerical child sex abuse case locally. It involved a popular woman in a local parish who arrived home one day in 1982 to find her son being sexually abused by a priest who was filling in while the parish priest was away. This locum priest had been visiting her husband, who was very ill. At first, when the story was exposed, I absented myself from reporting on it, telling news desk colleagues that I knew too many of the people involved. Throughout, Bishop Flynn took a narrow view of the case, along the lines of 'nothing to do with us. He's an order priest.'

When the abuse happened, the family went to their local parish priest, whom I also knew, when he returned from leave. The story came to light in 2003 and the mother concerned recalled how, when they went to this parish priest in 1982, the family 'got a very poor reception and were sent on their way with a comment such as "how dare a brat like my son make such an accusation against

121

a man of the cloth."' It was April 2002 before the abused man made a statement to gardaí. He received substantial compensation from the Kiltegan Fathers, the congregation of which the accused priest was a member.

After it came to light in 2003, the news desk at *The Irish Times* felt I should report on the case as I had a lot of background and local knowledge of it. I spoke to Bishop Flynn about it by phone. It was a very strained conversation. He insisted the first he had heard about the case was in November 2002. He was not aware the locum priest was in the parish and had not given permission for him to be there. He had told the family the case had nothing to do with the diocese as the priest involved belonged to a religious congregation. It was none of the diocese's business, he told them.

I asked Bishop Flynn whether he had reported the case to gardaí when he heard about it, in accordance with Church child protection guidelines. He had not. 'When dealing with adults, why should I go to the guards with allegations when there are responsible people there with evidence? They are not simple people,' he told me.

The accused priest had disappeared years before, he said, and he 'couldn't see him as a threat to anybody in the area'. He also said that, where victims of abuse were concerned, 'the media causes greater suffering than the original incident. That is the view of quite a number of people, including victims.' It was their view, too, that, in dealing with such cases, the media had already made up their mind when priests were involved. 'They put a twist on what they hear,' he said, which he described as 'anti-clerical'. He had not apologised to the family concerned, which they had requested, because 'it is awfully hard to apologise for something you had nothing to do with'.

Bishop Flynn and I never discussed that case again, and whenever we met afterwards we were just as civil and cordial to each another as before, though I always believed that from then on he saw me as a wolf in sheep's clothing.

A review of child protection practices in Achonry diocese in June 2013 (six years after Bishop Flynn retired in 2007; he died in 2015) found that, since 1975, eleven priests there had faced fifteen allegations of child sex abuse. None was convicted, with one, then retired, still alive. The review, conducted by the Maynooth-based National Board for Safeguarding Priests, found that in Bishop Flynn's time 'the diocese did not have a safeguarding policy and procedures document' and 'little evidence of any systematic process for filing or managing information about allegations relating to child abuse in the diocese'. There was 'scant evidence' that Bishop Flynn had shared allegations with the civil authorities 'as required in the [Church] policy and procedures'. There had been 'numerous examples' where 'there were long and unacceptable delays in communicating information about possible child abuse to An Garda Síochána or the HSE Child Protection service and in managing cases appropriately'. There was also 'an absence of appropriate response' by Bishop Flynn 'to allegations of risk, or to victims. In one case the reviewers noted that a priest was allowed to remain in ministry even after the previous bishop [Flynn] had received an allegation, which was not reported or addressed. Six months later the priest retired, with still no evidence that the allegation had been put to him. He has since died.'

The safeguarding review covered Flynn's entire period as bishop from 1976 to 2007. When it came to child protection it was a very poor record, but by no means exceptional where bishops of his generation were concerned. In general, when it came to accountability, those men adopted an attitude not dissimilar to that of the patrician Cabots of Boston, of whom it was said that, whereas everyone spoke to them, they spoke only to God.

7

Insurance and a
Medieval Monk

Of all the stories that emerged, one – above all others –
illustrated the mindset of the Catholic Church authorities
in Ireland when it came to protecting the institution and its assets
from the consequences of how they had dealt with allegations of
the sexual abuse of children by their priests. It was the revelation
that all the Irish bishops did in the early years was take out
insurance when alerted to what might be coming down the track.
That was in 1987. It would be almost another decade before they
published guidelines on child protection: a booklet, *Child Sexual
Abuse: Framework for a Church Response*, commonly referred to
as 'The Green Book', was produced in 1996.

In establishing that all the bishops did initially was take
out insurance policies, I was guided by a source who remains a
mystery to me but who, clearly, knew where the bodies lay buried,
particularly in Dublin's Catholic archdiocese. He and I (and I have
always assumed it was a 'he', probably a priest) communicated
irregularly, generally when he felt like it, for over seven years until
early 2010, when I received the last email.

The initial contact was in early 2003, when he sent me typed details in two brown envelopes, one with a Cnoc Mhuire (Knock, County Mayo) postmark and 'A souvenir from Knock' written on its back. Both were marked 'Private & Confidential', the two words underlined, and in one case starting with 'Strictly'. And at the end of both, printed in black ink and capitals, was 'FIAT JUSTICA ... ET RUANT COELI' (Let justice be done ... though the Heavens fall). Both letters, sent to me at *The Irish Times*, were signed 'LAZARUS', in capitals and black ink. I have no idea as to the significance of this, but I was very familiar with the Latin phrase. A variation of it is written over the entrance to the Bridewell Garda Station in Dublin, where Nicky Kelly and others had false confessions beaten out of them following the 1976 Sallins mail train robbery, then the biggest such robbery in the history of the Irish State. I had written about the case in *The Irish Times* and elsewhere, and later wrote the book *While Justice Slept* (2007) about the gross miscarriages of justice involved.

In later email contact 'Lazarus' referred to himself as 'Cadfael' and sometimes as 'Grand Inquisitor'. Cadfael was a twelfth-century Benedictine monk detective who was the main character in a series of novels by Ellis Peters, published between 1977 and 1994 and dramatised on ITV between 1994 and 1998. A Grand Inquisitor was, for a long time, the Catholic Church's lead figure for inquiring into alleged heresy. The title could also be a reference to a character in the Dostoevsky novel *The Brothers Karamazov*, where the Grand Inquisitor argues that Jesus was wrong in resisting the temptations of the Devil in the desert, thereby conferring on humanity more freedom than it could bear.

It was the initial information from 'Cadfael' in early 2003 that led me to the most damning revelation in those years about how the Catholic Church in Ireland really saw allegations of clerical child sexual abuse. They were just a threat to them. Cadfael supplied me with details of how, in the later 1980s, the

Irish bishops had taken out insurance with Church & General, later taken over by Allianz, as protection against compensation claims arising from child sex abuse by their priests. He also told me how the insurers became so anxious about the accuracy of information about abuser priests supplied by the bishops that they bought themselves out of the initial agreement in two hard-fought negotiation sessions in the 1990s. In other words, the insurers had been misled by the bishops.

I put the facts relayed to me by Cadfael to the bishops and the relevant insurance company, leading to the story which appeared in *The Irish Times* on 5 February 2003. In their statement then, the bishops confirmed that 'between 1987 and 1990 most dioceses obtained separate insurance policies from Church & General against the eventuality of legal liability accruing to a diocese from acts of child sexual abuse by priests'. They also said that since 1999 the bishops had had in place a €10.6 million fund to cover such claims. The origin of that €10.6 million, which the bishops did not explain then, would be revealed later. It resulted from the bishops not disclosing to the insurer that they already had abuse cases on their files when they first approached Church & General in 1987. The insurers bought themselves out of the 1987 deal for the €10.6 million, but still agreed to cover them for cases that arose from 1996 onwards.

The Church & General insurance company was formed by the Irish bishops at the beginning of the last century and in 2003 they still had a 'nominal' share in the company. Neither the bishops nor Church & General would tell me when questioned in 2003 what the 'serious legal issues' were that the bishops claimed had arisen between them in 1995. However, this was clarified in November 2009, when the Murphy Commission reported. On the issue of insurance it said, 'serious consideration was first given in 1986 to obtaining specific insurance cover' where possible claims arising from clerical child sex abuse might happen. An approach was made to Church & General Insurance, principal insurers for the Catholic Church in Ireland and part of the Allianz Group since 1998. 'Church & General understood that the impetus for this approach came from a visit by [then Archbishop of Dublin] Archbishop Kevin McNamara to the USA where he learned of difficulties in an American diocese arising from allegations of sex abuse by priests of that diocese.'

The report continued, 'It need hardly be pointed out by this Commission that the Archbishop's understanding of the need for insurance came from events much closer to home than the US. At this time, the Archdiocese had knowledge of approximately 20 priests against whom allegations of child sexual abuse had been made, or about whom there were suspicions or concerns.'

On 2 March 1987, according to the report, Church & General issued a policy for the archdiocese, wherein 'the stated insured was Archbishop McNamara and "his predecessors or successors in that office".' There was 'no indication given by the Archdiocese during the negotiations for the policy of any facts that would indicate that the Archdiocese had any prior experience of allegations of child sexual abuse by priests,' it said.

This was pretty shocking. Clearly, Archbishop McNamara's experience as a teacher of moral theology at the national seminary – St Patrick's College, Maynooth – did not impinge on his decision as Archbishop of Dublin to hide such relevant information from Church & General at the time. The Murphy Report said that under the terms of this initial policy, the archdiocese did, however, undertake to notify Church & General immediately it became aware of a priest whose behaviour might give rise to a claim. The policy agreed with Dublin was then made available to all other twenty-five Catholic dioceses in Ireland and was taken up by twenty-four of them. I never did find out which was the only Catholic diocese in Ireland not to take out insurance in this context.

Murphy continued that 'by 1994, Church & General was becoming concerned' about its financial exposure in the context. In February 1995 it sought renegotiation. As outlined above, talks took place with the Church, culminating in eventual agreement that the insurers would pay €10.6 million to the Stewardship Trust and so be free of all liability for claims arising from abuse incidents in the twenty-five dioceses before 1996. Each diocese then took out new cover for any claims arising from incidents of clerical abuse which took place after 1996.

There was no mystery about Cadfael's attitude to bishops and archbishops. Early in our correspondence he let me know his opinion of then Archbishop of Dublin, Cardinal Desmond Connell: 'So concerned is his eminence about the present crisis affecting his diocese that he has gone to Bari in Italy for a holiday!' That was tame compared to the consistent wrath he reserved for Archbishop Diarmuid Martin, who succeeded Cardinal Connell in April 2004. 'Cadfael', to put it mildly, did not like the new archbishop.

Apart from the insurance tip-off, much else of what he corresponded with me about were his grievances and those of some priests in Dublin at the approach of their new archbishop, who eschewed the paternalistic style of his predecessors. Archbishop Martin behaved towards them more like a chief executive and was less 'fatherly' towards his priests, whom he treated as adults. Or attempted to. Many were not used to that. Further, he had been out of Ireland for thirty years. Where some Dublin priests were concerned, his background at the Vatican's Council for Justice and Peace, where he had been secretary, then in its diplomatic service, culminating in his being its permanent representative at the UN in Geneva, did not cut the mustard. For his part, and probably to be more effective generally, Archbishop

Martin kept a distance from the Dublin clergy too – except for a small coterie of priests and lay staff with whom he surrounded himself at Archbishop's House in Drumcondra.

Martin had a difficult job. He was appointed to Dublin in 2004 in the direst circumstances. In October 2002 RTÉ had broadcast *Cardinal Secrets*, a damning television documentary by the late Mary Raftery that exposed the vile abuse of children by priests in Dublin and its cover-up by the hapless Cardinal Connell and his predecessors. The furore that followed led to a new law, the Commission of Investigation Act, passed in 2004, which allowed for more efficient and less costly State inquiries. The Dublin Archdiocese Commission of Investigation, the Murphy Commission, was established in March 2006 under that Act to investigate the handling of clerical child sexual abuse allegations in Dublin's Catholic archdiocese. This commission had legal powers of compellability, but its success would depend greatly on the new archbishop's cooperation. This he gave, 100 per cent, passing to the commission over 80,000 files from archdiocesan archives, including more than 5,000 documents that Cardinal Connell had deemed personal to him and over which the latter initiated a High Court action to stop their being passed to the commission. Eventually Cardinal Connell was persuaded by Church authorities in Ireland and Rome to drop this action. None of this made Archbishop Martin popular with his priests in Dublin or his brother bishops across the island.

Understandably, Cadfael felt strongly for innocent priests who were accused of abuse. But the issue was also a handy stick with which to beat his archbishop, as happened in April 2006, when, just weeks after the setting up of the Murphy Commission had been announced, Cadfael emailed me about a particularly sad case:

Out of the glare of the public eye, and in the privacy of St Kevin's Chapel in the Pro-Cathedral a strange scene unfolded after the Chrism Mass on Holy Thursday. Diarmuid Martin 'publicly' restored to ministry Fr —, a parish priest. Fr — had been 'stood down' following an allegation of child sexual abuse going back some thirty years. It turns out that the allegation was unfounded and he has been restored to Ministry. It was a sad scene, a priest with an unsullied reputation had been subjected to the humiliation of a public removal despite the Archbishop's insistence of his voluntary stepping aside, and his good name and reputation dragged through the mud. Even sadder still was the spectacle of this poor man thanking his tormentor for his restoration. Such is the loyalty of these older men that they will allow themselves to be used as a doormat and thank the offender for the experience. Privately he speaks of the pain and injustice of it all. Offenders need to be outed and have no place in the clergy – but the innocent need protection. Any priest can find himself in Fr —'s position on the most spurious of allegations. His Archbishop, it seems, doesn't give a shit. Oh yes he spoke of his 'losing sleep' over Fr — and his plight in quivering tones, but we have seen enough of him now to know that he can turn that on at will … This man is a politician par excellence not a shepherd. Shepherds care for their sheep. Politicised shepherds care primarily for themselves and their careers. His desire to be squeaky clean in the public perception is costing him the loyalty of his clergy who feel sold out.

This was an illustration of the broader anger felt by priests at how any of their number could be dealt with by bishops confronted with abuse allegations and whose policy then was immediate removal from ministry until the allegation was investigated, stood up or established as false. Certainly, some innocent men suffered greatly as a result, but the sad fact, as established through experience and various studies, is that few child abuse allegations are false.

It would be over two years before I had any further messages from Cadfael. In August 2008, after I wrote a piece reflecting the anger of some priests in Dublin with Archbishop Martin's style, Cadfael couldn't restrain himself in his enthusiasm. 'I am amazed by your piece in today's *Times* ... you have been firmly in his Grace's pocket for so long,' he emailed. 'The men in black are furious with his high-handedness.' He continued, 'Thank God someone has had the good sense to shout "The Emperor has no clothes", up to now you and others have written eloquently on the fine cut of them. Cadfael.'

This irked me and I responded typically, if excessively:

Cadfael, Well, well. I had thought you were dead! So many attempts to contact you since our last correspondence proved fruitless. Then it must've been that rather thick fabric in His Grace's pocket which prevented the signal getting through! Yes, there have been complaints about His Grace's 'style' vis-à-vis his priests, almost from Day 1. Few have been expressed directly, none have been on the record. Indeed one of the earliest expressions of such 'disquiet' was from your good self, but it too was not for public eyes. In such circumstances it is very difficult for the likes of those of us in His Grace's pocket to make reference, solely on the basis of rumour, innuendo and hearsay, without it being construed as gratuitous pursuit of mischief and which others among your colleagues would be among the first to shout about to the heavens. Indeed, is it not significant that the priest who has raised this issue has done so anonymously?

The fault therefore, dear Cadfael, is not with those of us comfortably residing in His Grace's pocket so much as with those smarting men who complain among themselves, do nothing, and blame others for not doing something about their ongoing predicament. Let them help themselves and you might then find that His Grace's pockets are suddenly not as crowded. With best regards and (truly) good to hear from you again.

The 'thought you were dead' phrase was crass but not without context. That name 'Cadfael' stopped me dead in my tracks at a funeral in January 2007, that of the late author, broadcaster, passionate Gaeilgeoir, bon viveur and general all-round decent man Seán Mac Réamoinn. He was part of the distinguished team of Irish journalists who had reported on the Second Vatican Council in the mid-1960s. Seán, in whose company it was my good fortune to revel many times, was given to the pithy phrase. He once remarked that 'everything in the Catholic Church is either forbidden or compulsory'. But my favourite was his description of himself in later life, as 'like a census form, I am broken down by age, sex and religion'.

I went to pay my respects at his removal and there Seán lay in an open coffin at Fagan's funeral directors on Dublin's Aungier Street. It was some time before I noticed a book had been stuffed into the coffin beside his right hand. It was one of the Cadfael chronicles. I was stunned. 'Seriously?', I muttered to myself. I shut up abruptly, realising I might be heard, not least by (the late) Monsignor Tom Stack who, inevitably, was there too. Parish priest in Milltown, Monsignor Tom shared that alleged divine quality of being everywhere present. He missed little and I did not want to arouse his curiosity. I calmed down. The more I thought about it, the more I realised the Cadfael who had been in contact with me could not be Seán because he would have spoken to me directly about such issues. Despite frequent emails to Cadfael about all of this around the time of Seán's funeral, there was no response then. On this occasion, however, it seemed my 'thought you were dead' line provoked an urgency on his part. He was back to me within an hour, writing:

> It is somewhat difficult in my position to maintain a regular contact, but I will endeavour. It's dangerous to lead a charge when you can never be sure how many will follow or whether you will be left charging alone. The fact that the object of your criticism can determine your life circumstances for years to come also has a certain dampening effect. As you well know priests are generally a docile lot, not really through cowardice but through loyalty. When you give your life in service to the church you develop a love for it, warts and all. Bishops could presume on that loyalty when priests felt that the Bishop, despite his human shortcomings, was basically a man of faith trying his best to be a father to his priests and people.
>
> DM [Diarmuid Martin] has exhibited a worrying disregard for his priests, most clearly shown in his stance on those accused of child abuse, the presumption of innocence to which every human being is entitled is withdrawn from an accused priest and he is pilloried by the church that he serves. Talk to Fr — parish priest — of his nightmare of false accusation, or Fr — parish priest —, although they are probably so wounded that will simply want to forget the sorry episodes.

He added, 'Patsy, "the king is in the all together" and I predict will soon realise it when he begins to feel the chill, so at least stop. Cadfael.'

I contacted the two priests he referred to but neither would speak to me. Subsequent emails from Cadfael in 2008 concerned monies going missing in a parish, which I wrote about when the archdiocese acknowledged it in a brief statement. His acute displeasure at the archbishop never wavered. In November 2008 he emailed about Archbishop Martin that the 'boys in black are seriously pissed off with this little Hitler, and his henchman Fr — who carries out Il Duce's orders. Good will is down the pan.' By coincidence I met said 'henchman' on Nassau Street in Dublin one evening around then, as he left a reception where a glass or two of wine had been imbibed. Our paths hadn't crossed before, nor have they since. He cast a cold eye on me, said he never read, watched or listened to Irish media, and passed by.

Cadfael's optimism was unconfined in the early days of December 2008:

> Very strongly rumoured in Roman circles these days that DM is to be appointed in the coming days as President of the Pontifical Council for Justice and Peace. The present incumbent Cardinal Martino [Martini] has reached retirement age and is about to step down. Martin already served there as Secretary of the council. This would mean a return to Rome, where his heart is, and a new man for Dublin ... Those close to DM have detected a distinctly upbeat mood in recent weeks ... he must have got the heads up on it ... Salve!

Cadfael's optimism proved unfounded and was followed by a silence.

In November 2009 the Murphy Report was published with its damning findings on the sexual abuse of children by priests in the Dublin archdiocese and its cover-up by previous archbishops over decades. In early December 2009 I contacted Cadfael to sound out his response to the report. It was two months later, February 2010, before he replied: 'Sorry I have been silent for so long. Circumstances make it difficult for me sometimes. Since we last communicated the Dublin Diocese is in meltdown.' There was

> a lot of seething anger amongst the men in black ... Diarmuid is no longer the darlin he once was and many are hoping and praying for his recall to Rome as soon as possible. Your piece this morn captured well the spirit of the Manresa meeting [a meeting of some Dublin priests at Manresa, the Jesuit centre in Dublin's Clontarf, following publication of the Murphy Report], although the language used there was far more direct than you have reported.

He said, 'Respect for Diarmuid has evaporated and has been replaced by a deep sense of hurt and injustice.' Cadfael had clear views on the Murphy Report too, writing:

> [It] cannot be taken as the fifth gospel; and while its core revelations are beyond doubt substantially true and shame all the men in black, it also deserves a considered professional analysis of its methodology and content. This is not denial, it is the response of mature men anxious for justice for all implicated whether 'by association' or commission. DM sees such an approach as tantamount to denial and it sends him into a frenzied attack on its proponents.

Three days later he was back again. The Manresa Meeting had been, he said:

unique in the history of the Diocese and voices were unanimous in their condemnation of DM. The men who called the meeting are sound[,] balanced men, well regarded by their peers and it took a deal of courage to initiate it. Unfortunately, time ran out, the room had to be vacated for another group, so the resolutions were not voted on. Among them was a request to the Congregation for the Clergy in Rome to investigate the lack of support for the priests of the diocese following the report. There are rumblings of another meeting being called by invitation to every priest in the diocese, but whether this actually happens remains to be seen. Bye for Now.

It was my last communication from Cadfael. I hope he's still with us and in a happier frame of mind. Despite his earnest wishes, Diarmuid Martin would remain Archbishop of Dublin for another ten years, until 2020.

✠ ✠ ✠

As Cadfael believed accurately, I had a different view of Archbishop Martin. Without doubt he was the most impressive religious leader I dealt with in my twenty-six years as Religious Affairs Correspondent of *The Irish Times*. I 'marked' him for almost seventeen years, from his appointment as Coadjutor Archbishop of Dublin in 2003 until our last interview in January 2021 – since when I have left the man alone to enjoy his retirement. We had a professional relationship, always at a remove. I believe that is necessary with public figures if journalists are to do their job properly and be free to critique, if necessary. I had also seen colleagues, mainly in the political arena, get too close to influential figures, only to rise – and fall – with those same personalities. Admittedly such distance was easier to maintain in Religious Affairs because clergy, in general, tend to have a consistent view of the media – to be avoided, unless absolutely necessary! It was also my experience that strong news stories rarely come from those in authority.

Diarmuid Martin was different. While he did not court attention, he was relaxed around media people in a way very few other Church or faith leaders were. It may have helped that he had close friendships among journalists while at the Vatican and that his older and only sibling, Séamus, was also a journalist – in his case, with *The Irish Times*. Séamus was a senior colleague of mine at the paper, who worked abroad for much of my period as Religious Affairs Correspondent. He never attempted to influence me when it came to reporting on his brother, nor did he ever discuss that with me. Some of Archbishop Martin's critics in the Church, and he had many, felt he got a soft time from the media because of these relationships, suggesting a touching naiveté in their understanding of journalists, who can be among the least collegial professionals when it comes to one another, of necessity, owing to the competitive nature of media organisations.

The truth, from a media perspective, is that Diarmuid Martin always came across as honest and straightforward, and he didn't trot out pre-cooked phrases prepared for him by communications professionals. Indeed, at times, he could seem almost incoherent in interview. Usually this indicated that he was thinking on his feet. It was unpolished and refreshing. His unequivocal commitment to child protection was a stand-out feature of his period as archbishop, as was his immense patience with abuse survivors, some of whom can be demanding. This may be understandable, but many find it exhausting. Among survivors, no other Catholic Church leader came higher in their esteem than he did. He was passionately, consistently supportive of them and was central to making the Irish Catholic Church one of the safest places for children. This came at a cost, where his relationship with brother bishops and his priests was concerned. They never really trusted him.

Martin was culturally different too, much of that due to his being in Rome for thirty years before his appointment to Dublin. He moved with ease at the highest levels in the Vatican, something alien to his brother bishops in Ireland. He was an outsider in other senses too. Alone among his brother Irish bishops, his background was 100 per cent Dublin working class: that section of Irish society which suffered most from clerical child sexual abuse and not least in Ballyfermot, where Martin grew up. Previous archbishops of Dublin had moved abuser priests into such areas, where the loyalty of the people meant they were less likely to complain. Martin's family had thirteen addresses as he grew up, including a single room in a tenement building on Digges Street in Dublin's city centre. Eventually they moved to Ballyfermot and his father got a job at the CIÉ works in Inchicore. After primary school in Ballyfermot, Martin attended the Oblates in Inchicore, then the Marist Brothers at Marian College in Ballsbridge. It wasn't your usual passage to the Catholic episcopacy in Dublin, which, generally, included education at a private fee-paying college run by one of the more prestigious religious congregations.

His immediate predecessor as archbishop, Cardinal Desmond Connell, was educated by the Jesuits at Belvedere College and had been UCD's Dean of the Faculty of Philosophy and Sociology before becoming archbishop. *His* predecessor, Archbishop Kevin McNamara, had been vice-president and Professor of Dogmatic Theology at St Patrick's College, Maynooth, then Bishop of Kerry before his appointment to Dublin – while *his* predecessor was that other 'Belvedere boy', Dermot Ryan, who had been Professor of Oriental Languages at UCD before, in 1971, succeeding John

Charles McQuaid, a 'Blackrock College boy' educated by the Spiritans (formerly the Holy Ghost Fathers). All these men had abysmal records when it came to clerical child sexual abuse. The Murphy Commission found that they had all 'handled child sex abuse complaints badly' and that 'not one of them reported his knowledge of child sexual abuse to the gardaí ... until November 1995'.

In the main, of course, Dublin's priests liked and respected their archbishops. To them it seemed important to have someone they could 'look up to', both academically and class-wise. So too did the other Irish bishops, it seemed. They liked the idea that Ireland's major diocese would be run by a figure of some intellectual and class standing. As Archbishop Martin's brother, Séamus, recalled in his 2008 autobiography, *Good Times and Bad: From the Coombe to the Kremlin – A Memoir*, Diarmuid 'completed his doctorate in moral theology [in Rome] but never got round to doing the public defence of his thesis that is part of the continental system. He is probably not entitled, therefore, to be described as Dr Martin, but Irish newspapers insist that all bishops are automatically "doctored".' According to reliable sources, Diarmuid Martin did not defend his doctoral thesis publicly in Rome because he was advised by a senior colleague not to do so as, in the latter's opinion, it was 'too liberal'. Otherwise, he may not have had as impressive a career at the Vatican.

After ordination in Dublin in 1969, he studied moral theology at the Pontifical University of St Thomas Aquinas (the Angelicum) in Rome and was curate in Dublin at Cabinteely for a brief period in 1973–4 before going to Rome. There he lived next door to St Peter's Basilica at the Teutonic (German) College, as Archbishop McQuaid did not want his priests to become part of an Irish ghetto in Rome but to have a larger experience of the Catholic world. In 1976 he entered the service of the Holy See at the Council for the

Family, becoming under-secretary of the Council for Justice and Peace in 1986. In 1991 he helped draft Pope John Paul II's great social justice encyclical *Centesimus Annus*, becoming secretary at the council in 1994. In that role he represented Rome at various UN international conferences as well as to the International Monetary Fund and the World Bank, dealing mainly with debt and poverty reduction. He was flying high.

So when Pope John Paul II asked him to go back to Dublin he demurred. The pope had to ask a second time and, finally agreeing, Diarmuid Martin was appointed Coadjutor Archbishop (with a right to succeed) of Dublin in May 2003.

From the beginning there was resistance to him among some Dublin clergy. His approach was a little too direct, too cut and dried; he did not do 'pamper'. Through it all he retained his 'Dub' working-class humour, as evident after Masses outside the Pro-Cathedral in Dublin when he spoke to the people leaving. As archbishop he lived simply in a small apartment at Archbishop's House in Drumcondra, where he did his own cooking (after doing his own shopping).

Whatever the attitudes to him were within clerical circles, he was soon the most respected Church leader among the wider public in Ireland. This extended to his relationships with Protestant churches in Dublin which, ecumenically, were probably the warmest since the Reformation. Similarly with other faith groupings in the city and with his reception by members of the LGBTQ+ community in Dublin, whom he treated with compassion and without judgement.

This meant that when he stood down in January 2021 the news was met with remarkable tributes from political, Church and faith leaders as well as abuse survivors. What made this all the more surprising is that just ten years previously, such was the rage of the Irish people at findings of various statutory reports into clerical child sexual abuse in the Catholic Church that then Taoiseach Enda Kenny, a practising Catholic, won almost universal praise for his evisceration of the Vatican in an extraordinary Dáil speech in July 2011. Then too there was almost unanimous public support for the government decision later that year to close the Irish Embassy to the Holy See.

My own respect for Archbishop Martin was very much in my mind at the press conference at Dublin's Mater Dei Institute in 2009 when the Murphy Report was published. He had cooperated fully with the commission that prepared the report. At the press conference an emotional Archbishop Martin was at the top table with other senior clergy in a room full of media. I had just read the report before leaving the *Irish Times* newsroom and was livid. This was not because of any surprise at the report findings, so much as shock at seeing what I had long since concluded myself outlined there in lucid language. I remember just one thing before I stood up: a determination to exclude Archbishop Martin as far as possible from whatever words I was about to direct at the Church representatives sitting at the table before us. I said my bit and sat down with no memory of my words and no notes. It came from the gut. Other media colleagues then stood up to vent their anger too. We were a chorus of the enraged. It was, strictly speaking, unprofessional of us all. But then it has been said that the function of a journalist is to comfort the afflicted and afflict the comfortable, and we were in afflictive mode.

It was some weeks later before I found out what I had actually said at that press conference. My then colleague Mary Fitzgerald had taped proceedings, and she transcribed what I had said at my request the following month, after journalist Vincent Browne wrote about that Mater Dei press conference in the *Sunday Business Post* newspaper. It sounds flat on the page. What is missing is the fury. Addressing Archbishop Martin I said:

Nobody doubts your sincerity, sir, and indeed the report as we see today compliments your cooperation with it, and it wonders whether the child protection measures put in place can survive your leaving this diocese ... so don't take this question personally: How can the Irish people be expected to ever trust this institution again after what we found out this year through the Ryan Report and through this report today? How can the Irish people be expected to trust the Catholic Church when as recently as 2006 the Commission wrote to the Congregation of the Doctrine of the Faith [at the Vatican] looking for information, and it didn't even reply? How can the people be expected to trust the Church when it wrote to the Papal Nuncio here in September 2007 looking for information and he didn't reply, and wrote to him again earlier this year when they were drafting the report and he didn't have the courtesy to reply to a statutory authority set up by the Government of this State ... why should we trust the Catholic Church again in Ireland?

What Vincent Browne wrote was flattering, if testament to one of my probable failings: a tendency to erupt. He reflected how:

A mere 40 years ago, a former holder of the office of Archbishop of Dublin, John Charles McQuaid, was arguably the most powerful person in the country. He commanded awe and trepidation, he decreed which universities Catholics could attend, he was believed to have been the one who decided the licensing hours, the books we could read, the form of the health service we could access, the films we could view – even, on one occasion, the football match [against communist Yugoslavia] that we could not see. Yes, there were functionaries who, theoretically, decided these matters, but the belief was that power lay in the palace at Drumcondra. People knelt on one knee on meeting him to kiss McQuaid's ring, which he proffered almost disdainfully. His attire of soutane and cape, both tinged with red, heralded his importance, his eminence. And he was punctilious about that eminence, reminding the Papal Nuncio of the time of his status in the Church hierarchy. Deference was his expectation, and he was greeted with deference, his utterances received with deference.

But by 26 November last, there was no trace of any lingering deference. The office of archbishop had diminished in power and eminence, not least because of the revelations of McQuaid's conduct during his reign from 1940 to 1972, during which time he covered up abuse of girls by a priest in Our Lady's Hospital for Sick Children in Crumlin. The old arrogance had gone, too. [Archbishop] Martin's tone was diffident, apologetic, defensive.

But what happened next was what marked a very different Ireland. The religious affairs correspondent of *The Irish Times*, Patsy McGarry, stood up abruptly. McGarry is a polite, modest man. There is no side to him, no affectation, no grandstanding. But he was almost apoplectic that afternoon, apoplectic over the abuses chronicled in the Murphy Report, apoplectic over the calculated cover-ups and lies.

It was on the behaviour of the Papal Nuncio and the Vatican that he focused the brunt of his ire, demanding an explanation for the Vatican's and nuncio's refusal to cooperate with the Murphy Commission. He was persistent, angry, even confrontational vis-à-vis the Archbishop of Dublin. It was a magnificent, commanding performance.

Immediately afterwards, Nell McCafferty rose, incandescent [McCafferty does incandescence brilliantly]. She ridiculed the now-cowering clerics flanking the archbishop for their presumption in calling themselves 'Father' or even 'Reverend Father'. She focused on the archbishop himself for his presumption in having himself called 'Your Grace'. [Actually, this charge was misplaced, for Martin does not stand on titles]. What was holy about it, she demanded. She was followed by the normally polite religious affairs correspondent of RTÉ, Joe Little. Another modest, diffident man. I assumed the tone would change. It didn't. Another spectacular, and informed, onslaught. It must have been excruciating for the clerics – and particularly for Martin. His prepared statement had been generous and contrite, but his response to the onslaught was defensive and evasive. But it was the spectacle of the doyens of the media assailing the Catholic Archbishop of Dublin that was so extraordinary, after decades [centuries?] of deference, bowing, scraping and ring-kissing. When John Paul II came to Ireland in 1979, there was a special audience arranged in a convent in Cabra for the media. When the Pope eventually emerged on a balcony overlooking the hall where hundreds of journalists were crowded, a scene of mass hysterical subservience unfolded. Several hardened hacks were crying. Almost all the journalists sang, over and over again, 'He's got the whole world in his hands'.

Were that Pope's successor to return now, there would be questions, insistent questions, about his and the Vatican's roles in the cover-up of the abuse of children both in Ireland and around the world by clerics of his church. I don't think there would be much communal singing. As a non-believer, I could be expected to rejoice in that, but isn't it healthy that we have toned down the deference thing?

✠ ✠ ✠

Cadfael's observation about the docile nature of priests was something I identified very early in my period as Religious Affairs Correspondent of *The Irish Times*. I alluded to it in an article published in October 1999, which drew on my head the wrath of no less a person than Cardinal Cahal Daly, former Catholic Primate of All Ireland, who had retired three years previously. The article followed my attendance at a meeting in All Hallows College in Dublin of the since defunct National Conference of Priests of Ireland, set up by the bishops as a forum for priests. There was a discussion among a panel of priests on the platform of the auditorium and when it was opened up to the couple of hundred of priests in the seats below there was not one taker, just the sound of silence. By coincidence, that evening I attended the annual synod of the united Church of Ireland dioceses of Dublin and Glendalough at Taney Hall, Dundrum, where it was hammer and tongs in debate involving male and female clergy, male and female laity, on every subject on the agenda.

I wrote an article contrasting what I had witnessed at the National Conference of Priests of Ireland meeting and at the Church of Ireland synods in Dublin later that day. In a lengthy letter to me, Cardinal Daly took exception and said what I had written was like 'an obituary for the Catholic Church and good riddance'. I was furious. I believed that my card was being marked. I thought to myself, *this is how these guys operate behind the scenes*. Daly, by then, would have known everything about me – seed, breed and education at the junior seminary for Achonry's Catholic diocese, St Nathy's College, Ballaghaderreen, where the then Bishop of Achonry, Tom Flynn, had taught me.

Daly would also, then, have been familiar with my trenchant criticisms of the bishops' handling of the Mary McAleese Communion episode at Dublin's Christ Church in 1997 and of their subsequent 1998 'One Bread One Body' document, which set out that Catholics must never take Communion in a Protestant Church and Protestants could be allowed to do so in a Catholic Church only *in extremis*, even as the ink was not yet dry on the Good Friday Agreement of April 1998. I had also, by then, started to be very critical of the Church's handling of clerical child sexual abuse allegations.

I replied to Daly, stating that I had simply reported on the facts of the two events I had attended that same day, and concluded my letter as he had his: 'and I hope you will take this in the spirit in which it is intended'. There was no response.

We 'broke bread', so to speak, the following year when we both were on the panel at a discussion in St Mary's College Belfast, where the then president was Father Donal McKeown, the current bishop of Derry. The cardinal and I did not discuss our earlier correspondence but found common ground over Keadue, County Roscommon, where his father was from and whose annual O'Carolan Harp Festival he had opened on many occasions. It helped.

Also in attendance at St Mary's that day was Bishop Patrick Walsh, successor to Cardinal Daly as bishop of the Down and Connor diocese, which takes in most of Belfast and Antrim. He wrote me a letter afterwards saying, 'the format of the evening was very pleasing to the priests and they all enjoyed and benefited from it. Thank you for your contribution.' He added, 'I will now be able to put a face to your reports in the *Irish Times* which I do read carefully.'

To my surprise, Cardinal Daly resumed correspondence with me soon afterwards. One letter I recall had to do with a new book he brought out in 2004, *The Minding of Planet Earth*, dealing with 'the urgent need to confront these enormous challenges if crises of cosmic dimensions are to be averted'. He invited me to the launch and wondered whether *The Irish Times* would be interested in an article on its themes. I commissioned a piece from him for publication in the paper's weekly 'Rite and Reason' column.

I continued to be surprised at correspondence from some bishops. A man I greatly admired as a human being is the now retired Bishop of Killaloe, Willie Walsh. (The diocese takes in most of Clare and parts of Tipperary.) A deeply compassionate person, he was a bishop who 'smelled of the sheep' long before that was preached as desirable among clergy by Pope Francis – himself elected in 2013, three years after Bishop Walsh's retirement.

In a Catholic Church context Bishop Walsh was before his time, and courageously so during the chilly papacies of John Paul II and Benedict XVI, when he expressed an openness to discussion on the ordination of women, mandatory celibacy for priests, same-sex issues and birth control. He also believed Protestants should be welcome at Communion in Catholic churches and, most particularly, he was very sensitive towards abuse survivors. This I found out directly when dealing, off the record, with a troubled man from Killaloe diocese to whom Bishop Walsh could not have been more generous, considerate or helpful.

An incident at Maynooth in April 2002 illustrated for me the character of the man. About thirty bishops had gathered for an emergency meeting after the resignation of Bishop of Ferns Brendan Comiskey. That followed a BBC documentary *Suing the Pope*, wherein survivor Colm O'Gorman outlined his abuse as a child in Ferns diocese (consisting mainly of County Wexford) by Father Seán Fortune. The atmosphere at Maynooth that day was fraught as the bishops arrived, but this was added to greatly by a very angry abuse survivor, Gerry Kelly, there to protest. He had spent his childhood in Artane industrial school, where he said he was sexually abused. He had suffered a stroke and limped, using a stick for support. That, and his generally aggressive attitude, intimidated arriving bishops.

He jostled then Auxiliary Bishop of Dublin Martin Drennan and confronted Bishop of Meath Michael Smith when he arrived in his car. Then papal nuncio Archbishop Giuseppe Lazzarotto practically ran to get away from him. Behind the scenes it was decided to move a planned press conference with the bishops to a different location in case Kelly might disrupt that too. However, as all the other bishops rushed away from Kelly, Bishop Willie Walsh went directly to him. No doubt his many years coaching Clare hurlers was a help. The two men spoke, with the bishop an attentive listener. When a distressed Kelly began to weep, Bishop Walsh put a hand on his shoulder and spoke what must have been consoling words. Kelly calmed down. The encounter spoke more than any words could.

It was no surprise in 2010 that when it came to Bishop Willie Walsh submitting his letter of resignation to Rome, having reached the age of seventy-five, it was accepted with comparative speed. Many would say that was the greatest tribute of many that came his way then.

In February 2008 Bishop Walsh had taken me to task in a letter written from Knock, which he was visiting at the time. I had written an article criticising the bishops who, I said, had not learned anything when it came to dealing with sexual abuse and whose instinct was to reach for lawyers when confronted with it. He insisted that, though this may have been the case in the past, 'I honestly believe it is not being done today.' He 'would be very saddened if one of my colleagues did so ever again'. He was mainly concerned that survivors would be put off by my article. They needed 'to know that we want to do all in our power to help them on the journey towards healing'. He continued, 'If I am wrong, then truly "we have never learned".'

A year later, in March 2009, the Bishop of Cloyne, John Magee, announced that he was standing aside as bishop there following revelations that led to the setting up of a commission to investigate the handling of clerical child sexual abuse allegations in the mainly east County Cork diocese. Bishop Willie Walsh wrote to me again soon afterwards and recalled how in his previous letter he had protested at my suggestion 'that our [the bishops'] handling of child sexual abuse issues was still flawed'. He continued, 'In the light of recent events I now accept that my protest was unjustified.' I quote this not to make me look good but to make him look good, and I can only imagine the personal despair he felt when writing these words in February 2009. It would not have helped that Bishop Magee had also been the only man in history to be secretary to three popes: Paul VI, John Paul I and John Paul II. No doubt Bishop Walsh's upset was compounded with publication of the Ryan Report in May 2009, the Murphy Report in November 2009 and the Cloyne Report in July 2011.

In the context of their dealings with clerical child sexual abuse, some bishops and religious superiors had much in common with the peace of Yeats's 'Lake Isle of Innisfree': learning, for them, came 'dropping slow'. When the Cloyne Report was published in 2011, with its repeat of shocking findings of cover-ups there too, I rang the Catholic bishops' spokesman Martin Long to discuss it. I said to him, 'When will these fuckers ever learn?' Later, he told me he had been on speaker-phone when I called with, beside him, the recently resigned Bishop of Cloyne, John Magee. So be it.

A favourite episcopal letter I received came from the then Bishop of Kilmore (mainly County Cavan), Leo O'Reilly. He wrote to me in December 2008 following a profile I had written about him and his handling of his role as education spokesman for the bishops. He found the article 'very positive and fair', adding, 'I hope getting a letter like this from a bishop will not make you ask yourself are you doing your job properly!' It didn't.

8

Icarus

Throughout most of the early years in my role as Religious Affairs Correspondent of *The Irish Times* there was persistent background 'noise' surrounding the abrupt departure in 1994 of Monsignor Micheál Ledwith as president at St Patrick's College, Maynooth, Ireland's national seminary. It all suggested that there were sex abuse allegations involved; that a substantial financial settlement had been made; that the monsignor resigned his post because of the allegations; that the seventeen trustee bishops of the college were all aware of these circumstances; and that none of them would talk about it, ever!

Considering Ledwith's central role in the Irish Catholic Church and his rapid ascent in Church affairs, followed then by that even speedier descent, I felt impelled to establish what had really gone on.

A priest of Ferns diocese, Ledwith flew up the academic ladder at Maynooth, from Professor of Dogmatic Theology in 1977 to its president eight years later in 1985, when he was only forty-two. He was also appointed by Pope John Paul II as a member of the International Theological Commission, which advises the Vatican on matters of doctrine. At any one time this commission has a membership of no more than thirty theologians and is closely linked to the Vatican's Congregation for the Doctrine of the Faith, which, essentially, determines all matters of faith and morals for Catholics.

In 1988, with the death of then Archbishop of Dublin Kevin McNamara, Father Ledwith was one of three names submitted to Rome as a possible successor – the other two being the then Auxiliary Bishop of Dublin, and later Bishop of Limerick, Donal Murray, and Professor Desmond Connell, then Dean of the Faculty of Philosophy and Sociology at UCD, who was eventually appointed. It was following this that the title monsignor was bestowed on Professor Ledwith by Rome. Then Monsignor Ledwith resigned as president of Maynooth six months before his term of office was to end. Newspaper reports at the time described this as 'a surprise development', while he said himself that he was doing so, in April 1994, with effect from June of that year, to avoid disruption in the middle of an academic year. He planned to take a leave of absence to pursue research and writing interests, he said. It was later reported that he had gone on a fundraising trip for St Patrick's College to the US.

Monsignor Ledwith's departure from the college presidency was thereafter surrounded by mystery. A senior Church source told me at the time it was not possible to discuss the matter 'for legal reasons'. This was rumoured to be because of a confidentiality clause in an agreement involving a third party, a clause that it was believed had been included at the behest of the college board of trustees and involved seventeen of the Irish Catholic bishops.

In April 2002 queries I submitted as to the circumstances of Monsignor Ledwith's departure from Maynooth, and as to his whereabouts then, were referred by a spokesman for the then Archbishop of Dublin, Cardinal Connell, to the press office of the Irish Bishops' Conference in Maynooth, since 'it has nothing to do with us' (despite Cardinal Connell's position on the Maynooth

College's board of trustees that dealt with the Ledwith case in 1994).

When the query was put to the Irish Bishops' Conference press office in Maynooth, it was referred to the president's office at St Patrick's College, because it (the Bishops' Conference press office) did 'not represent St Patrick's College or the trustees'. Finally, on 22 April, contact was made by phone with Monsignor Dermot Farrell, Monsignor Ledwith's successor as president of St Patrick's College and now Archbishop of Dublin.

I put my queries to him over Ledwith's departure verbally and he requested that they be emailed to his office. This was done, but garnered no response, so, following further contact with his office, they were emailed again to a different address, as requested by his secretary on 29 April. There still was no response. In a further phone call on the matter to the bishops' spokesman, the late Father Martin Clarke, he said he would convey the queries to the relevant party. A subsequent phone message indicated that this had been done. But there was still no response from the president's office at St Patrick's College, Maynooth.

It was classic runaround stuff, all of which I reported in the paper. I had hoped the publicity would flush out a response. I had a very good contact in Maynooth itself, but the agreement was that, while he would tell me nothing, he would keep me on the right track by confirming what was true and what was not of whatever I dug up or which might come my way.

It seemed I had hit a wall. Then I got a remarkable break. One afternoon in the newsroom, as I struggled to come up with new ways to get the bishops to talk, I idly googled the name Micheál Ledwith, expecting little. I almost fell out of my seat at what came up on my computer screen. Could it be true? Google was still something of a new phenomenon and I began to doubt what was before me. But soon it all stacked up.

There was Monsignor Ledwith in all his glory being described as a guest lecturer with a New Age movement on the west coast of the US, while he was still listed in the *Irish Catholic Directory* 2002 as a priest of Ferns diocese in Ireland. According to the New Age movement website, he was a part-time lecturer at the Ramtha's School of Enlightenment, founded in 1988 at Yelm in Washington state. He was 'Dr Miceál Ledwith' and 'one of the most fascinating speakers in the world today'. Included was an accurate biography of his career in the Catholic Church in Ireland. He, it said, 'clearly shows us how shackled we are by religions having gotten so far "off the mark", what we have not been told that is so important not only to our understanding, but to our mental and emotional well-being'. The website asked, 'Does anything about the religion, or beliefs that you were brought up with … or ran away from, trouble or confuse you? In Miceál Ledwith, we have a trusted source to go to for answers that your soul recognises as truth.'

My soul was somewhat astonished at the human story of a man who was a Catholic theologian of international standing and an adviser to the Vatican on matters of faith and morals just eight years previously, and who was now a leading advocate of a New Age movement devoted to a 35,000-year-old being called Ramtha the Enlightened One.

We published the story in a front-page report on 8 May 2002 with some background on Monsignor Ledwith himself and his previous high-flying career in the Irish and international Catholic Church, noting that he had been born in 1942 at Taghmon, County Wexford, and attended St Peter's College in Wexford town before going to St Patrick's College, Maynooth, where he had excelled academically. He had studied in Paris, Salzburg and at Bad Reichenhall, Bavaria, then taught at St Peter's in Wexford before becoming a lecturer at Maynooth in 1971. Professor of

Dogmatic Theology there in 1976, he was made head of the department in the following year, appointed college vice-president in 1980, and the college's twenty-fifth president in 1985. And still only forty-two! Heady stuff.

I submitted a list of questions to the authorities in Maynooth. There was no immediate response, but I knew that this time they would have to reply, if under some duress. It took them over three weeks to do so. That was on 31 May, the Friday of a bank holiday weekend, a great time to release 'bad' news. On that day the office of the president of St Patrick's College, Maynooth, on behalf of its seventeen trustee bishops, issued a statement confirming that an allegation of 'sexual abuse of a minor' had been made against Monsignor Ledwith in 1994. He had been informed of the allegation and had denied it strenuously. The allegation was made known by the Monsignor's bishop, Bishop of Ferns Brendan Comiskey, to both the gardaí and the health board, it said. On the basis of legal advice, Monsignor Ledwith had decided to enter into discussions with the complainant and both parties had reached a private settlement, without admission of liability. The statement also said the settlement agreed was funded entirely by Ledwith and without any assistance from the Catholic Church or the college at Maynooth. It was further disclosed that in 2000 the college authorities were informed of another allegation against the Monsignor, made by a former student who studied at Maynooth between 1992 and 1994.

All this took place against a background of Bishop Comiskey himself having resigned the previous March following the rebroadcast of *Suing the Pope* on RTÉ television. Its focus, Father Seán Fortune, took his own life in March 1999 while awaiting trial for the abuse of twenty-nine boys. In the documentary, Colm O'Gorman told his grim story of abuse at the hands of Fortune with powerful conviction. As well as the resignation of Bishop

Comiskey, the documentary led to the setting up of the Ferns Inquiry, which reported in October 2005, detailing findings of the extensive abuse of children by priests and its cover-up by local Church authorities. It was the first statutory inquiry to report on the abuse of children by Catholic priests in Ireland.

It was Bishop Comiskey who had proposed Monsignor Ledwith, one of his priests, for the presidency of St Patrick's College in 1985.

During the long May silence that followed publication of our report on Monsignor Ledwith's newfound role with the Ramtha School of Enlightenment, and the eventual response from Maynooth, I was contacted by two former Maynooth seminarians – one a priest – who wanted me to meet them and the former Senior Dean at St Patrick's College, Father Gerard McGinnity. Father McGinnity had been removed from the post some years previously when he tried to alert the bishops to Monsignor Ledwith's alleged activities with younger men, as relayed to him at the time by six senior seminarians when Ledwith was vice-president of St Patrick's College. These included the two men I met with Father McGinnity at a hotel near Dublin Airport. It was the beginning of revelations about another atrocious cover-up saga where the bishops were concerned, and which involved the destruction of Father McGinnity's clerical career. Former deans at Maynooth were usually destined for higher things in the Church. One, Michael Harty, went on to become Bishop of Killaloe. Father McGinnity, however, ended up being sent on sabbatical for a year and was then 'exiled' to a remote parish in Northern Ireland as a curate.

There was no doubting the deep sense of injustice felt, on his behalf, by the two men accompanying Father McGinnity on the day we met. They wanted the matter investigated and rectified. A gentle, refined man, McGinnity was then parish priest at Knockbridge, County Louth. He and I would meet regularly over the following years as he updated me on or responded to developments in the case. Clearly, he had been another man whose talents were quickly identified at a young age in Maynooth. He was appointed junior dean at St Patrick's College when twenty-six and senior dean in 1978 when he was thirty-two. Predecessors in the post would, generally, have been much older. From 1973 Father McGinnity taught communications at Maynooth and completed a doctoral thesis on the theology of St Ambrose. He conducted retreats for diocesan clergy, contributed to RTÉ religious broadcasts, and published a number of books, including *Christmen: Experience of Priesthood Today*, a bestseller in 1985.

On 5 June 2002, less than a week after the Maynooth authorities confirmed, eventually, that an allegation of 'sexual abuse of a minor' had been made against Monsignor Ledwith in 1994, which he denied strenuously, I reported in the paper what had been done to Father McGinnity at Maynooth in the mid-1980s when he tried to alert the authorities there to concerns surrounding Ledwith. The article stated how over a period in 1983–4, six senior seminarians at St Patrick's College were so concerned about the behaviour of Ledwith towards their junior colleagues that they 'did the unthinkable', as one put it, because 'it was not done [for seminarians] to meet bishops'. The six, five of whom were later ordained and three of whom were still priests, arranged separate meetings with the then Catholic Primate Cardinal Tomás Ó Fiaich and other bishops, including then Bishop of Down and Connor Cahal Daly (a cardinal when this emerged), Bishop of Ferns Brendan Comiskey, Bishop of Galway Eamonn Casey and Bishop of Derry Edward Daly. The seminarians met the bishops in groups of no fewer than two. One bishop advised them to 'go back and say your prayers'. That was when the seminarians approached Father McGinnity. They had become concerned about their own futures by then, because, having reported their anxieties about Monsignor Ledwith to their own bishops too, with no action following, they began to feel vulnerable. So, they sought Father McGinnity's protection, as well as his help, in alerting the bishops to their concerns about Monsignor Ledwith.

Later in 1984, following these representations by the seminarians, Father McGinnity contacted the college bishop trustees himself to express concern about the alleged behaviour of Ledwith. It was also in that year that Father McGinnity was consulted by the then Papal Nuncio to Ireland, Archbishop Gaetano Alibrandi, as to the suitability of Ledwith for the then vacant position of Bishop of Ferns. Father McGinnity conveyed to the nuncio the concerns expressed to him by the seminarians about Ledwith and in the end it was Bishop Brendan Comiskey, then an auxiliary bishop in Dublin, who was appointed to Ferns.

All these efforts by the senior dean were to have little effect. Instead, Father McGinnity was persuaded by the bishops to take a sabbatical for a year and was soon told he would not be returning to Maynooth. He was posted as curate to a rural parish in the Armagh archdiocese. Back in Maynooth, Monsignor Ledwith became president at St Patrick's College, a position he held until his abrupt departure in June 1995.

Following publication of these matters on 5 June 2002, Cardinal Cahal Daly and three other bishops wrote to *The Irish Times* disputing the claims that they had been approached by the senior seminarians with complaints about the behaviour of Ledwith. Cardinal Daly – as well as then retired Archbishop of Tuam Joseph Cassidy, retired Bishop of Derry Edward Daly and Bishop of Ardagh and Clonmacnoise Colm O'Reilly – claimed the seminarians' complaints had, instead, been about the former college president's 'extravagant' lifestyle. But members of the group of six seminarians subsequently repeated to *The Irish Times* that they had made explicit to the bishops at the time precisely what they were talking about. There was no confusion on the matter as far as they were concerned. The accounts were in direct conflict.

For his part, Monsignor Dermot Farrell, then president of St Patrick's College, told me that there was nothing in the college records to show that any formal complaint had been made about Monsignor Micheál Ledwith by Father McGinnity. He also said they had received no complaints directly from Father McGinnity. When it was put to him that Father McGinnity had said he had been 'demoted and humiliated' at the college in 1984 for his efforts to protect the seminarians who had complained to nine bishops about Ledwith's behaviour, Monsignor Farrell said there were 'many, in fact, who retired from the College and went to parish ministry, including people involved in the formation process and other people, including professors'. At least half a dozen had done so in his own time at the college, he stated. He also said that Father McGinnity's description of what had happened to him, as having been 'demoted and humiliated', was 'his view of the matter'. What had happened was 'twenty years ago, long before my time. We do not have anything on the records of the College to indicate that that's the case,' he concluded. As for the six seminarians who sought Father McGinnity's protection at the time, he said the college had no way of compelling them to come back and take part in an interview about the matter. Pressed as to whether an inquiry into the matter was required, Monsignor Farrell said that was a matter for the bishop trustees, but he did agree that it would certainly be to the benefit of the college if the matter was cleared up.

These comments by Monsignor Farrell did not go down well with the relevant former seminarians, one of whom described them to me as 'the same old smokescreen really'. Another said it was 'past time for the truth to come out and to stop this shadowboxing. There were many good and holy priests in Maynooth at the time, and there still are. The bishops have a duty to such men to come clean,' he said. He also said they must clarify what funds in each diocese supplied money to Monsignor Ledwith's pension fund. 'Was it a case of parishioners contributing to pay off a man they [bishops] themselves were investigating?' he asked.

Another of the six rejected Monsignor Farrell's comment that Father McGinnity's account of events at the college in 1984 was 'his view'. It was also the view of the six. 'And I would feel [it is] the view of the great majority of Gerry's classmates and co-diocesans', who 'would be aware of the kind of derogatory spin put on events of that time, emanating from Maynooth'. This was a reference to rumours about Father McGinnity, suggesting that 'his health broke down', which circulated in Maynooth and elsewhere after his sudden departure from the national seminary in 1984 and his later posting to a rural curacy. One of the former seminarians described these rumours to me in June 2002 as an illustration of what he felt was the cynicism employed by Church authorities in dealing with Father McGinnity. That same month the same rumour was repeated to me by a senior Church figure, who said that Father McGinnity had a nervous breakdown and that this was why he was sent on sabbatical and removed from his post as senior dean at St Patrick's College.

I asked Father McGinnity if this was true. He was shocked at the question, but far more shocked to hear that this particular rumour had been circulating about him for eighteen years. At my request, he secured a letter from the County Armagh medical practice where he has been a patient since birth on 5 April 1947. According to his doctors, throughout his lifetime, 'there has been absolutely no record of psychological or mental problems' where Father McGinnity was concerned.

I reported this in July 2002.

Another of the former seminarians concerned was 'quite appalled at the lack of response of the bishops then, who not only ignored what we told them but promoted to president the man we spoke about'. It horrified him that, because they were not listened to, 'other people suffered abuse'. Himself a married man with a family by then, he was 'not bitter, just incredibly disappointed for those other people'. He was also annoyed that he and his colleagues, all mature students who had worked for many years before entering Maynooth, were treated so dismissively at the time.

By then, relations between myself and Monsignor Farrell were less than cordial. This manifested itself particularly in my regular contacts – mainly by email – with him, because it was through him, as president of St Patrick's College, that all my queries about Monsignor Ledwith were channelled. Throughout the weeks leading up to the bishop trustees' 31 May statement released by him, and particularly afterwards, I was swamped with credible allegations – some alleging sexual impropriety involving seminarians, others alleging misappropriation of funds, some containing further allegations against Monsignor Ledwith. These I put to Monsignor Farrell in a lengthy email on 26 June, almost a month later. Altogether there were twenty-one questions. His response on 1 July 2002 was brief and of the 'I have no information ...' or the 'not prepared ... to comment on specific disciplinary issues regarding individual students' variety. The last two questions, however, clearly made him see red.

Aware of the sensitivity involved in posing those two questions, I had begun:

> I am sorry to have to pose these two more personal questions, but in the context of what is suggested about Mgr Ledwith's

way of doing things I feel there is no way out of doing so. (xx) You are said to be a relative of Mgr Ledwith's. Is this true? If so, how close is the blood relationship? (xxi) It has also been said he created a new role in his [president's] office for you when you arrived at the College. Is this so? If so, what was the title of the new role? Assistant to the president?

The background to both questions was simple. Monsignor Farrell began lecturing at St Patrick's College in 1989, was appointed executive assistant to Monsignor Ledwith (then president there) in 1990 and became a vice-president in October 1993. This rapid ascent was noted, and not with pleasure, by some staff at Maynooth. When Monsignor Ledwith stood down in 1994, he was succeeded by the then senior vice-president, Monsignor Matthew O'Donnell, who died two years later in 1996, aged sixty-four. He was succeeded as president by Monsignor Farrell.

Through sources, I had established that Monsignor Farrell was related to Monsignor Ledwith. But in 2002 Monsignor Farrell was in no mood to confirm any of this. In his 1 July reply he made his position quite clear:

> My response to queries xx and xxi is this. If you and/or your newspaper publish any matter which suggests, directly or by inference or by innuendo, that the offices I have held in St Patrick's College, Maynooth, and the manner in which I was appointed and have discharged the duties attaching to those offices have made me complicit in any way with the wrongdoing and conduct alleged against Monsignor Ledwith[,] I shall, without any further notice to you and the *Irish Times*, take all measures available to me to demonstrate the falsity and malice of such [a] suggestion. Yours sincerely ...

In normal circumstances such aggression would be all the encouragement I and colleagues would have needed to ensure publication of whatever caused such a response, not least because the facts were the facts. This I made clear to a solicitor who contacted me on behalf of Monsignor Farrell to discuss the matter. He asked to see me and I called to his offices in Dublin where I also made clear that I had established the simple facts of the matter, which were beyond any legal action on which Monsignor Farrell might decide. I left the solicitor with the impression that what I had established would be published.

But I was undecided. The facts were the facts, but I felt that by reporting them – even while making it clear that there was no evidence to link Monsignor Farrell in any way with the alleged wrongdoing of Monsignor Ledwith, or that he had any knowledge of such alleged wrongdoing – there might still be a risk of causing damage by association owing to the overall context. I had no reason to believe that Monsignor Farrell was anything other than a totally innocent party in all the Ledwith business, and I did not want to be party to an injustice that would not be dissimilar to what I was by then convinced had been perpetrated on Father McGinnity by the Church authorities at Maynooth.

For this reason I decided against reporting even the facts as I had established them, but I did waver in that decision some months later. On 5 November 2002 I wrote to Monsignor Farrell concerning further allegations that had been put to me about how the Ledwith business was handled at Maynooth. In similarly aggressive mood, he replied:

> As you will know from my previous correspondence, I am determined to protect my personal good name and reputation. I trust that you will appreciate your own

responsibility as a journalist to treat sensational, wild and inaccurate allegations with the scepticism they deserve. Given my response to this letter, and given previous correspondence, I would have to consider it malicious of you and/or your newspaper if you publish any matter which suggested directly or by inference or innuendo that the matters which you raise in this email and which pertain to me as true.

It really was not a moment for any senior Irish Catholic Church figure, particularly at Maynooth at that time, to lecture any journalist on his/her responsibilities. But I bit my tongue, for almost twenty years, until January 2021. That was when I interviewed the new Catholic Archbishop of Dublin, Dermot Farrell. He was an altogether different man, clearly not under the same pressures as during our torrid exchanges in 2002. He confirmed that he was 'a distant cousin' of Monsignor Ledwith and that the first time he became aware of the allegations against him was in 'May 2002, when trying to assemble what the facts were' following media queries. An inquiry into the matter by Senior Counsel Denis McCullough was held, which reported in June 2005. 'I think I was the one who asked for an inquiry,' he said, continuing:

I wasn't aware of why he [Ledwith] stood down in '94. I wasn't involved. I was there obviously. The reason that he gave for stepping aside to people at the top, people in the leadership at the College at the time, was that Maynooth's bicentenary was coming up and everybody was anticipating his retirement and he was going to go basically ahead of time. Subsequently I became aware, long after, of the allegations. Obviously somebody knew about them [allegations]

163

because they emerged later, if you look at McCullough and Murphy.

Supreme Court Justice Frank Murphy conducted an inquiry into the handling of child sexual abuse allegations by Church authorities in Ferns diocese. His report was published in October 2005. Monsignor Ledwith, who had been laicised in 2005, gave evidence to that inquiry as a priest of Ferns diocese. Archbishop Farrell said both reports showed that Ferns diocese was aware of the allegations against Ledwith. 'But I can certainly tell you the leadership of the College, and I wasn't the president at that time, I was vice-president, I wasn't told by anybody, neither by Bishop Comiskey nor by Cardinal Daly nor indeed by any of the other trustees, and I am not too sure when the trustees actually became aware of those allegations.'

He had had no contact with Ledwith since 2002. 'The last time I spoke to him was when that statement was issued. I was asked by the trustees to contact him and to alert him that statement was coming out.'

The McCullough Inquiry, to which Archbishop Farrell alluded, was established by the seventeen bishop trustees of St Patrick's College in June 2002 to investigate the claims of the six senior seminarians that in the period 1983 to 1984 they had approached nine bishop trustees at the college with complaints about alleged sexual impropriety involving Ledwith and junior seminarians there, and when their claims were dismissed, they then went to Father McGinnity.

Father McGinnity refused to cooperate with the McCullough Inquiry because he felt 'an inquiry which is not independent but conducted under the auspices of that body undergoing inquiry is wrong in principle, it seems to me'. However, four of the former senior seminarians did cooperate, as did Cardinal Cahal Daly,

Bishop Edward Daly, Bishop Colm O'Reilly, Archbishop Joseph Cassidy, Bishop Eamonn Casey, Bishop Brendan Comiskey, former college president Monsignor Michael Olden and Monsignor Ledwith.

McCullough's report was published in June 2005. I have never met him, but, on the very day of his report's publication, we passed each other on Dublin's Halfpenny Bridge and nodded to one another in acknowledgement – we have not met since. The report found it 'very difficult to reconcile' accounts in the Father McGinnity case given by Bishop Casey and Bishop Comiskey 'with the almost complete lack of knowledge of these events on the part of the other bishops'. It found an investigation by Bishop Casey into Father McGinnity's complaints had been 'abrupt and truncated'. It said that 'concerns of apparent propensities rather than accusations of actual crime or specific offences' had been communicated to a number of bishops by Father McGinnity. It also concluded that it 'does appear that to have rejected Father McGinnity's concerns so completely and so abruptly without any adequate investigation may have been too precipitate although, of course, to investigate in any very full or substantial manner a generic complaint regarding a person's apparent propensities would have been difficult'.

A remarkable revelation from the report concerned Ledwith's 'lavish lifestyle', which also concerned the seminarians. This involved 'his expensive holidays in Florida and elsewhere in America and his ownership of an aeroplane, a boat on the Shannon and a summer residence on the shores of Lough Derg in County Clare'.

Following publication of the report, then Catholic Primate Archbishop Seán Brady and the other trustee bishops at the college apologised to Father McGinnity and the relevant former seminarians there. 'We are satisfied that Fr McGinnity and those seminarians who expressed concern in the early eighties were acting in good faith. We regret any hurt felt by those involved and that the investigation in 1984 was not more thorough,' they said.

The McCullough Report was the first report on clerical child sexual abuse-related matters in Ireland. Four months later, in October 2005, the Ferns Report was published. It was the first Irish State inquiry into such matters and had also investigated the Ledwith affair. Father McGinnity cooperated with this investigation, conducted under the chairmanship of former Supreme Court judge Frank Murphy. It found that 'by any standard the concerns as communicated by the seminarians and expressed by Father McGinnity were inadequately investigated. They also appear to have been wholly misunderstood.' It found as 'entirely understandable Fr McGinnity's feeling that he was victimised as a result of the concerns of the seminarians which he expressed. Punitive actions of that nature could only deter bona fide complaints to Church authorities which should be valued as providing information for the control of those having access to young people.'

Clearly the Catholic bishops had not anticipated either McCullough's findings or those of the Ferns Report. In a letter to me, dated 21 October 2003, Cardinal Cahal Daly made this clear. He had written to congratulate me on an article I had written on 'the problem of false allegations of child sex abuse', as he put it, a frequently expressed concern by Church authorities and allies at the time. 'It does take courage at this time to point to that danger, and I should like to congratulate you on having that courage and to thank you for your article,' he wrote.

He went on to challenge 'allegations made about me in the [RTÉ] *Prime Time* programme on Tuesday 14 October', saying, 'May I avail of this letter to tell you, for your own information' that the allegations 'are false'. Continuing, he said:

The words alleged to have been spoken to me by students in 1984 were not spoken to me (or indeed to any of the bishops who were approached by seminarians in Maynooth at that time and who signed a joint letter to *The Irish Times* rejecting the claims made by some seminarians). The words alleged to have been spoken by me to those students who came to me were emphatically never spoken by me. I do not suggest that people are deliberately lying; but the phenomenon of 'transferred memory' is well recognized, and these allegations may be an example of that syndrome.

He continued, 'My own recollection of these events is very clear; and it is corroborated by contemporaneous notes which I made of the gist of the conversations between the seminarians and myself. It is corroborated further by the independent recollection of the other bishops who were approached by seminarians at the time.'

Where the McCullough inquiry and a preliminary investigation by then Senior Counsel George Bermingham (now a judge and president of the Court of Appeal), which preceded the Ferns Inquiry, were concerned, Cardinal Daly said that 'all of these matters were examined thoroughly' by both. He had 'made a comprehensive, detailed and dated submission to each of these enquiries on the entire sequence of the relevant events and I have preferred to remain silent until the conclusions of these enquiries are made known'.

It was also the case that 'I did not simply decline to take part in the *Prime Time* programme or declare myself simply unwilling to take part; I let it be known to *Prime Time* through my secretary that I am convalescing from a recent illness and am at the moment away from home, and, for these reasons, could not be available for interview for the programme.' Wishing me well, he concluded, 'I wanted to convey these facts to you for your private information only.'

In 2016 Father McGinnity retired as parish priest at Knock-bridge, County Louth, an event marked by a Mass concelebrated by sixteen priests and celebrations at the local community centre, attended by over 300 people. He has never been offered any form of redress by the Irish bishops, despite the findings of both the McCullough Report and the Ferns Report that the inadequacy of their investigations into concerns he conveyed to them about Ledwith led to their destruction of his once-promising clerical career.

9

Drumcree, O Drumcree

It was like a scene from an epic movie on the grand scale – such as, perhaps, the parting of the Red Sea in Cecil B. DeMille's 1956 film *The Ten Commandments* – a once-in-a-lifetime sight to behold. But there was no Moses leading the way, nor was there a Promised Land ahead, just Portadown. Immediately before us was the nationalist Garvaghy Road and behind was the Church of the Ascension at Drumcree. The local Orangemen were taking their traditional route down the Garvaghy Road, which stretched in front of us. On either side it was lined with hundreds of soldiers; behind them were lines of armed police in riot gear, behind them lines of Saracens, behind *them* a line of jeeps and behind all that insulation were the outraged, hemmed-in residents of the Garvaghy Road, standing and sitting on walls, on roofs and hanging out of windows, all ferociously banging dustbin lids against the nearest wall while shouting drowned-out obscenities at the top of their voices. The Orange parade was being forced down the road against their will.

It was Sunday, 6 July 1997 and, to everyone's surprise, then Northern Secretary Mo Mowlam had decided that the Orange parade should be allowed back that way to Portadown after attendance at the traditional first Sunday of July service at the

Church of the Ascension in memory of young men from the area killed at the Battle of the Somme from 1 July 1916. It was the last time the Orangemen were allowed take their 'traditional route' to Portadown.

In 1995 the Orangemen had been ordered not to take that route for the first time in 188 years. This had provoked violence and rioting at Drumcree and across Northern Ireland. The decision was reversed and, after lengthy talks with local nationalists, the Orange parade was allowed to take place. Up to 500 Orangemen walked silently down the road led by Ulster Unionist MP David Trimble and DUP MP Reverend Ian Paisley. When the parade reached Portadown, Paisley and Trimble held their hands aloft in triumph, which provoked deep anger on the Garvaghy Road, where it was decided that the Orangemen would never pass that way again.

The following year, in July 1996, police decided the parade would not be allowed down the Garvaghy Road. Thousands of Orangemen and supporters gathered at the bridge in a dip on the road between the Church of the Ascension and the rise to Garvaghy. Barbed wire and barricades were erected. Once again, violence broke out, not just locally, but throughout Northern Ireland, targeted mainly at Catholics.

Police and civilian casualties at the Drumcree barricade grew throughout that July, with angry Orange crowds estimated to be about 10,000 strong at times. A Catholic taxi driver, Michael McGoldrick, was murdered near Portadown by loyalist paramilitaries. It was enough to make the authorities change their minds and once again allow the Orange parade down the road. This led to rioting in Garvaghy and throughout nationalist Northern Ireland.

Relations between the Churches in Northern Ireland deteriorated, with the Catholic Primate, Cardinal Cahal Daly, and the Church of Ireland Primate, Robin Eames, in whose archdiocese of Armagh Drumcree is based, falling out over that 1996 decision to allow the Orangemen to parade down the Garvaghy Road. Cardinal Daly was aggrieved because he believed his Church of Ireland counterpart had been informed in advance by the RUC that the parade would be permitted to take place, but that Archbishop Eames had not trusted him with this information.

And so there we were in 1997, my first Drumcree of eight. Eight summers with the length of eight long winters, déjà vu again and again. In 1997 it was widely believed the parade would not be allowed. Then, almost at the last minute, Mo Mowlam was saying she had not made up her mind. We now know that had she not allowed the parade that year, more than likely David Trimble and his UUP colleagues would have withdrawn from ongoing peace talks, which would have meant no Good Friday Agreement nine months later in April 1998. That agreement seemed very unlikely in July 1997. The decision to allow the parade to proceed outraged nationalist opinion once more.

On that Sunday 6 July, at about 3.30 a.m., thousands of soldiers and policemen sealed off and sealed in the Garvaghy Road residents in preparation for the parade later that morning. Hundreds of residents staged a sit-down protest and were roughly manhandled off the road by police. Stones and petrol bombs were thrown, and as many as eighteen people injured by plastic bullets and batons. It was rough.

After a few hours' sleep, later that July morning I found myself on the Garvaghy Road, Orangemen behind me, with, on each side, row upon row of soldiers, police, jeeps, Saracens and outraged residents creating an ear-splitting din. Coursing through my mind was the line from Psalm 23: 'Though I walk through the valley of the shadow of death, I will fear no evil.' It was impossible not to feel fear. My press pass would hardly spare me – or the Orangemen I had decided to accompany as Religious Affairs Correspondent – from a petrol bomb or stray bullet.

Another reason why I was at Drumcree had to do with the fact that the Church of Ireland was at the centre of what so frequently seemed an impossible situation. The Church of the Ascension there, its rector, Reverend John Pickering, and its local vestry were Church of Ireland. The tensions generated in those years almost split that Church in two, along Northern Ireland and Republic of Ireland lines. That would have been a tragedy, because the Church of Ireland is a unique institution across the two jurisdictions. Its members include substantial numbers of unionists and nationalists who worship side by side and, generally, agree to disagree amiably on political matters.

A couple of hours earlier the Orangemen had gathered at Carleton Street in Portadown for a 9.30 a.m. start to their parade. It was a warm, bright Sunday morning as the scattering of men in dark suits stood outside the Orange Hall there, some holding folded collarettes. Inside, a plaque on the wall commemorated those 'who died as a result of terrorist action against Ulster'. One man said he has been walking the route 'every year' since 1958. He had no desire to give offence, he said.

Pastor Kenny McClinton, a former member of the Ulster Defence Association and the Ulster Freedom Fighters who had served time for two murders, during which imprisonment he found God, told an American television crew that people on the Garvaghy Road were trying to set up 'a pocket of the Republic inside sovereign territory which is British, and having failed to do it with the bomb and bullet for thirty years they are now setting out to do it by stealth'. He said he represented the Ulster Civil Rights group and was there as a supporter of the Orangemen's right to parade.

At about 10.30, District Master Harold Gracey addressed the approximately 1,200 Orangemen outside the hall. They 'merely want to come from the church [of the Ascension] as we have done for two centuries', he said. Nothing must be said, he insisted, which could be the cause of valid complaint. Reverend Dwane Russell thanked God for the beautiful day, appealed for His protection and urged that nothing be done that would bring 'disrespect or discredit on our colours' along the way.

The parade set off for the Church at Drumcree to applause from onlookers, taking a route through Portadown to the countryside where it was situated, with the intention of returning to the town via its traditional 'circular' route through the Garvaghy Road. It was led by a colour party of three, one carrying the Portadown standard and two with ceremonial swords. Crowds lined the streets, mostly families, with cameras and dogs, clapping as the Orangemen marched at a quick pace to music from the Edgarstown Accordion Band. A young girl, standing on the pavement with a camera to her face, called 'Dad, Dad' to a man in the parade. An Orangeman waved at her. As they turned into the Corcrain Road, an RUC woman said into her walkie-talkie that they estimated there were 1,800 in the parade, and two bands.

As the parade passed an estate, an old man on crutches and wearing an Orange sash stood stiffly to attention. The green opposite him was full of materials for an Eve of the Twelfth bonfire. Just across was Obins Street, where nationalist residents were hemmed in by lines of police and army personnel as the parade passed. Farther on, Craigwell Road was blocked off by soldiers too. The windows on Corcrain Orange Hall were boarded up and the letters 'I R A' had been scrawled across three of these ground-floor barricades.

The music stopped as the parade approached St John's Catholic Church, with soldiers and police standing along the route. Drumcree Church could be seen across the fields, behind St John's. The music started again as the parade headed up Drumcree Road into open country. When it arrived at the Church of the Ascension, UUP leader David Trimble was there to meet it, as was Reverend Pickering. Bowler hats and umbrellas were lined up inside the door. Green Party TD Trevor Sargent was in the church as an observer, sitting on his own. 'An Irish-speaking Protestant, I'm disliked by everyone,' he joked to me.

The service began with Reverend Pickering reading a statement from Archbishop Robin Eames urging those present to reflect the ethos of their culture with dignity. Then all sang 'O God Our Help in Ages Past, Our Hope for Years to Come'. After the Creed, they prayed for members of the royal family, the prime minister, the secretary of state for Northern Ireland, members of the security forces and lasting peace 'in this area, in Garvaghy, in Portadown, in our country, and all the world'.

In his sermon Reverend Pickering said Drumcree was where 'this country nearly came to the brink of something awful in 1996', but that he would like to think of it being 'a turning point for Northern Ireland, where peace would begin and spread to every corner of our country'. He urged the congregation to imagine they are walking on water to Jesus, not to be 'full of fear and sinking, like Peter'.

Collection plates were passed around as they sang 'Will Your Anchor Hold in the Storms of Life?' David Trimble took up the collection in one part of the church. After a rendition of 'God Save the Queen', Harold Gracey expressed particular gratitude to Reverend Pickering, saying he was 'like a rock standing at the top of this hill'. Gracey appealed for no demonstration of triumphalism and explained that only members of the Portadown Lodge were walking back down the Garvaghy Road. They would meet up with everyone else 'when we arrive safely at the other side', at Shillington Bridge, he said.

Outside, the Portadown District Orangemen formed up six abreast. David Trimble saw them off. A helicopter hovered above. 'Left, left, left, right, left,' shouted a voice and they were off. Riot police and soldiers had sectioned off a side road as the parade headed towards the Garvaghy Road. All was silence, but not for long. Soon we were making our way through an ear-splitting cacophony along the entire length of the road with the heavily armed presence to our left and to our right. It seemed to take for ever but, anxious and uncertain, all eventually arrived safely in Portadown, where the Orangemen were greeted by wildly enthusiastic crowds as conquering heroes who had passed bravely through the valley of death, fearing no evil.

There was no such warm greeting for media. I was slapped about the place by an angry woman on the footpath, who shouted abuse at me and sent my notebook flying. 'Tell the truth. Why don't ye tell the truth?' she screamed at me. They hated us in Portadown and made no secret of it. At the beginning of the parade there one year, ahead of the parade itself, I was once again slapped about the place by another incensed woman, who was just as passionate about the truth. My notebook was sent flying then too. As I tried to retrieve it, I almost ended up under the Orangemen's feet as they caught up with me.

Violence was never far from the surface at Drumcree. Coming up to midnight there one year, a colleague, Marie O'Halloran, and myself were doing a final survey of the night on Drumcree Hill for the news desk in Dublin when we were approached by a local Orangeman who, hearing our accents, cocked one hand into pistol form, pointed at our heads individually and went 'bang, bang, bang'. Thereafter, we knew him as 'Bang, Bang'. You could never be sure just how seriously to take such gestures. A few days after that I saw Bang Bang in his Royal Black Preceptory (a sort of upmarket Orange Order) uniform at nearby Scarva, County Down, where they also stage an annual parade. Seeing me, he had the grace to look appropriately abashed.

✠ ✠ ✠

The worst of times at Drumcree occurred in July 1998, when it became a focal point for those opposed to the Good Friday Agreement of the previous April. In the dying hours of Monday 13 July that year, following days of rioting as the Orangemen were stopped by a barricade, the British Army and the RUC, from going down the Garvaghy Road, Reverend Ian Paisley made an appearance. Standing at the front door of the parish hall in Drumcree as midnight approached, he roared his half-truths at an eager crowd. He had arrived in the gathering dusk and – in the church grounds, which the Church of Ireland had declared were out of bounds to all – he addressed the crowds in incendiary language about the parade being blocked, about the sell-out that was the Good Friday Agreement and about the evil media. I slipped my notebook out of sight and made myself as inconspicuous as possible, convinced I was about to be beaten to a pulp by a crowd enraged beyond control. I was saved by the descending darkness.

Early on the previous day, Sunday 12 July, news broke about the deaths of three Catholic children (Jason, Mark and Richard Quinn) following an Ulster Volunteer Force (UVF) firebomb attack on their home at Ballymoney, County Antrim a short time after 4 a.m., an event linked to the violence at Drumcree over the previous week. Three UVF members were named later as being responsible, with one, Garfield Gilmour, sentenced to life imprisonment. Files released by Northern Ireland's public records office in 2022 offered a sobering perspective on the violence at Drumcree between 4 and 12 July that year, where the RUC recorded 598 attacks on security forces, which injured seventy police officers. The police responded by firing 751 plastic bullets and arresting 254 people. When the violence subsided, 2,237 petrol bombs were recovered. The night of 9–10 July that year saw 'the worst violence of the standoff to date' at Drumcree itself, the police records stated, with similar levels of violence reported on the following night, while the Portadown Orangemen were 'in bitter and hostile mood and had shown no signs of flexibility'. The disorder halted abruptly early on Sunday 12 July following news of the three Quinn children's deaths.

The killing of those children prompted the Orange Order chaplain and Presbyterian minister Reverend William Bingham to tell his congregation in Pomeroy, County Tyrone, that Sunday morning: 'I'm not ashamed to say that I wept as I heard of the loss of three little boys in Ballymoney ... I have to say this: that after last night's atrocious act, a fifteen-minute walk down the Garvaghy Road by the Orange Order would be a very hollow victory.' The attack on the Quinn home in Ballymoney was 'exactly the opposite of what Orangeism stands for. It is anathema to Orangeism and it ought to be so,' he said.

Bingham's sermon that Sunday was not a rare courageous act on his part. An impressive man, whom I had interviewed a number of times by then, he had officiated at the funerals of six of his congregation killed by the IRA. Most were members of the security forces. He had been outspoken at the funerals and was frequently praised for his warmth in comforting the bereaved. He received death threats from republicans, which meant that he and his young family had to move out of their house in Pomeroy several times. Yet his sermon about the Quinn children earned him the odium of some on his own side, who now considered him a pariah. They dragged him by his collar from the Orange parade in Pomeroy the following day and threw him into a ditch for his comments.

An evangelical Protestant, Bingham was also a deeply compassionate man, and compassion is not usually the first word that comes to mind about anyone described as evangelical. His understanding of Orangeism was very useful to Southerners such as myself in gaining an insight into how Orangemen and women of goodwill saw themselves. Speaking to a New Dialogue fringe meeting at the British Labour Party conference in 1997, he recalled, 'My first experience in the Orange Order was on parade with my family on the Twelfth of July 1969 in Markethill, County Armagh ... I was five years of age, hand in hand with an elderly uncle.' The Order, he said, 'stresses the values of family and community. It brings together the past, the present, and the future, grandparents, parents and children, as part of the one tradition, strengthening the family, enhancing respect and toleration between the generations when there is much in society to pull them apart.' And whereas Orangeism, he said, was committed to reformed Christianity (Protestantism), 'that is not to say by definition that a true Orangeman is in any way antagonistic towards Catholics or people of other faiths'. Paraphrasing from the 'Qualifications of an Orangeman', he said an Orangeman should abstain from all uncharitable words, actions or sentiments towards Roman Catholics.

It was a theme he returned to in his sermon following the killing of the Quinn children. You might say that Reverend Bingham represented the acceptable face of Orangeism as I had witnessed it among the majority of the membership in Portadown over those eight long years. These were decent people who would be hard to distinguish in the crowd at any GAA match in the Republic. Similar people with deeply held, if different, allegiances.

If Reverend Ian Paisley put the fear of God into me that 1998 July night in Drumcree, I would also see another side to his character soon afterwards. Just five months later, in December 1998, while reporting on a session of the European Parliament, I went in search of the offices of then EU Agriculture Commissioner Franz Fischler, where a significant meeting about Northern Ireland was taking place. Following a labyrinthine journey through the innards of the European Parliament building, I was told by Fischler's secretary that the meeting there – involving John Hume, Ian Paisley and Ulster Unionist MEP Jim Nicholson – was still under way.

It was just a week after John Hume had received the Nobel Peace Prize along with David Trimble in Oslo. The three politicians were there to plead a case for Northern Ireland's pig farmers following a disastrous fire at a bacon factory in Ballymoney, which had had a hugely destructive effect on the local pork industry. Fischler promised to send an expert to see what could be done. Suddenly I heard an outburst of raucous laughter from the meeting room. Pigs, no less, had brought the three Northern Irish politicians together as one.

Afterwards, when I approached an initially suspicious Reverend Paisley, he became animated as he related how badly off Northern Ireland's pig farmers were as a result of the fire and how they had to be helped. Jim Nicholson explained that British Agriculture Secretary Nick Brown said he might be able to assist as well, and John Hume said they'd all better rush off or they would miss an important vote in the parliament. And off they went, three colleagues looking after their voters. Considering what had gone before, it seemed an impossibly hopeful situation, the stuff of fantasy even.

Almost ten years later, in March 2008, when Reverend Paisley was the Northern Ireland First Minister, there was a centenary event at Queen's University in Belfast. The attendance included President Mary McAleese and Queen Elizabeth. It was the first time both heads of state met publicly on the island of Ireland. Queen Elizabeth unveiled a centenary stone to mark the occasion, with lines from a specially commissioned stanza by Seamus Heaney engraved on its plinth. Heaney read the stanza to the gathering: 'Still red brickwork / Remains our bulwark: / Here exercise / Of mind has stood / To us, for us / These 100 years / And will, for good.' Dr Paisley greeted President of Ireland Mary McAleese civilly. There was never any love lost between them.

In the Black and White Hall, before a marble statue of a pensive Galileo, the queen and Prince Philip greeted dignitaries, beginning with President McAleese and her husband, Martin. Later, in the university's Great Hall all three – Dr Paisley, President McAleese and Queen Elizabeth – sat at the top table for a centenary lunch, under an enormous portrait of the killing of St Peter the Martyr, beside which was a portrait of a young Queen Victoria, while other portraits on its walls included President McAleese and Seamus Heaney, both graduates of the university.

The assortment of approximately 100 guests also included then Northern Secretary Shaun Woodward, Seamus Heaney and other QUB graduates, such as poet Michael Longley, former UUP leader David Trimble, former Catholic Church Primate Cardinal Cahal Daly, former Church of Ireland Primate Archbishop Robin Eames, then SDLP MLA Dr Alasdair McDonnell and former *Irish Times* journalist Conor O'Clery. That mixum-gatherum was behind Dr Paisley's comment to me, as he left the university later, that it 'was some crowd in there today … liquorice all-sorts'. He laughed. I laughed. It was Paisley at his best, and that humour!

None was in evidence that July night at Drumcree in 1998 when he was at his absolute worst. With menace and misinformation, he stoked the angry crowd. The deaths of the Quinn children had nothing to do with the blocked Orange parade at Drumcree. He knew that, he said. Ballymoney was in his constituency. Just let people wait as the saga at the Quinn house unfolded, he said. 'There's a lot of dancing on those young fellows' graves for their own advantage.' Drumcree would continue as it had before, he said. It was 'too serious to be picked off by any happening in our country ... Is this country going to be ruled by Dublin? Is it going to see the Protestant people wiped out, as they had been in the South?' he said. And the media. Why was it so 'bitter and arrogant to Protestants and gentle and kind to Catholics?' He continued in such vein before concluding with the hymn 'O God Our Help in Ages Past'.

As he left, youths with scarves across their faces flowed through the crowds to the barricade below, carrying bottles of petrol, which they set on fire. They threw these up and over at the RUC and flowed back through the crowd of mainly middle-aged farmers and their wives to get more for the next barrage. Shots were fired too, as the petrol bombers ran up and down from tents in a field across from the Church of the Ascension, shielded by these older men and women from the Armagh countryside. It was this latter fact that shocked me most; to see ordinary middle-aged men and women shielding petrol bombers was not something I had expected, nor was the fact that no one tried to stop them. Not one of the Portadown District Orange Lodge marshals was anywhere to be seen.

Plastic bullets were fired as another shower of petrol bombs went over. One local youth was hit in the foot. He fell. An outraged crowd gathered round him. A Portadown District marshal appeared from nowhere and, with another man, linked the casualty to the first-aid centre at the parish hall. As the injured youth was helped up the hill, people on either side burst into applause for their local hero. A small group of Orangemen stopped myself and a colleague, demanding identification. They told us to clear off. Perhaps cheekily, we told them we were walking on the queen's highway. They reminded us we were 'Free State bastards' and that we had massacred Protestants.

A lot of the violent talk at Drumcree was just bluster. Still, in our night-time surveys of the hill for reports back to Dublin, we media from the Republic learned not to speak so our accents wouldn't betray us. But it must be said, most of the violence there did not come from the Orangemen themselves but from thugs attaching themselves to their cause. I had deep sympathy for Reverend John Pickering and his wife, Olive, who were caught in the middle of it all, but I was soon fed up at the paralysis of the Church of Ireland leadership, whose hand-wringing as deaths mounted was not impressive. The unity of the Church was threatened as bishops and members in the Republic were driven to desperation and shame seeing one of their churches feature on TV screens across the world as the epicentre of violence in Northern Ireland over those years. Three southern Church of Ireland bishops – Archbishop of Dublin Walton Empey, Bishop of Cashel and Ossory John Neill and Bishop of Meath and Kildare Richard Clarke – caused deep anger among Church members in Northern Ireland when they visited Reverend Pickering at Drumcree, where, it was believed, they tried to pressure him to call off the July Sunday Orange service. In general, Northern Church of Ireland members were prone to saying it was easy for those at a safe distance to criticise the Church for its stance on Drumcree, while some Southern members tended to dismiss Orangemen as bigots.

Meanwhile, killing followed killing. Drumcree played a direct role in the deaths of ten people, nine of them Catholic. They were Michael McGoldrick (1996), Robert Hamill (1997), Billy

Wright, the leader of the Loyalist Volunteer Force (1997), Adrian Lamph (1998), RUC Constable Frank O'Reilly (1998), the three Quinn children, Richard (10), Mark (9) and Jason (8), solicitor Rosemary Nelson (1999) and Ciaran Cummins (2001).

In May 1997 Robbie Hamill, a twenty-five-year-old Catholic, was attacked and beaten to death by loyalists in Portadown in full view of an RUC patrol, which did nothing. His grave near St John's Catholic Church on the Garvaghy Road had to be sealed off behind wire during the Drumcree protests of subsequent years, as it was defecated on. That just blew my mind. I could not comprehend a hatred so deep that someone would do that on a grave. It seemed beyond depravity. Even the dead were not safe at Drumcree. Soon St John's Church itself, its grounds and graveyard had to be sealed off behind high razor-wire fences during the Drumcree 'season' every year.

✠ ✠ ✠

My first encounter with the grief that flowed in such torrents from Northern Ireland was in 1993. In this instance the victim was Catholic too, but grief respects no faith. It concerned twenty-year-old Julie Statham of Dungannon, County Tyrone, who died by suicide in February that year. I reported on her funeral. She and Diarmuid Shields had been going out together for four years when he was murdered by the UVF a month previously. He too was twenty. The couple had planned to get engaged on 6 March that year, his twenty-first birthday. Neither lived that long. On 3 January Diarmuid and his father were the first victims of the Northern Ireland conflict that year. A UVF gang called to their two-storey house-cum-grocery-shop at the crossroads in Lisnagleer, near Dungannon. The Shields family were not political, but they had a deep interest in Irish music and Gaelic

183

football. It is believed the UVF gang intended killing them all but failed when Mrs Bríd Shields barricaded herself with a daughter and son into a downstairs room. Diarmuid and his father could not get away. Both were shot dead. Another brother, Davóg, was seriously injured.

Julie was distraught. A student at Queen's University, in the weeks following Diarmuid's death her life began to disintegrate. She visited his grave every day, sometimes spending hours there, playing tapes of albums and songs they both loved. On Monday 1 February she went to the Shields home for the month's mind Mass for Diarmuid and his father. The following morning, when her father called her, she did not respond. She had overdosed. 'On Candlemas Day the light went out in their lives,' the priest said of her parents at the funeral. Julie was an only child.

As sometimes the job demanded, I found myself having to do things which felt deeply uncomfortable. Like calling to the Statham home the night before Julie's funeral, in case either parent might wish to speak. Her mother was too upset. I was advised to talk to Julie's father. He was upstairs, where she was laid out. I couldn't do it. I left. Earlier, accompanied by a photographer who knew the way, I had visited the Shields home in the countryside near Dungannon. It was while a series of bolts were being drawn back on the front door, one by one, that I felt this too was going too far. But it was too late.

Bríd Shields was a small woman, polite and gentle. The realisation that someone like her had had to endure the horror she did seemed such an elemental violation. I regretted immediately having troubled her. She was kind and said little, but it hardly mattered. I could hardly bring myself to ask her anything.

The photographer with me was as moved. He was Protestant and based in Belfast. He told me about a Catholic girl he had been going out with and how she had ended the relationship on discovering he was a Protestant. The implacability of Northern Ireland was making itself felt. And its mourning. 'There is an ocean of grief,' said Father Denis Faul, then president at Dungannon Academy, where both Julie Statham and Diarmuid Shields had attended school, 'and a big lake of pain and injury which touches everyone here'. He continued, 'the ugly factions of Italy caused the deaths of Romeo and Juliet and now the ugly factions of Northern Ireland have taken the lives of these two young lovers'.

In the Dungannon area alone, over twenty young people had been killed in the previous two and a half years, including a twenty-eight-year-old man killed on the eve of Julie Statham's funeral Mass. At that Mass a friend of hers read Psalm 23, 'The Lord is My Shepherd', with the congregation responding, 'though I walk through the valley of death, I fear no evil'. It is why I remembered Julie and her funeral as I walked with Orangemen down the Garvaghy Road that July Sunday five years later.

At her funeral Mass there was a poignancy to the mood of the congregation as of a community doomed. So much so that, as they sang and prayed for Julie, it felt as if they were singing and praying for themselves too, for who among them might not be next? As her coffin was carried down the aisle, they sang that beautiful Protestant hymn 'Abide with Me', filling the church with its resonance and its significance for all the living and the dead of Northern Ireland.

Walking to the graveyard that day, an esteemed colleague – the late Mary Holland, there in a personal capacity – wept for both communities and their 'abandonment' by Britain and the Republic. Standing by the graveside, while the priest sprinkled clay on her coffin, intoning those comfortless words of dust and ashes, Julie's mother howled her anguish. It touched all hearers to the very marrow. Soon the grave was covered in a mound of

185

flowers and wreaths with their tender messages of love and loss, for so many decades a repeated image of Northern Ireland.

And there we were at Drumcree, all those years later, creating more funerals, over and over again, as immovable object and irresistible force met with ferocity. In my commentary on Drumcree I was very critical of both sides, in particular of the Orange Order leadership and that of the Church of Ireland. The latter wrung its collective hands in anguish while doing exactly nothing – apart from passing cosmetic motions at its General Synod in 1999, for instance. I also had little time for the intransigence of Breandán Mac Cionnaith, who spoke for the Garvaghy Road residents and seemed beyond the influence of even the Sinn Féin leadership.

I was being so critical of the Church of Ireland in commentary that a senior Church figure in Dublin asked me whether I had a problem with his Church. I did not and I do not. Similarly, an Orange Order leader in Portadown took me apart on one occasion and, eventually, announced it didn't matter what I wrote anyway as 'only three copies of *The Irish Times* are sold in Portadown, and two of those go to the RUC'. There could hardly be a worse condemnation at the time, because the RUC was at the lowest rung in the Orange Order pecking order at that point. I never did find out who was buying that third copy of the paper in Portadown back then.

One senior Church of Ireland figure in the Republic told me that 'one of the comforts that you bring to my life is that there is no question that the Orange Order and Drumcree people hate you even more than they hate me! It is some comfort but not a great deal!'

By then I was frustrated at the tribal nature of Ireland's Churches in general, which was always held to, even as murder reigned. Yes, there were extraordinary and courageous individuals within each Church who took great risks for peace, but as institutions they were quite useless when it came to dealing with violence.

✠ ✠ ✠

The tribal nature of the Churches in Ireland is not unique. You might say it is universal; that all religions are tribal, as illustrated more recently with the stance of the Russian Orthodox Church following the invasion of Ukraine by Vladimir Putin on 24 February 2022. From the beginning, Russian Orthodox leader Patriarch Kirill of Moscow gave his blessing to Moscow's invasion of Ukraine, seen as the cradle of the Rus civilisation.

I interviewed Patriarch Kirill when he came to Dublin in 2001 as Metropolitan Kirill of Smolensk and Kaliningrad. He was in Ireland to complete Russian Orthodox Church plans to take over a former Church of Ireland church in Harold's Cross to cater for its growing membership in Dublin. Territory was important to the patriarch then too. He said at the time that his Church opposed Pope John Paul II visiting Moscow as Catholic priests were actively seeking converts from the Russian Orthodox Church and that, in western Ukraine, Christians affiliated to Rome had used force and civil law against his Church in disagreements about property, despite an earlier agreement to resolve such problems peacefully.

In March/April 1999 I encountered the same tribalism in what is now North Macedonia, while reporting on the influx of thousands of Muslim refugees from Kosovo, driven out by Serb forces then undertaking an ethnic cleansing of Kosovo. They drove the Muslim Kosovars across the border to predominantly Christian Orthodox North Macedonia, crossing at Blace near the capital, Skopje, where they were not wanted by a local population sympathetic to the Serbs, who were also Christian Orthodox.

Hundreds of the Kosovars ended up sleeping on graves in a Muslim cemetery near Blace, as enormous refugee camps were being built by UN and NATO troops. NATO headquarters was in nearby Skopje for the duration. Reports of atrocities by Serb forces were emerging from Kosovo, with claims of mass killings in one village, while, in another, four truckloads of bodies were said to have been buried with one truckload burned. Meanwhile, tens of thousands of ethnic Muslim Kosovars were trapped by Serb forces in central Kosovo and threatened with starvation. Soon there were about 44,000 refugees in the camps near Skopje, with another 60,000 dispersed throughout North Macedonia.

On Good Friday that year I decided to check out how all this was being addressed in ceremonies at the Orthodox Church of St Kliment Ohridski in Skopje. In that crowded, colourful, incense-filled space it was as if the Kosovar refugees in camps a few miles away did not exist. Worshippers brought eggs to a highly ornate table, covered by a curtained canopy. A gospel with gilt covers rested on it, as did elaborately painted eggs and bank notes. Each person, as they approached the table, kissed the gospel, donated an egg or whatever money they could afford, then crawled beneath the table to be blessed with holy water by one of two priests on the other side.

The parish priest, Father Methody, remembering some English from his years in Melbourne, Australia, gestured to the crucified Christ being kissed by the crowds and said, quoting His words on the first Good Friday, 'Lord forgive them, for they know not what they do.' He was referring to the bombing of Serb forces in Kosovo by NATO, not the ethnic-cleansing policies of Serb leader Slobodan Milošević. The priest explained how Kosovo was very important to Serb Christians. It was 'the heart of their culture', he said. Most of the main monasteries in the

Serb Orthodox Church were based there, while the Patriarch of the Serb Orthodox Church was elected in Kosovo, not Belgrade (capital of Serbia), he continued. And lots of Serbs who had to leave Kosovo in the early 1980s had been replaced by (Muslim) Albanians, said Father Methody. As for Milošević, whose policy of ethnic cleansing had led to the thousands of Kosovar refugees arriving in North Macedonia, and who was already being accused of the genocide and war crimes, for which he would later face trial at The Hague, Father Methody believed him 'one very big leader'. The Serb, Russian and Macedonian Orthodox Christians 'like [him] as leader', the priest said.

Father Methody had nothing whatsoever to say about the ongoing suffering of Muslim Kosovars, nor did it strike him that there was anything wrong with this silence. The Muslim Kosovars belonged to another tribe, which had crossed the border into his country to escape slaughter by Serbs and now, in their destitute thousands, even as they cowered in camps within a few miles of his church, they did not matter. They were not of his tribe.

Just a month after I returned from North Macedonia, in May 1999, the Church of Ireland General Synod passed resolutions regarding Drumcree, which they knew in advance were a waste of time. They requested that Reverend Pickering and the vestry at Drumcree decline to extend an invitation to the Portadown Orangemen to attend the July service there again if they did not agree to three pledges: to avoid any action that would diminish the sanctity of the service; to obey the law before and after the service; and to respect the integrity of the Church of Ireland by word and action and not use Church property or its environs in any protest. They also passed a resolution banning the flying of flags other than the cross of St Patrick or that of the Anglican Communion from its churches. All these resolutions were without consequence if ignored.

I spoke to Reverend Pickering immediately after those resolutions were passed at the General Synod that day and he told me they would not be honoured at Drumcree, something the Church's bishops were aware of by then too. Their paralysis before Drumcree seemed morally bankrupt as murder followed murder, but it did mean the Church did not split, which it could so easily have done then. I have never been able to establish to my own satisfaction whether this paralysis was brilliant strategy or just ineptitude.

All Churches, all religions, are essentially tribal. At their best they act as a repository for the higher moral and spiritual values of their tribe, which they carry from generation to generation. That is seen as their role within the tribe. In situations of conflict, the best they can hope to do is moderate the extremes, particularly the violent ones, but frequently they are just impotent in that context, as we in Ireland know. Loving your enemy is all very well, but that too may have to be moderated if you are not to lose your tribe.

The Catholic Primate Archbishop Eamon Martin put it well in an interview we did in April 2023 to coincide with the twenty-fifth anniversary of the Good Friday Agreement. Real dialogue on reconciliation between the communities in Northern Ireland was 'not happening on the ground and our communities are still very segregated,' he said. 'Everybody is still tribal. Cultural tribalism still exists here which we haven't been able to break out of. It's not easy to break out of ...' So it is with religions worldwide.

✠ ✠ ✠

By July 2000 senior colleagues at *The Irish Times* regarded me as something of a Drumcree veteran, so when one of my favourite people at the paper, Róisín Ingle, was sent along to write 'colour' pieces about events there that year I was asked to make sure she was safe. Along with most media, we were based at the Seagoe hotel in Portadown. Róisín, then in her twenties, had met a young Orangeman who was in a band and decided to write 'a day in the life' article on him. I wasn't fazed when she said she had met him at a riot in Portadown earlier that day. Or that he had told her he would drive us to Drumcree hill for the final post-midnight report. On the hill that night we were silent, as usual. Having established that the situation was likely to be quiet for the night, I decided to leave. But Róisín wouldn't budge. She was going to stay on the hill among all those angry loyalists, with Jonny the Orange bandsman, whom I'd never met before. What was I to do?

I consulted journalist colleagues Marie O'Halloran and Audrey Magee. 'She won't budge. I can't leave her here. With her Southern accent anything could happen. And she's a woman. On her own. But she won't budge.' The two women pointed out, pertinently, 'She's an adult and he seems a nice guy.' I was not reassured. I tried again to persuade Róisín, but she was not for turning. I was about to plead, when she insisted she would be fine. Jonny just smiled. There was no choice but to return to the Seagoe where I hardly slept as my nightmares lined up, one by one, to present me with the very worst possible scenarios.

Next morning the RUC reported a quiet night; nothing out of the ordinary. Further relief came with the knowledge that Róisín was to return to Belfast that day. I didn't see her again until our staff Christmas party, five months later. She came up to me there and asked, 'Do you remember that lad who drove us to Drumcree hill that night?' I certainly did. 'Well, we've been together since,' she said, with a happy laugh. I was floored and dubbed myself to Róisín as 'the fool on the Hill'.

Róisín and Jonny Hobson have been together since and have lived happily ever after in Dublin. Róisín wrote, '[We] first met in the middle of a riot in Portadown. A car in flames on the railway tracks. Stones hurtling through the balmy July air. I managed to get his phone number before the army closed in. Love at first riot, as my colleague Patsy McGarry said, of those heady days on the hill at Drumcree. Twenty years later the fire still burns.'

Almost twenty-four years later, on 29 February 2024, that fire burned as strongly and Róisín proposed. Beforehand she sent me a text: 'It's a Leap Year. And I am going to ask a certain former Orange man a big question tonight. I thought you should know.' Later she sent me a photograph of the blissful two, with Jonny holding a knotted tie to the camera for illustration. 'He said yes he'd tie the knot!' texted Róisín. As if it was ever in doubt.

It seems love stories, too, can begin at Drumcree.

10

An Irishwoman Abroad

Her name was Mary, and she was with child.

It was the early 1950s when she arrived in London with her fiancé. They left Ireland because of her pregnancy. Both were from rural Roscommon; neither had ever been abroad before. They got jobs, she in a branch of W.H. Smith on Oxford Street. Soon he was gone. He fled to the US. Mary was in despair, forsaken. One day she lay down in a park, her swollen belly obstructing the sun, and pleaded with God to take her and the baby. He didn't. As she said years later, it seemed He too had abandoned her. Noticing her distress in W.H. Smith's one day, a colleague, an older woman, approached and asked her what the matter was. Mary broke down and wept out her sorry story. Deeply moved, the English woman embraced and consoled her. She brought Mary to her large house in south London. There she showed her its bright basement apartment, which she offered to Mary.

It was Mary's home for more than three decades. She reared her son there, paying the kind English woman a nominal rent. Mary had very little to do with the Irish community in London except for an unorthodox couple who owned a picture-framing shop near where she lived. She began to work there. She loved it and its clientele, who were mostly theatre people. She enjoyed their instinctive tolerance, their joie de vivre, their penchant for gossip, their (by the standards of the time) outrageous personal arrangements. Beneath all that 'luvvy' stuff, she recognised an honesty about people and relationships that was absent in mainstream society.

Mary attended Mass for the sake of her son, though her own faith was badly shaken. She visited Ireland rarely but kept in contact with one brother, who helped her out and would come over to see her. But even he was pushed to the limit when she visited Ireland. He would ask her to hide in the back of his car, behind the front seats, so neighbours would not see her and ask questions. When her son accompanied her to Ireland, he too had to cower in the back seat.

Much worse was the attitude of Mary's mother, an instinctively kind and warm woman who was very devout. Mary did attend Mass when in Ireland, but her mother would not sit in the same pew. Mary accepted these humiliations as her due. For she had sinned against what was also her own moral template. A lifetime in exile was as it should be. She did not blame her mother, her fiancé, the Church or Ireland. At least not with conviction. There was no self-pity, just hints of self-loathing. She was never with another man after the father of her child went to the US, where he married and raised a family. How could she expect any man to want a relationship with her when she had a son? How could she ever tell a man such a thing? How could she face rejection again? She believed it was better not to get involved at all. So she didn't.

Mary sent her son to Catholic schools in London and hoped he would be treated well: her badge of shame, her little star. She hoped all those kids from regular families would not humiliate him for her sin. She hoped he would not feel humiliated when he realised the truth. As he grew up he became religious, as well as curious and confused about his national identity. Was he Irish or English? It was difficult for her to encourage him to assume an Irish identity, not that she ever spoke a bad word about Ireland. Eventually her son went to live in North America but had no contact with his father.

In the early 1990s Mary returned to live with her brother in Ireland. In time she became ill and, over the years, declined painfully. She died in 2000 as unobtrusively as she had lived, well-liked – loved even – by those of us who got to know her.

When I met Mary, that student summer in early 1970s' London, her story was a blow to my green vision of Ireland. I was a little older than her son. One summer I stayed with them. She even organised a job for me on a building site not far from where they lived. She and I grew very fond of one another. One evening, as a treat, I took her to see the musical *A Little Night Music* in the West End. We both agreed it wasn't very good, but we loved its main song, 'Send in the Clowns'. It became our theme tune. Afterwards, in our many moments of levity, she would sing the first verse to me, and I'd respond, 'But where are the clowns / Send in the clowns / Don't bother … we're here!' Some duo. Mary was my aunt.

She was known in the family as 'Babs' and I wrote about her in *The Irish Times* on 16 January 2021, four days after publication of the Mother and Baby Homes Commission Report. The timing was not accidental, because I believed that had she and her fiancé not gone to London when they discovered she was pregnant, she would have ended up in just such a home to save the family from shame – possibly the nearest and most infamous one at Tuam, County Galway: St Mary's Mother and Baby Home, which remained open until 1961.

By January 2021 my ninety-two-year-old mother, younger sister of Babs, was in the nursing home in Ballaghaderreen with dementia. She died the following June. It would have been too much for her had I written about Babs in earlier years. Despite being a hugely tolerant woman, she too carried within herself traces of the shame her generation would have felt at having a sister who got pregnant out of wedlock.

Shame was why women ended up in Magdalene laundries or Mother and Baby Homes, and why it was arranged that so many children born out of wedlock were adopted abroad, far away – usually by white Catholic couples in the US. Because my aunt went to London, her son, my cousin, escaped that fate. Both were saved from separation, shame and stigma in Ireland by Babs's decision to go to London, and by the kindness of a decent English woman.

I am in no doubt that, had she stayed in Ireland, my grandmother would have insisted that Babs should go to the Tuam Mother and Baby Home and, from there, have her son adopted. My grandmother would have done so for the sake of the broader family, to avoid the stigma that would have followed the family had it been revealed that her eldest daughter had become pregnant out of wedlock, and to also address 'the problem' of her illegitimate child. Tuam could offer Babs a second chance in life too, were it kept secret. It was a way out for everyone.

Personally, I never have had any doubt about the source of that shame in Ireland. It was due to a peculiar hybrid of Catholicism, which, unlike the version in continental Europe, was seemingly obsessed with sex. It appeared to be the only sin. The root of this obsession was Victorian prudery, promoted by the remarkably faithful (for a member of the British royal family) Prince Albert but driven mainly by Protestant evangelicals, the people who really brought down Parnell because of his adultery with Katharine O'Shea. Such sexual puritanism was dominant in Britain, of which Ireland was then part, during the later nineteenth century and extending into the twentieth.

Ireland's Catholic Church, then finding its feet after centuries of persecution, was seemingly anxious to be seen as the most respectable of them all in the Britain of the day. It was determined to move the Irish people from the comparatively lax view of sex, which saw their numbers reach 8.2 million in 1841, a figure never reached since. Denunciation and shame were its weapons of choice when it came to shaping the faithful into 'happy' little Catholic Irish boys and girls – that, and corporal punishment, which, throughout most societies in those times, helped ensure that children were seen and not heard. Economics was a major factor too, in that the subdivision of small-holdings in Ireland was ended after the Famine, with most children emigrating while the eldest son inherited and then, usually, only when his elderly parents died. It meant heavy restraints on sexual activity. Soon, in parts of rural Ireland, there were more bachelors and spinsters than married couples. Fertility rates plummeted.

By 1922 the Catholic Church controlled education and health-care in Ireland. To all intents, by the later nineteenth century it had evolved into an alternative civic State in Ireland within the larger British State. With independence, and following a civil war, the financially exhausted Irish Free State became hugely dependent on the Catholic Church to provide what education and healthcare there was. This helped persuade the new State's politicians to outlaw divorce in 1925, for instance, and set about creating through its laws a Catholic State for a majority Catholic people, ignoring the beliefs of its small Protestant and other faith minorities. It took little persuasion, because those same politicians were of a similar conservative Catholic mind. It should not be forgotten that all the 1916 leaders were Catholic – including socialist James Connolly, who received the last rites of the Church before he was shot in May 1916. So well might Kevin O'Higgins, a member of the new Free State government, say in

1923, 'we are the most conservative-minded revolutionaries that ever put through a successful revolution'.

The Ireland they presided over 'was a cold harsh environment for many, probably the majority, of its residents', the 2021 Mother and Baby Homes Report found. This was particularly so, it said:

> during the earlier half of the period under remit [from 1922 to 1998]. It was especially cold and harsh for women. All women suffered serious discrimination. Women who gave birth outside marriage were subject to particularly harsh treatment. Responsibility for that harsh treatment rests mainly with the fathers of their children and their own immediate families. It was supported by, contributed to, and condoned by, the institutions of the State and the Churches. However, it must be acknowledged that the institutions under investigation provided a refuge – a harsh refuge in some cases – when the families provided no refuge at all.

Not surprisingly then, when I was a student in Galway and subsequently, my Aunt Babs's experience greatly informed my interest in and support for women's right to control their fertility, to financial independence and to equality in all things. Nor can it be a surprise that I had a particular interest in Magdalene laundries as well as Mother and Baby Homes.

Patricia McDonnell was probably the first person with whom I had dealings in connection with the Magdalene laundries. Her sister-in-law, 'Mary' (a pseudonym), spent twenty years at the Sisters of Mercy Magdalene laundry in Dún Laoghaire, County Dublin. There were still Magdalene laundries operating in Ireland when Patricia established the Magdalen Memorial Committee in the early 1990s. The last such laundry in Ireland closed in Dublin on 25 October 1996. It was located on Dublin's Seán

McDermott Street, named after the 1916 leader executed eighty years earlier.

Patricia's Magdalen committee was probably the oldest such group in Ireland. She set it up after reading a 1993 report in *The Irish Times* about the exhumation of women buried near the High Park Magdalene laundry in Dublin's Drumcondra. The Sisters of Our Lady of Charity were selling land to a developer and wanted the 133 remains removed to Glasnevin cemetery. During the exhumation process, twenty-two additional and unidentified remains were found. The Magdalen Memorial Committee arranged for a seat to be placed in Dublin's St Stephen's Green in memory of all the women who had been in the laundries. In 1996, even as the laundry on Seán McDermott Street was still open, then President of Ireland Mary Robinson unveiled the seat, erected on a site arranged by then Minister for Arts and Culture, and later President, Michael D. Higgins. A plaque on the seat reads, 'To the women who worked in the Magdalen laundry institutions and to the children born to some members of those institutions – reflect here upon their lives.'

Patricia's sister-in-law came from a well-off farming back-ground in County Galway. In the late 1930s Mary's parents died. Two of her brothers, who were nineteen and seventeen at the time, took over the farm, while she looked after the house. The smaller children were sent to relatives. The local priest told Mary's brothers that he felt she was in moral danger. He knew a nice family in Dublin where she would be safer. Mary's brothers were not convinced, but the priest and his housekeeper persuaded them otherwise.

The priest drove Mary to the Dún Laoghaire Magdalene laundry and asked her brothers not to contact her, to allow her settle in. Every time Mary's brothers inquired, the priest warned them off. Over time they stopped asking.

When Mary's younger brother, Patricia's husband, went in search of his sister, he eventually found her at the laundry in Dún Laoghaire. The first time he saw her, 'beside a robust nun, she looked like someone from Belsen', he said. Patricia was 'horrified at her condition. She was painfully thin. It took her family a year to find her,' she told me. 'Most were young girls when they started in the laundries. My sister-in-law started when she was sixteen. Some thirteen- and fourteen-year-olds were sent to the laundry as punishment, and then left there. And at the time the age of majority was twenty-one,' she said.

Her husband threatened the nuns with legal action if Mary was not released. A time and date was set. When he arrived to pick her up, Mary was on her knees scrubbing a floor. He asked a nun why this was the case and was told, 'Do you want us to have a riot? No one has ever left this place.'

That was in 1960. It took time for Mary to adjust to life outside, her only query ever being why she was detained at the laundry at all. In the late 1990s Patricia McDonnell and her husband began inquiries about Mary's time in Dún Laoghaire. They contacted the Sisters of Mercy. 'They denied the laundry existed,' Patricia said, 'even though it was there in *Thom's Directory*.' So she rang RTÉ's Joe Duffy, and *Liveline* was inundated with calls from people confirming the laundry's existence.

Contacted again, the Sisters of Mercy said they had no records from the laundry. Later they supplied the McDonnells with a copy of an electoral register, which proved Mary had been in the laundry between 1951 and 1959. The Sisters of Mercy were unable to provide the government's Inter-Departmental Committee, set up to establish the facts of State involvement with the Magdalene laundries (it reported in 2013) with records for either of their two laundries, in Galway and Dún Laoghaire.

In 2002 and 2003 Patricia wrote to the Department of Education asking how Mary could have been detained, and for so long. It responded that the laundry was a privately run institution over which the State had neither a supervisory nor a regulatory role. The Inter-Departmental Committee Report found there had been 'significant State involvement' with the laundries.

From 1922, ten Magdalene laundries were operated in the Republic of Ireland by four religious congregations: the Sisters of Mercy (at Galway and Dún Laoghaire); the Sisters of Our Lady of Charity (at Drumcondra and Seán McDermott Street); the Sisters of Charity (at Donnybrook and Cork); and the Good Shepherd Sisters (at Limerick, Cork, Waterford and New Ross).

I remember Patricia McDonnell's outrage at a special service of 'prayer and healing' for people in such Catholic-run institutions organised by then Archbishop of Dublin Desmond Connell at St Andrew's Church on Westland Row in May 1998. The service was strong on symbolism, as such services tend to be, but less so where concrete restitution or justice might be concerned. There, surveying the packed congregation of mainly religious and well-meaning members of the faithful, what came to mind were those damning lines from Yeats: 'Players and painted stage took all my love / And not those things that they were emblems of' ('The Circus Animals' Desertion').

Down the years, in reporting on the abuse issue and the Church's response to it, those lines kept intruding on my mind without invitation, but that St Andrew's service was something of a stand-out moment. At its beginning Archbishop Connell spoke of 'the pain of those who often cried in vain for help and of those who could not even name their anguish'. There were biblical readings and members of the congregation lit candles from a large 'Candle of Healing' on the altar and were blessed with the Sign of the Cross 'as a gesture of healing'. Afterwards, all adjourned to what was then still known as Archbishop Ryan Park on Dublin's Merrion Square, where a rose bed was inaugurated, in which a sign was placed to say that it was dedicated to all those who had been 'physically, mentally, emotionally, or sexually abused'. It did not specify by whom. The rose bed has long since disappeared. That happens to symbols.

The park had originally been named after Dr Dermot Ryan, who succeeded John Charles McQuaid as Archbishop of Dublin from 1971 to 1984. He donated it to the city of Dublin. It had been acquired by the Catholic Church early in the twentieth century with the intention of building a cathedral there. When that was deemed no longer likely, Archbishop Ryan handed over the park to the City Council, which then named it after him. His name was removed from the now Merrion Square Park after publication of the Murphy Report in 2009, which was very critical of previous archbishops of Dublin, including Dr Ryan, for their handling of clerical child sex abuse cases.

Even before that rose garden event followed the St Andrew's service, it was already clear that this entire exercise in symbolism had fallen flat on its would-be worthy face. It was crashed by Christine Buckley and Carmel McDonnell Byrne, who had spent their childhoods at the Goldenbridge orphanage in Dublin run by the Sisters of Mercy. Both women had featured two years earlier in a 1996 RTÉ documentary *Dear Daughter*, which exposed the shocking abuse of children at the orphanage. They had not been invited to the service.

Christine told me she became aware of the event through the media. She did not light her candle and wondered why the readings of stories of violence had to be taken from the Old Testament, when they could have been taken from her experience at Goldenbridge. Carmel wondered why there were no representatives of the religious orders there to say 'I'm sorry';

why no one from the Church had said 'sorry'. She was 'absolutely appalled' at the service. Christine said she heard two nuns present remark, on seeing her, 'Would you look at that brazen hussey.' Patricia McDonnell, who was not invited either, contacted me immediately before the service to say had she known about it she would have organised a picket.

✠ ✠ ✠

Mary Norris had spent much of her young life in a Magdalene laundry. A gregarious good-humoured Kerry woman, it was in October 2002 when she and I went to see Peter Mullan's *The Magdalene Sisters*. Halfway through, it had not seemed such a good idea. She wept and wept. 'The reality was even worse,' she said. 'I see now how they dehumanised us.' But she did not want to leave. Leaving was not something she was used to. It certainly was not an option back then when all she could do was pray and slave in that brave new Ireland, which had many such people in it.

Mary was born in Kerry, in 1933, the eldest of eight children. Her father died, leaving a young wife with two boys and six girls aged between six months and twelve years. They coped. Then a man began visiting their house, occasionally staying at night. The children noticed that their mother was 'a little bit happy' again.

One morning a garda and a man from the Irish Society for the Prevention of Cruelty to Children arrived to take the children away – 'the Cruelty Man' as Mary and others referred to him, without irony. It had been decreed that the woman of the house was an unfit mother. 'Everyone was screaming,' Mary recalled. They were even going to take the baby, but realised she was being breastfed, and left her. (She too was taken, when weaned.) The other seven children were brought to Sneem Courthouse and committed to 'a place of safety' by the judge.

In Mary's case, that was a Killarney orphanage. As she cried hysterically, she was given the routine disinfectant bath on arrival and ushered to a dormitory under the supervision of Sister Laurence, who was not impressed. 'I don't know what you are crying for. Your mother's a tramp, an evil woman, and I hope you don't turn out like her,' she said. To her undying shame, Mary responded, 'Yes, sister.' She began to wet the bed and was made to carry the mattress on her head to the drying room every day. At bath time every Friday, as the wettings continued, Sister Laurence would beat her with a belt around the lower back (where the weals would not be visible). There was no education, except for Christian Doctrine, and they were kept apart from 'the town children' at the school there.

At sixteen, Mary got a job as a servant to a retired school-teacher in Tralee, a brother of one of the Killarney nuns. There she did all the cleaning for him, his two nephews and his blind sister, for 2s 6d a week. She was allowed out once a week. The film *My Wild Irish Rose* arrived in town and she wanted to see it. She was told 'No' but sneaked out to see it anyway. The next day 'the very same Cruelty Man' came to take her away again. She was told she had been 'a very bold girl' and was brought back to the Killarney orphanage. 'I knew you were a tramp. I knew you'd turn out like this,' Sister Laurence told her, and dispatched Mary to see a local doctor. He examined her intimately, painfully, and told the woman sent along to supervise the visit, 'I don't know what's wrong with the nuns. This young woman is intact.' No one explained to Mary what he meant.

The nuns sent her to the Good Shepherd Magdalene laundry in Cork. Back at the orphanage, 'the Good Shepherds' had always been the ultimate threat. Mother of Our Lady O'Mahony greeted her there. 'We can't call you that here,' she responded when Mary gave her name. Instead, she was named 'Myra'. An older resident stripped Mary. Her bra was replaced with a piece of buttoned-down calico which flattened her breasts. Her long dark hair was cut short. She was given a grey dress, boots and a white cap, and brought to the sewing room where she sat 'among these old women, crying and making scapulars'.

At supper she saw 'all these young pretty girls' coming from the laundry and heard them refer to her, beneath their breath, as 'the new sheep'. No talking was allowed, and even during recreation time discussion to do with life outside was forbidden. Just saying the rosary, over and over again, sometimes singing hymns, and prayers were read to them by a nun at mealtimes.

They got up at 6 a.m., went to Mass, had breakfast, began working in the laundry at 8 a.m., broke for lunch at 12.30 p.m., resumed at 1 p.m. and finished at 6 p.m. They had an hour's recreation until 7 p.m., when, in theory, they were allowed talk, but there was not much to talk about. Not least as 'particular friendships' were forbidden. Few of the approximately 130 women there were unmarried mothers. Most were from orphanages.

Mary was told she couldn't write to her mother. Only to Sister Laurence. She did so, begging to be taken out of the laundry. There was no reply. Following a petty misdemeanour one night, Mary was punished after prayers in the dormitory. She was made to lie on the ground between two lines of praying girls, repeating 'through my fault, through my fault, through my most grievous fault' again and again until the nun conducting the prayers finally announced 'You are forgiven.' She was allowed to resume her place among her praying colleagues. Once, she faked a toothache in a half-baked plan to run away. The dentist removed the perfectly good tooth. She was so desperate, she even considered suicide.

Later, she discovered an aunt of hers in the US had been enquiring, in letters with money enclosed, of Sister Laurence about why Mary was not getting in contact. She was told Mary had a job in Tralee, had left it and no one knew where she was. Sister Laurence then got Mary a job in a laundry at Newcastle, County Limerick, but soon Mary was back in Kerry, in Sneem, where she worked for two years before heading off to England. She remained there until 1993 before returning to County Kerry with her husband, Victor.

Her mother had married the man who had been visiting, but it was not a happy affair. She too had gone to London and lived on the same street as Mary for eight years, dying in 1989 surrounded by many of her children.

I had asked Mary to come with me to see *The Magdalene Sisters*, to establish what she thought of it and its accuracy. This was in preparation for an article I would later write for the paper. Mary was high in her praise of the film's accuracy and was 'very glad it was done' and 'grateful to the man who had the courage to do it'. She demurred at some scenes where the girls had contact with outsiders other than a priest; that did not happen where she had been. She was also unsure about what she felt was an excessively humiliating strip scene but agreed that could have happened in other laundries.

'Maybe now Irish people will begin to believe,' she said, and continued, 'Wasn't Our Lady lucky? If she was in Ireland, she'd have been put in a Magdalene laundry and Jesus would have been adopted!'

In 2009, less than a month after publication of the Ryan Report in May, then Ombudsman and Information Commissioner Emily O'Reilly, now European Ombudsman, said, 'we all emerge … somewhat lost, unbalanced, the touchstone of our former beliefs and certainties cast adrift'. The report followed a nine-year investigation into the treatment of children in orphanages, industrial schools and reformatories run by eighteen religious congregations. It uncovered appalling stories of neglect and physical punishment in those residential institutions for children and found that the sexual abuse of boys was endemic.

O'Reilly, who was the first journalist to report in 1984 on the death of fifteen-year-old Ann Lovett, found at a grotto in Granard, County Longford, with her dead infant son beside her, continued, 'We stood exposed, not as an island of charming saints and chatty, avuncular scholars but as a repressed, cold-hearted, fearful, smugly pious, sexually ignorant and vengeful race of self-styled Christians.' Following publication of the Ryan Report, she noted how '"we didn't know", is the constant refrain'. Speaking at a conference in Dublin, which I reported on, she said:

> Certainly, very few knew of the systemic nature of the abuse, of the near unbelievable extent and depravity of the sexual abuse in particular; of the political, bureaucratic and clerical cover-ups – but no adult living in Ireland throughout the period in question did not, in broad terms, know. If things were hidden, they were hidden in clear sight: the crocodile lines of boys and girls that streamed out of the institutions; the certain knowledge that corporal punishment [was] at the very least practised therein; the incarcerated Magdalene women in their Madonna blues and whites who walked the open streets of towns and villages in church processions. Judges knew, lawyers knew, teachers knew, civil servants knew, childcare workers knew, gardaí knew. Not to know was not an option.

Noting that the religious congregations had borne the brunt of criticism following publication of the report, she said this was 'no surprise'. She continued that 'the hands and fists that descended on the bodies of the children were those of the people who worked in or who had access to the religious-run institutions'.

'Yet', she said, 'the forces that enabled the abuse or turned blind, indifferent eyes to it ranged way beyond the institutions' walls, [were] present within the plusher offices of State, and the boardrooms of so-called charitable institutions as well as within the dank, depressing, and frequently terrifying dormitories of the institutions themselves'. Abuse thrives 'when society remains indifferent to the abuse because it is by and large indifferent to the abused'.

Even then, in the summer of 2009, when so much had already emerged, there was no move on the part of official Ireland to investigate what had happened in the Magdalene laundries. This was despite the indefatigable efforts of such bodies as the Irish Human Rights Commission, the Justice for Magdalenes group, the National Women's Council of Ireland and the Magdalene Survivors Together, and also the work of Professor James Smith of Boston College in the US, whose 2007 book *Ireland's Magdalen Laundries and the Nation's Architecture of Containment* was very influential. In 2006 Maureen Sullivan helped set up Magdalene Survivors Together. She had been in the New Ross, County Wexford, Magdalene laundry run by the Good Shepherd Sisters. She was from a poorer family and there was abuse in the home. She confided in a nun who 'sent for my mother and told her about this school in New Ross where I'd get a good education'. When she arrived at the 'school', Maureen asked a nun where the classrooms were. 'She laughed.' There was no schooling, just the laundry every day, from 6 a.m. to about 9 p.m., with cleaning duties in the evening and at weekends. They made rosary beads and Aran jumpers in the evenings. She was twelve when she arrived in the early 1960s, so young she was hidden in a tunnel 'under the church' when inspectors arrived. Once, when she was fourteen, she was forgotten about in the tunnel and left there. She became hysterical. 'It took days to get over it.'

After that she was moved to another laundry in Athy, which was smaller but 'the very same ... cold, callous' atmosphere. Again it was 'no talk, no friends'. She 'often got a box [blow]' from the nuns – particularly when she didn't respond to the name they gave her, Frances.

In November 2009 Maureen was among five women who had been in Magdalene laundries who attended the Department of Justice in Dublin, where they met then Secretary General Seán Aylward and Assistant Secretary James Martin for a two-hour meeting. The other women were Mary Smith, Marina Gambold, Maureen Taylor and Kathleen Legg. They told the officials about their experiences in the laundries. Compensation for the women and a State apology were among topics discussed. They were accompanied by Steven O'Riordan, director of the film *The Forgotten Maggies*. I accompanied them but was not allowed to attend the meeting. I stayed around to hear how they got on. They explained to me how they had told Aylward and Martin about conditions in the laundries and how the State had a responsibility for the women held in such institutions.

A spokesman for the Department of Justice said afterwards that the meeting with the women had been 'very constructive and helpful'. So it seemed, until that meeting was spoken about at the UN Committee Against Torture (UNCAT) in Geneva two years later. There was general surprise when, on 25 May 2011, Department of Justice Secretary General Seán Aylward told UNCAT how he 'personally' had met 'a deputation of women who had sad experiences to account of their early childhood in these institutions'. Indeed, he told the committee, 'I think we were the first Department to agree to meet them.' From this first meeting, he told the committee, he learned that 'the vast majority of women who went to these institutions went there voluntarily or, if they were minors, with the consent of their parents or guardians'.

Back in Ireland this was greeted with outrage by the women who had spent so long in the laundries. I wrote in the paper how Aylward's statement to UNCAT was 'quite remarkable. This reporter was present at the Department of Justice that day, 4 November 2009, when Mr Aylward and other officials met the deputation of women survivors of the Magdalene laundries he was referring to.' I added how on the day I had established, from the women he had spoken to, that 'not one of those five women entered the laundries voluntarily or with the consent of parents or guardians'. I explicitly recalled how Mary Smith had said she told him that she 'cried and cried' on being committed to the Good Shepherd laundry in Cork by 'the Cruelty Man'. How 'once that door was locked, never, never, were you going to get out of there'. Steven O'Riordan said he found it 'quite ironic' that Aylward should tell UNCAT that the women entered the laundries voluntarily 'when he himself met with members of Magdalene Survivors Together and was told that the girls did not enter voluntarily and were kept against their will while forced to carry out work they did not want to do'. O'Riordan concluded, 'clearly the Government is not or has not been listening to the Magdalene survivors'.

Earlier that May, the Irish Human Rights Commission (IHRC) president, Dr Maurice Manning, had been in an uncompromising mood about various departments of State when it came to the Magdalene women. He called for a statutory inquiry into the Magdalene laundries but also for prosecution of those who had abused the women. He said an IHRC report on the matter, published in February 2010, had been met by a 'wall of official indifference' and railed against 'the official indifference and indeed hostility [to the Magdalene issue] which has been there for such a long time'. On 10 May, prior to Seán Aylward's presentation to UNCAT, Dublin human rights lawyer Maeve O'Rourke of the Justice for Magdalenes group, which had fought a long-running campaign for an inquiry into the laundries, presented a strong case for this to the UN body in Geneva.

Subsequently, UNCAT produced a scarifying report on the issue.

On 14 June 2011 then Minister for Justice Alan Shatter announced that the government was to set up an interdepartmental inquiry to investigate the State's role in relation to the laundries. The previous week, the four religious congregations concerned had agreed to cooperate with any such inquiry. An estimated 30,000 single mothers and other women were detained in the laundries between 1922 and 1996. In the Dáil, after that interdepartmental inquiry report was published (in February 2013), Taoiseach Enda Kenny delivered a heartfelt apology on behalf of the Irish people to the women who had been in the laundries.

11

Travels With the Pope

The unexpected, they say, is what happens when you're looking the other way. You meet the strangest people when reporting on papal visits. One I had not expected was the 'pink lady' with her four-foot-high statue of the Virgin Mary, or the 'dark-eyed beauty of the low life'. But then, this was Cuba. It was January 1998 and Pope John Paul II was the first pontiff to visit the island in what was billed as an encounter between 'the two last great autocrats of the 20th century', himself and Fidel Castro. It could hardly have gone better, with Castro even letting it be known how much he owed to the ethic instilled in him by his Jesuit educators.

That these two titans should meet at all caused great excitement: Castro, the last remaining leader of a communist regime in the Western world, and a pope whose election in 1978 and subsequent visits to his homeland of Poland helped collapse communist Eastern Europe and the Soviet Union.

It helped that in 1992 Castro had removed a commitment to atheism from Cuba's constitution and, just the previous month, he had also allowed the reinstatement of Christmas celebrations on the island. It helped too that the Vatican had consistently opposed economic sanctions against Cuba. In 1998 there were about 250 priests on the island, where almost half of its then 11 million population still considered themselves Catholic, despite Castro's closure of Catholic schools, his nationalisation of Church properties and jailing/expulsion of priests following the 1959 Revolution.

Pope John Paul's visit precipitated the biggest 'invasion' of Cuba by Americans since the Bay of Pigs incident in 1961. US citizens were banned from visiting there but accreditation to report on the papal visit was agreed by Washington, with presenters, reporters and television crews descending on the island in their thousands. It was estimated that approximately 3,000 media personnel covered the event.

Not all Cubans welcomed the visit. Ray and Lenin, for instance. ('Yes, that's my name,' Lenin said, with a weary shake of his head.) On a potholed side-street they were selling cigars on the black market. The pope's visit was interfering. 'There are two million people in Havana, and this week there are one million police,' an unhappy Ray told me.

As yet another Westerner fascinated with Cuba, I had visited the island in September 1997 en route to Ecuador, where I had hoped to interview Bishop Eamonn Casey. I travelled extensively on the island and found it an altogether depressing experience. The poverty was oppressive and all-pervasive. Struggle was everywhere, in the countryside and along the shabby streets, with their splendid buildings falling down. The people seemed passive and resigned, stagnant, just getting on with it.

There was no romance there, just an unforgiving reality and a two-tier economy: the expensive one for tourists in luxury hotels, and that of the streets. Yes, Cuba may have had a healthcare and an education system that should have been the envy of the rest of the world, but it was at a great price to its poorest people. Of course, economic sanctions, particularly by the US, played a big role in the all-pervasive depression. In the countryside I was reminded of subsistence living in the rural world I grew up in during the 1950s and 1960s: the seemingly eternal struggle of people, then and there, just to exist.

In January 1998 this was not uppermost in the mind of a beautiful young woman in Havana as she drew her scarlet fingernails slowly along my inner left thigh, her intent absolutely clear. 'My dark-eyed, brown-skinned beauty of the low life, I am a reporter,' I attempted to say. 'My vocation is to observe life's feast, not to take part in it.' I might even have tried, 'Sorry. I'm an Irish Catholic agnostic; Catholic by background, agnostic through lack of conviction, but the guilt never goes away you know.' However, my mouth was full of spaghetti, with one strand that seemed to have accumulated the combined length of the Shannon, the Tiber, the Appian Way and the road to kingdom come joined end to end.

I had been sitting at the counter of what approximated to the city's only fast-food restaurant when she sat down at the counter beside me, all grace and elegance and aged about twenty-two. By the time I had swallowed, her nails were in retreat, heading for the safer lowlands of my kneecap, where they rested casually. 'I lub hangsome fat men with blue eyes,' she said. It touched a nerve. 'My dear satin eyes, it's the sweatshirt I'm wearing,' I was about to say. 'Beneath it lies the svelte body of an athlete. Besides, I've just had a plate of spaghetti.' Then I remembered I was in a country where 'fat' is attractive, and that her supermodel slimness probably had more to do with a scarcity of food than vanity.

She delved into a handbag and took out a photograph. It was of a child, a small, curly-haired version of herself, about eighteen months old, and she began talking about her daughter in that seductive, lisping Spanish/English where the 'v's become 'b's, and the 'g's are strangled. I was about to advise her that, if she was ever to be a success at her trade, she should never try to entice a man through his conscience, when she reached for the sachets of sugar on a saucer beside my coffee. 'For her?' she said, indicating the child. I nodded. She put them in her bag, and I didn't feel so 'hangsome' any more.

A young Canadian man was sitting farther along the counter. Earlier he had told me he had come to Havana from the Cayman Islands, where he had spent three months working. He was in Cuba for a few days before setting off to tour Europe. He could not take his eyes off my oak-tinted companion, which she noticed, and was soon curled around him as tightly as ivy on an old ash tree. It was said then that approximately 30 per cent of young women in Havana between the ages of eighteen and twenty-five were engaged in prostitution. This was hardly surprising. A prostitute could make more in a night than a teacher or government official, on $7 to $8 a month in the late 1990s, might make there in three or four months. And it is a part of the world where the attitude to sex is very relaxed by European standards.

It was in that same Havana restaurant that I met an older woman of a very different hue, and for the second time. She too was looking for dollars. We had met that first time just days beforehand at the airport in Santiago de Cuba, both returning to Havana after the pope had said Mass there. Santiago de Cuba, at the island's southernmost tip, was where we media burned under a merciless sun, doing our best to huddle in the slight shadow of a single bare tree while Pope John Paul visibly wilted as he said Mass. It was excruciating to watch the struggle as this ailing seventy-seven-year-old man with Parkinson's disease battled through the impossible heat, aided only by his indomitable spirit. The huge congregation responded anxiously to his obvious suffering. That emotion came to a head at the shrine of St Lazarus in Havana the following night, as he went among the sick and the infirm, blessing them. Many of those he touched seemed in far better shape than him – with his stick, his slow walk, his laboured speech, his tired, tired face and one eye almost completely closed. Watching him from the choir, as he shuffled along among the sick and infirm, two young girls began to cry.

Checking in at the airport in Santiago de Cuba en route back to Havana, this older woman made felt her presence and that of her ever-silent but conspicuous companion. The woman – pink powder on her face, pink lipstick, a pink scarf, a pink cardigan over a dress that was a lighter shade of pink – looked like a refugee from a 1950s' Doris Day film but was really from Toronto. She was accompanied by the large statue of the Virgin Mary, all vanilla and blue. The 'pink lady' had more (miraculous) medals on her chest than any army reservist, while a set of rosary beads dangled from her neck. She plonked her statue at the check-in desk. On impulse, and foolishly, I asked whether the Virgin Mary was paying. Recognising my accent, it was as if she had discovered, at long last, another devout Catholic like herself, and she pounced on me like a cumbersome St Bernard dog flaunting warmth, welcome – and pink.

She dug a hand into one of her many bags and drew out a photo album to show me all the bishops, archbishops and cardinals she had photographed with the Virgin Mary statue. Her ambition, she said, was to have every major Church figure in the Americas photographed with it. The Virgin Mary seemed unmoved as her chaperone waited for the airline seat, which she assured me 'the Lord would provide' – and He did, courtesy of Cubana, the national airline of that atheistic State. Others in the queue distanced themselves from the pink lady, who seemed oblivious and begged me to go to daily Mass for the souls in Purgatory and to pray for the conversion of Fidel Castro, even as he was providing free airline seats for herself and the Virgin Mary.

I wasn't too happy some days later when she sat down beside me in that Havana restaurant. She had no money, of course, but the Lord would provide once again. This time, it seems, He had chosen me as agent without prior consultation. Having delivered accordingly, I absented myself as soon as decently possible, setting off for the international press centre nearby to get accreditation for the next major papal event, the set-piece Mass in Havana's Plaza de la Revolución the following morning. Darkness was falling and some of Havana's most beautiful young women stood along the footpath. They grabbed passing men by the arms, giggling, laughing, making gestures of intent. Among them was the dark-eyed lady, lovely as before, and probably still looking for 'hangsome, blue-eyed, fat men'. With dollars.

No one anticipated the mass exodus of American media on the morning of the Mass celebrated by Pope John Paul II in Havana on Sunday, 25 January 1998. Our press area, presided over by the huge seven-storey outline in steel of Che Guevara – one of the leaders of the 1959 Revolution – with the quotation 'Hasta la Victoria Siempre' (Until Victory, Always), seemed suddenly bereft. Monica Lewinsky had struck, prompting a sudden exit of US media to report on her allegations of sexual activity with then President Bill Clinton. One senior American television journalist assured me, with regret, that it was the end of Clinton. Despite his own disappointment, he was very excited at the scale of the story he was rushing back to cover. Journalists!

Hundreds of thousands attended the Mass that morning, including Castro and the 1982 Nobel Prize for Literature winner, Colombian Gabriel García Márquez. I was a fan of the writer and was then going through a phase of enthusiasm for 'magic realism', as exemplified in his novels, and had just read his *One Hundred Years of Solitude*. The atmosphere in the square was heady and the crowd kept interrupting the pope's homily with applause. He went off-script to acknowledge this. 'I am not opposed to applause,' he remarked at one interruption, 'because when you applaud, the pope can rest a bit.'

The homily, unsurprisingly, was mainly on religious themes. 'Every people needs to be religious,' he read, and 'an irreligious people will die, because nothing in it encourages virtue'. It was later that day, as he was about to leave Cuba, that he made his most significant comments on the US embargo. With Fidel Castro at his side, he said Cuba's 'material and moral poverty' arose not only from 'limitations to fundamental freedoms' and 'discouragement of the individual' but also from 'restrictive economic measures, unjust and ethically unacceptable, imposed from outside the country'.

✠ ✠ ✠

In the year 2000 Pope John Paul II visited some of the countries that had featured in the life of Christ two millennia earlier. His first such visit was to Cairo in February 2000, when the leading Egyptians were there to greet him, including Egyptian President Hosni Mubarak; everyone that is except the head of the Coptic Church, Pope Shenouda III. It was felt this was a quid pro quo for what had happened in 1973, when Shenouda became the first Coptic pope to visit Rome in over 1,500 years but was not met at the airport by Pope Paul VI. The great schism between Eastern (Orthodox) and Western Christianity took place in 1054, with both sides excommunicating the other over theological and structural differences. However, on this occasion Pope John Paul made a point of actually visiting his Coptic counterpart in Cairo, as I was reminded of for years afterwards every time I called to see my late mother. A photograph of the two popes walking side by side was published on the front page of *The Irish*

Times and there I am in the background. A colleague emailed me with his proposed (but unused!) caption for the photograph: 'The Pope from Rome. The Pope from Cairo. And the one from Ballaghaderreen.' My mother had the photograph in her hallway. The incongruity of that trinity appealed to her sense of humour.

The following month Pope John Paul was in Israel, where his reception was chilly. Suspicious of his overt sympathy for the Palestinians, his welcome to Israel was stand-offish, to say the least. It was clear this tired old man had a lot of work to do there, and he did it.

In contrast to his arrival, the reception was very different at the Mass he celebrated the next day on Manger Square in Bethlehem on the West Bank, just yards from the Church of the Nativity, where it is believed Jesus was born. The congregation included the (Muslim) President of the Palestinian National Authority, Yasser Arafat. In his sermon Pope John Paul forcefully affirmed his support for the creation of a Palestinian homeland and called for 'decisive actions' by world leaders to improve living conditions for the then 3.6 million Palestinian refugees. 'This is a place that has known the yoke and the rod of oppression,' he said. Afterwards he visited the crowded Dheisheh refugee camp near Bethlehem. A population of 9,624 Palestinian refugees lived there then, most of them Muslims who had fled or been pushed from their homes at the creation of Israel in 1948. Living conditions for the refugees, and another 2.4 million Palestinians who lived outside camps elsewhere, were frequently 'degrading', the pope said.

He did not exaggerate. I stayed on in the camp afterwards and spoke to a young man there who was helping the UN run it. He was in his mid-thirties, had been born in the camp and spoke angrily about the treatment of his deceased father, who had died a few weeks previously and whom the Israeli authorities refused to allow to be buried back in his home place in southern Israel, from where he and his family had been displaced in 1948. It astonished me that people could have lived in a refugee camp for fifty-two years.

The following day the pope met the country's president, Ezer Weizman, and blessed Israel, seen by many as a final Church recognition of their State. Later, during a visit to the World Holocaust Remembrance Centre, Yad Vashem, in Jerusalem, he said that 'as bishop of Rome and successor of the Apostle Peter, I assure the Jewish people that the Catholic Church ... is deeply saddened by the hatred, acts of persecution and displays of anti-Semitism directed against the Jews by Christians at any time and in any place'. He met Holocaust survivors, including several from Wadowice, his home town in Poland, and impressed the Israelis with his personal warmth. This, of course, was the first pope to have visited Auschwitz and to attend a synagogue in Rome.

But nothing Pope John Paul did on his visit to Israel that year could compare with his appearance at that most sacred Jewish site, the Western – or Wailing – Wall in Jerusalem. In one of his most dramatic gestures towards the Jewish people, he prayed at the Western Wall as would a Jew and, as is traditional with Jews, he placed his prayer in one of its crevices. It read, 'God of our fathers, you chose Abraham and his descendants to bring your Name to the Nations: we are deeply saddened by the behaviour of those who in the course of history have caused these children of yours to suffer, and asking your forgiveness we wish to commit ourselves to genuine brotherhood with the people of the Covenant.' The prayer was taken to the city's Yad Vashem Holocaust memorial hall, where it is on permanent display.

Being in Jerusalem that day was to witness a conversion in sentiment every bit as sudden and complete as happened to St Paul on the road to Damascus. A cool, suspicious people tripped over themselves to express their gratitude and affection. The then Israeli prime minister, Ehud Barak, who had recalled that when his people 'were led from all over Christian Europe to the crematoria and the gas chambers ... the silence was not only from the heavens', praised Pope John Paul personally. 'You have done more than anyone else to bring about the historic change in the attitude of the church towards the Jewish people, initiated by the good Pope John XXIII,' he said. Almost the entire Israeli cabinet took part in the official departure ceremony from Ben Gurion Airport. Most had been absent for the pope's arrival.

But I cannot leave the Jerusalem visit without mentioning my own experience of the miraculous there, and the tawdry too. The 'miraculous' concerned the first report I ever sent to the *Irish Times* news desk from a laptop, which was from Jerusalem on that trip. I was, frankly, astounded when, having just pressed 'send', I called colleagues in Dublin to discover that my report had already arrived. Not since, as a child on that Christmas morning, I saw the footprints of Santy Claus's boots in the ashes of our fireplace at home have I been as awestruck.

And then the tawdry. That was the 'Way of the Cross/Via Dolorosa' in Jerusalem, along which Christ allegedly made his way to Calvary. Nothing quite prepares you for all those crowns of thorns on sale. Real ones, reasonably priced. Made from finest olive wood, with thorns that could be used in keyhole surgery. Fittings are free! In shop after shop along the so-called 'Way of Sorrow'. You might prefer a plug-in statue of the Virgin Mary that glows in the dark? Or 'genuine' Jordan River water? Those 'Ecce Homo' carpets? The Church of the Holy Sepulchre at its end – where, it is believed, Jesus was crucified, buried and rose from the dead – may be one of the most sacred places in Christendom, but it has to be among the least holy. With crowds everywhere, some even Christian, it is shared by six Christian denominations who cannot agree, so the key to the church has been held by a local Muslim family since 1192. Allegedly discovered in the third century by Empress (and later saint) Helena, mother of the first Christian Roman emperor, Constantine, scholars believe the Via Dolorosa is about as authentic as much of the merchandise on sale along its route. The Church of the Holy Sepulchre, however, is believed to be the real deal.

Back where our family originally come from in Mullen, County Roscommon, there is a short bog road of less than a mile in length which is known locally as 'the St Helena Road'. I never did find out how it got its name, but I doubt she was there. After all, *those* Romans never came to Ireland.

For myself, the most memorable moment during Pope John Paul's trips to Egypt, Jordan and Israel in that most significant year took place on 26 February 2000, when his pilgrimage took him to Mount Sinai – the place where it is believed Moses conversed with God and received the Ten Commandments. The pope flew from Cairo to Sinai, made a private visit to the Orthodox Church of St Catherine in the Monastery of St Catherine there, and had hoped to celebrate Mass in the monastery. Owing to ongoing differences between Orthodox and Western Christianity, this was not possible. Instead, he led a prayer service in the monastery garden attended by a few hundred people, accompanied by the wails of children and loud conversations at the back, such as would be familiar in a parish church anywhere. Delivering one of his most sublime homilies, he referred to Mount Sinai as

a soaring monument to what God revealed here. God shows himself in mysterious ways, as the fire that does not consume, according to a logic which defies all that we know and expect. He is the God who is at once close at hand and far away; he is in the world but not of it. He is the God who comes to meet us, but who will not be possessed. He is 'I am who am', the name which is no name. 'I am who am': the divine abyss in which essence and existence are one. The God who is being itself.

Even in my unbelief I was moved by this and wondered in admiration at the mind that could conceive such an ethereal thought.

When Pope John Paul II had visited Galway in 1979, I was there too, with most of my old friends in 'the Galway Gang'. (We remain even older friends all these decades later!) Three years previously, in 1976, most of us had been among the estimated 250,000 at a Rolling Stones concert – with Lynyrd Skynyrd, 10 CC and more – at Knebworth in England's Hertfordshire. Where we were concerned, the visit of Pope John Paul to Galway was not dissimilar to Knebworth or some such rock concert, even if the headline act was somewhat unusual for us. We prepared accordingly and in the small hours of that morning headed from Galway city to Ballybrit Racecourse with thousands of others, well laden with liquid and other supports. I have always found it revealing how the great majority of the 'gang', all from the West of Ireland and Catholic backgrounds, were no longer believers by then. One of our main challenges at the time was that, liberal in outlook, we were confronted with returning to a society with which we were no longer compatible. Pope John Paul's words at Ballybrit brought us little comfort, but then we hadn't really expected them to. They were a throwback to the world from which we had become free, but which he consolidated. Still, we enjoyed the spectacle at Ballybrit, the atmosphere, the alcohol and each other's company, as always.

Another such spectacular involving Pope John Paul II, which I witnessed and experienced, was his funeral in 2005 and it was yet another occasion to marvel at St Peter's and the Vatican complex. Nothing quite prepares you for St Peter's Basilica; photographs and film eliminate that vital sense of scale. You have to *be* there. 'Magnificent,' said a still idealistic friend, 'but is it Christianity?' Being in St Peter's is to feel the presence of so much tumultuous history. Its very construction split Western Christendom, an event that continues to plague us in Ireland. The levy imposed to pay for it was the straw which prompted the great reaction against Rome, led (in 1517) by Martin Luther. Some side chapels are closed off by huge drapes for private prayer, while the embalmed remains of popes at rest are visible through glass in the front of side altars. Also behind glass is Michelangelo's *Pietà*. Near the great doors marking the entrance to St Peter's, it has been sealed off since a man attacked it with a hammer in the 1980s, knocking off one of Mary's arms, which was later reattached. What is most remarkable is that its creator was just twenty-four when he chiselled it out of marble. And another way of appreciating one's own insignificance is to behold the list of all 265 previous popes – Francis is 266th – high on a wall just inside a great side door to the basilica. Realising the tiny space taken by the popes who have lived during one's own lifetime is like seeing time in eternity.

Outside St Peter's the eponymous square seems not as big as it can appear on television, but the stonework of its magnificent circling Bernini colonnade is splendid. It proved a dramatic setting for the epic funeral that was Pope John Paul II's in April 2005, which was attended by millions, many of them young Poles who had slept overnight on surrounding streets. We media were high up on top of the Bernini colonnade, in my own case beside the statue of St Sebastian perforated by arrows. All of us were affected by the gravity of the occasion and that sense of the passing of a great figure of the twentieth century. As someone not prone to finding significance where there may be none, I was taken aback when a breeze began to turn the pages of an enormous copy of the gospels placed on a dais near the altar in St Peter's Square as the funeral Mass was under way. I wondered, when those pages stopped turning, at what chapter it rested. A film-maker would have loved the scene.

Only the British can do ceremony as well as Rome.

✠ ✠ ✠

The election of Pope Benedict XVI subsequently took me by surprise. Not that he was elected pope, but that it happened so fast. His papacy caught me out twice, badly: at its beginning and at the end. When white smoke billowed from the Sistine Chapel at almost 4 p.m. on 19 April 2005, I was in an internet café near St Peter's Basilica filing my first reports of the afternoon to Dublin. It was the second day of the conclave. Wi-Fi at the press centre in the Vatican broke down intermittently, said to be due to interference from powerful security technology protecting goings-on in the Sistine Chapel. I found a small internet café not far from St Peter's and as I was writing there my phone rang. It was George Hook from Newstalk radio in Dublin. 'Have we a pope, Patsy?' he asked. I assured him and his listeners it was far too soon for that. Then I noticed a text from my sister Sinéad in Ballaghaderreen asking, 'Is that white smoke?' She was watching on television, about 1,700 miles away. Now seriously rattled, I noticed the crowds running past the café towards St Peter's. Resorting to language still rarely used by clergy, I gathered my things and ran to the Vatican, arriving in time to hear Chilean Cardinal Jorge Medina announce 'Habemus Papam' (We have a pope). So began the papacy of Benedict XVI.

When he announced its end almost eight years later, on 11 February 2013, I was in Dublin's Whitefriar Street Church, where the Catholic Church's marriage advisory agency, Accord, was presenting its annual report before the statue of St Valentine. The late Bishop of Elphin, Christopher Jones, a genial and fellow Roscommon man, was also there. My phone began to hop with queries from colleagues and radio stations asking whether it was true that Benedict had announced he was resigning. I assured them that of all the popes in history, Benedict was the last pope likely to make such a radical decision. Bishop Jones didn't think so either. Then, it was confirmed as true. Did I notice St Valentine wink?

I asked Bishop Jones whether he might consider running for the job. He would be the first Roscommon-born pope, I said, by way of encouragement. He was not having it and laughed. 'No, I'm too old,' he said. He was seventy-six. On his election the following month Pope Francis was ... seventy-six! Roscommon's loss, Argentina's gain.

I cannot say I was ever a fan of Cardinal Joseph Ratzinger, who became Pope Benedict XVI in 2005. As prefect at the Vatican's Congregation for the Doctrine of the Faith (CDF) from 1981 until his election as pope, his destruction of so many careers among clergy who disagreed with his rigid interpretation of Catholic teaching was ruthless and relentless. He helped to force closed many windows thrown open by Pope John XXIII and the Second Vatican Council in the 1960s. Nor was he especially impressive as pope. Indeed, the outstanding event of his eight-year papacy was its ending: he was the first pope to resign in 600 years.

But there was another highlight, his election itself, as a German who had been a member of the Hitler Youth. As a teenager, he was conscripted by the Nazis and had no say in the matter, but in 2005, after his election in succession to Pope John Paul II, there was no doubt about the impact this had on German people present in St Peter's Square that April day where his investiture as Benedict XVI took place. I spoke to some of them and was moved at what his election meant for them and their country. I had not expected it, which, on reflection, I probably should have. For them it amounted to a sort of forgiveness by the world.

For instance, there was Stefan Rieger, a thirty-seven-year-old fireman from near Regensburg in Bavaria, the region from which Pope Benedict himself hailed. I asked whether he was proud to be German that day. Stefan would not agree with the word 'proud'. 'It is difficult to say "proud", especially with our history. But I am happy that he is Pope. I am happy that this man is Pope,' he said. Stefan was taking photographs of his group of firefighters and gun club members, all dressed in traditional regalia from Pope Benedict's home ground in Germany. About twenty of them, men and women, posed behind a long banner that read *Pentling gratuliert seinem Ehrenbürger Papst Benedikt XVI*. Stefan struggled to translate. Pentling was the local large town. The rest read 'Congratulations to an honoured local man, Pope Benedict XVI' (or words to that effect). Their area was 'the home of the Pope. He was there for 25–30 years,' Stefan said, explaining that after the pope was ordained he lived there when teaching at Regensburg. 'He is very special, [we] all know him personally, [he is] very normal. He doesn't like such big events. He wants to read and write books,' he said.

Father Christopher Eichkorn was from Freiburg diocese in the Black Forest area near the German/Swiss border. He was carrying a large European Union flag with a smaller German one above it. 'We are very glad to have a pope from Bavaria – the first German one for over 500 years. From the country which started the Reformation, and which started two world wars. We now have a special chance to start a new time in our country,' he said. 'From the beginning of the twentieth century there had been two negative movements from Germany. From the beginning of the twenty-first century we should have a positive movement from Germany,' he said. The election of Pope Benedict had been 'good for the German people', he added, but he was 'shocked' when it happened. 'I couldn't believe a pope would come from Germany.'

As 'enforcer in chief' of orthodoxy during the long, almost twenty-seven-year papacy of Pope John Paul II, Benedict's papacy is seen as an extension of that of his predecessor, which began in 1978. In the CDF he had forcefully silenced the liberation theologians of Latin America, as well as dissenters, such as his old academic colleague Hans Küng and American Father Charles Curran. In his infamous *Dominus Iesus* document of 2000, he dismissed all reformed (Protestant) Churches as not Churches 'in the proper sense'. They were merely 'ecclesial communities'. All other faiths were 'gravely deficient'. In a 1986 document Cardinal Ratzinger described homosexuality as 'a more or less strong tendency ordered toward an intrinsic moral evil; and thus the inclination itself must be seen as an objective disorder', and he was believed to be central to the 1994 Vatican document which underlined the ban on the ordination of women to the priesthood.

For such reasons he became known as 'God's rottweiler'. It was also while at the CDF that in 2001 he wrote two letters to every Catholic bishop in the world, both in Latin – one asking that they refer to him all credible allegations of clerical child sexual abuse on their files; the second instructing that the correspondence be kept secret. This was why, during Benedict's papacy, the Murphy Commission in Ireland, then investigating the handling of clerical child sexual abuse in the Dublin and Cloyne dioceses, wrote to the Vatican seeking those files sent by Dublin and Cloyne to Rome in response to his 2001 correspondence. The commission never got the files. Yet, in his 2010 letter to the Catholics of Ireland, Benedict had no problem in, deservedly, excoriating Ireland's bishops for their role in covering up so much child sexual abuse while ignoring his own role in doing exactly the same. In later years, it would emerge that as Archbishop of Munich in Germany from 1977 to 1982 he was involved in the cover-up of such cases himself.

In person he was a shy, diffident man, a classic number two. Highly qualified academically, he was not at all suited to lead from the front. He was a scholar who wished to remain so but had high office thrust upon him. It was a mistake, and this became very clear within a year of his election as pope. The particular incident concerned Muslim–Catholic relations, where he could never be described as sure-footed. In September 2006 he delivered a lecture at his old university in Germany's Regensburg, wherein he quoted a medieval emperor as saying, 'show me just what Muhammad brought that was new and there you will find things only evil and inhuman, such as his command to spread by the sword the faith he preached'.

It was a PR disaster. One consequence was that nine out of ten Turkish people opposed a trip to their country that Benedict had planned for November 2006. Even as he arrived in Ankara, it was unclear whether Turkish Prime Minister Recep Tayyip Erdoğan would meet him. Up to the last minute, we media did not know whether Erdoğan would turn up. He did and, some days later in Istanbul, Benedict prayed at the Blue Mosque, in stockinged feet and as a Muslim would have done – something Cardinal Joseph Ratzinger would have found hard to approve. There could hardly have been a starker illustration of the difference between dealing with the 'real' world and how that world can be seen from the abstract heights of pure dogma/ideology.

Twice in major addresses during that visit, Benedict quoted comments made by his predecessor, Pope John XXIII, on the Turkish people. It is doubtful whether Cardinal Ratzinger, who had undone so much of what Pope John XXIII had set in train, would have done such a thing. Benedict recalled how another of my predecessors was in this country not as Pope, but as the Papal Representative, from January 1935 to December 1944, Blessed John XXIII, Angelo Roncalli, whose memory still enkindles great devotion and affection. He very much esteemed and admired the Turkish people. Here I would like to quote an entry in his *Journal of a Soul*: 'I love the Turks; I appreciate the natural qualities of these people who have their own place reserved in the march of civilization.'

The mention of Pope John helped mollify the Turkish people's view of his then less-than-popular successor.

So beloved is Pope John XXIII, and so popular was he while in Turkey as papal nuncio, that they named a street after him in Istanbul. It is called Papa Roncalli Sokak – which I found eventually. It was while walking its short length that I got a phone call from broadcaster Claire Byrne, then with Newstalk radio, to do an interview. With the arrival of the mobile phone, such interviews can take place in the strangest places. One I did in 2009 was with a Colombian radio station in South America while on a back stairs in Dublin's St Stephen's Green Centre, following publication of the Ryan Report. I was interviewed in English by a man who then translated what I said into Spanish 'live' on air, before I was questioned in English again.

Probably the most timely such interview was my announcement to Africa in March 2013 that a new pope had been elected. That would turn out to be Pope Francis. I was in the Vatican's Paul VI Hall, where thousands of the 5,600 media accredited by the Holy See press office to cover that papal election waited. It was Day Two and we were settling into the longueurs between each billowing blast of black smoke from the Sistine Chapel chimney. Covering a major news story is often like reporting on a war. There are long spells of boredom, punctuated by brief bursts of anxiety-inducing unpredictable excitement.

A friend had been working with BBC Africa in Nigeria and asked whether I would agree to do daily live reports on the papal election over the phone, gratis, for Africa. My interviewer in Lagos was a pleasant man, but his English was so accented that I had great problems understanding what he was saying at times. It meant that frequently, during these live broadcasts, I had to wing it, hoping I understood him correctly and was answering the questions he had asked. For most of the evening of 13 March, we in the Paul VI Hall had been watching the huge TV screens and waiting. A solitary white gull rested on the Sistine Chapel chimney while we tried to outdo one another with puns for a caption should the gull get caught in the next blast of expected black smoke. Then I got a call from my friend in BBC Africa. I went to my favoured spot near the hall's entrance, where the signal was better, and prepared to report on the day's non-events up to that point. As I began, smoke came from the Sistine chimney. It was a dull grey-black, as expected, and I began to relay this on-air. Then the smoke turned a milky white. I was astounded. I said something like 'Hang on, hang on', doubting my own eyes. Then media colleagues began to cheer, and I continued, 'It is white. The smoke is white. We have a pope. We have a pope.' And so, I announced to Africa the election of the man who would be Francis.

✠ ✠ ✠

A visit by Pope Benedict XVI to the UK in 2010 was an unexpected success, despite torrid opposition in advance. The crowds were not as big as when John Paul II had visited in 1982, but they were never expected to be. Even so, numbers were surprising, particularly in London. It was at the level of his engagement with British political and civic leadership that Benedict garnered most success. His Palace of Westminster address on the role of religion in society was something of an intellectual showstopper, which was accessible to all. It was received with resounding appreciation. This was reflected in British media coverage, which was positive, with particularly favourable editorials in the *Daily Telegraph* and *The Times*. Indeed, the degree of interest by British media in the visit was not expected, particularly where Sky and the BBC were concerned. It seemed too that the British people in general were surprised to discover that, in place of the ferocious 'panzer pope' they had been led to expect, they were presented with a smiling, polite, elderly gentleman who touched them in unexpected ways.

This was particularly the case when, during the ceremony in Crofton Park near Birmingham at which Cardinal John Henry Newman was beatified, Benedict recalled 'with shame and horror' the bombing of nearby Coventry through English spoken in a heavily German accent. The day marked 'a significant moment in the life of the British nation, as it is the day chosen to commemorate the seventieth anniversary of the Battle of Britain,' he said. 'For me, as one who lived and suffered through the dark days of the Nazi regime in Germany, it is deeply moving to be here with you on this occasion, and to recall how many of your fellow citizens sacrificed their lives, courageously resisting the forces of that evil ideology.'

Pope Benedict would say that his beatification of John Henry Newman (canonised in 2019) in September 2010 was a high point of his papacy. He was hugely influenced by Newman, and his idea of conscience as the 'connecting principle between the creature and his Creator', the 'guide of life, implanted in our nature, discriminating right from wrong'. Both saw conscience as an expression of the natural law of God written on the heart of every human being and encompassed in the Ten Commandments. In 1990, as Cardinal Ratzinger, when marking the centenary of Newman's death, the future pope recalled personally experiencing 'the claim of a totalitarian party, which understood itself as the fulfilment of history and which negated the conscience of the individual. One of its leaders had said: "I have no conscience. My conscience is Adolf Hitler." The appalling devastation of humanity that followed was before our eyes.' He also liked to quote Newman's words, 'To live is to change, and to be perfect is to have changed often.'

The irony in all this is that 'change' was not something anyone would associate with Cardinal Ratzinger/Pope Benedict when it came to his understanding of Catholic dogma, nor would respect for the conscience of others when it came to his disciplining theologians he considered to have deviated from his/Rome's interpretation of Catholic doctrine.

✠ ✠ ✠

By February 2013, when he announced his resignation, it was clear that Benedict had lost control of the Curia at the Vatican, with a series of scandals culminating in the leaking to media of his private papers by butler Paolo Gabriele in 2012. The election of Pope Francis in March 2013 was as brief as that of his predecessor. As soon as we saw white smoke from the Sistine Chapel chimney, there was a rush from the press centre to nearby St Peter's Square. It was not yet full as bells rang out and a damp drizzle fell, but it soon became very crowded as excited Romans taxied in from all over the city. People speculated on who the new pope might be and many thought that such a short conclave must mean someone like Cardinal Angelo Scola, Archbishop of Milan, had been elected. Indeed, that evening, the Italian bishops issued a press release congratulating him on his election. A hugely embarrassing mistake, the release was quickly withdrawn. Then he emerged, the man Paddy Power had at 50 to 1 and no one had given a second thought to because he was seventy-six and was said to have withdrawn his name at the 2005 conclave which elected Benedict XVI.

The name of Argentinian Jesuit Jorge Mario Bergoglio was proclaimed to the approximately 100,000-strong crowd in St Peter's Square. There was a silence, with few aware of who this man could be. Some thought, because of his name, he must be Italian. (His parents were.) But almost immediately he won the Romans over with his homely words 'Buona sera' (Good evening) and an explanation that his electors had gone to the end of the earth (Argentina) to find him. This, clearly, was a man with a sense of humour and one who was very comfortable in his own skin. We wondered then whether he might be the first Jesuit Pope. He is.

As soon as he left the balcony at St Peter's, I set off looking for 'colour'. Usually, on such a big story, there is a quirky humorous one as companion to all the dry fact. I wondered where I would find the like that evening, when I saw a sole Argentine flag being waved frantically way up St Peter's Square. I elbowed my way there, driven on by an ever-nearer deadline. And so I met the luckiest Argentinian Catholic family in the whole wide world that evening. Well, certainly in St Peter's Square. Seven of them, from Buenos Aires. The mother, Dolores, explained breathlessly how she knew Francis personally. You couldn't make it up and I thanked my good fortune for chasing after that Argentine flag. She said that the new pope was 'very honest. I think he is going to do big things for the Church.' Her son Francisco (20), a student of music and the one carrying the flag, knew the new pope too and pointed out that both he and Francis had the same name. He wondered whether, all in all, his election might even be as good as Argentina winning the World Cup in football.

Through all this excitement, I was nagged by a memory. As with all cardinal electors before the conclave that elected Francis began, Irish Primate and Archbishop of Armagh Cardinal Seán Brady had celebrated Mass at his designated church in Rome, that of Saints Quirico and Giulitta on Via Conti. He and his assistant, Father Tim Bartlett, had spoken briefly to us Irish media afterwards. Speculating about how long the conclave might last, Father Bartlett said Cardinal Brady didn't think it would take too long. I suggested it wouldn't do if the election was to happen on the Friday of that week, 15 March, the Ides of March, anniversary of the assassination of Julius Caesar. It was then that Father Bartlett said the election could be over as early as Wednesday 13 March. It was. I reported this to Dublin that night, but it was too late for publication. Remembering this in St Peter's Square that Wednesday evening I could have wept. What a scoop was there!

✠ ✠ ✠

One of the great privileges of being a journalist is the access it gives you to people. It is something I never get used to and never take for granted. I was on the plane with Pope Francis to and from Ireland in 2018. It was my first time to cover a papal visit from 'the inside'. It is normal for a number of journalists from the country a pope is visiting to be offered seats to travel with him and the Vatican press corps, as part of the VAMP (Vatican Accredited Media Personnel) on such trips. It meant five of us from Irish media and two cameramen were included in the seventy-four-person contingent on the papal flight with the security people and Pope Francis himself.

Most of us flew to Italy the previous Thursday on the 6.20

morning flight from Dublin to Rome. The following day we received our press accreditation at the Salla Stampa (Vatican press office) near St Peter's Square and collected our return tickets to Dublin a few doors farther down Via della Conciliazione. Tickets cost €1,277 each. Pricey, at half the price. Our advice was to be at Fiumicino Airport by 5 a.m. the following morning. It meant a 4 a.m. start, my second that week (the first was to catch the Dublin to Rome plane).

The trip to Ireland was on a very squashed Alitalia flight – 'Shepherd 1' as it was called. Pope Francis and his entourage were behind a curtain towards the front of the plane. The first many rows were full of mounted TV cameras on both sides, then there were the radio people and finally those of us print/digital journalists working for newspapers and magazines. I found myself sitting beside Gerard O'Connell, a veteran Vatican journalist originally from Cork, and his wife, Elisabetta Piqué. From Buenos Aires, she wrote one of the first biographies of Pope Francis following his election in 2013. She had known him for many years by then and, no doubt, this was a help in Gerry O'Connell being one of the very few journalists to predict, prior to the March 2013 conclave, that Cardinal Jorge Bergoglio was likely to be the next pope.

A short time into our flight Pope Francis came down through the plane to speak to us. He was very informal, chatty and relaxed, speaking to everyone and shaking hands with people individually. Clearly a very warm, genuine, good-humoured man, he spoke only in Italian. Most members of the Vatican press corps had English, so they translated for the rest of us when necessary.

Of course, he was particularly warm to his old friend Elisabetta and her husband, Gerry. And so he came to me who, having no Italian, could only smile back. People had been encouraged to talk to Pope Francis about personal matters and those close to their hearts, though it hardly seemed the environment to do so with so many of the world's media eavesdropping. But Martin Bashir, then Religion Editor of the BBC, did tell a clearly delighted Pope Francis how he had just got word that morning that he was a grandfather. Bashir had yet to be exposed for deceiving Diana, Princess of Wales into giving that infamous 'there were three of us in this marriage' BBC interview in 1995.

We had been told that it was protocol that none of us should send reports from the plane. The reason for this was never clearly explained, whether for safety or to prevent media trying to scoop one another, but we duly obliged. Still, as we came in to land at Dublin Airport, I couldn't resist sending a short video clip of Pope Francis talking to us en route from Rome to a colleague who was writing a live *Irish Times* blog on the event.

From the airport we were taken by bus and garda escort direct to Dublin Castle, where Pope Francis met Taoiseach Leo Varadkar, members of the government and assorted dignitaries. The pope then went to Áras an Uachtaráin before going to Dublin Castle. There was a small media contingent, mainly cameramen and photographers, at the Áras.

After speeches at Dublin Castle, we were taken to the Alex Hotel in Dublin's city centre, where our 'bubble' contingent would spend that night (€215 B&B). Those of us with the VAMP would not be allowed outside that bubble, for security reasons, until we arrived back in Rome. We barely had time to check in before being whisked to the Pro-Cathedral, where Pope Francis was to meet over 300 engaged or newly married couples. All was sweetness (too much) and light in the lead-up to his arrival there. Then, just as he was about to speak, we were whisked away to the Capuchin Day Centre, where Pope Francis was to meet homeless people and that living saint, the Franciscan Brother Kevin Crowley – a lovely event, which had barely got under way after Pope Francis's arrival when we of 'the bubble' were whisked away again.

From a media perspective this was infuriating, because Pope Francis is a man who rarely sticks to a script and whose off-the-cuff remarks are usually the most interesting. But, from the organisers' point of view, the priority was to ensure that we could get to events he was attending, so we had to be one step ahead all the way to avoid getting caught in traffic.

After the Capuchin Day Centre we were taken back to the hotel to unpack and get ready for the Festival of Families event in Croke Park that evening. Again, we were there before Pope Francis. I was surprised at the huge cheer that went up as actor Patrick Bergin began singing the great Leonard Cohen classic 'Anthem', until I realised Pope Francis had just arrived. For all of us the following hours of entertainment were a welcome wind-down. But we had not eaten since the flight that morning. Okay, I had grabbed a few sandwiches at the Capuchin Day Centre – of which I was reminded many times by colleagues during the rest of the visit, who insisted I had taken food from the mouths of the homeless. And there were sandwiches at Croke Park. After the festival there was a long delay in getting out of Croke Park, meaning many colleagues didn't get back to the Alex Hotel until the small hours. I was luckier. I was given a lift back after doing an RTÉ interview with Mary Kennedy.

Next morning saw another 4 a.m. rise as we had to pack and load our luggage for the return flight to Rome that evening. Then we were taken to Dublin Airport in the teeming rain for the flight to Knock Airport in Mayo. It was short but the landing was a bit shaky, with the plane swaying side to side as it came in. Pope Francis met gangs of delighted school children before being taken by speedy motorcade in the mist to Knock Shrine. Most of us media stayed at the press centre in the airport because available media places were very limited at Knock. We were on board the plane again before Pope Francis left Knock Shrine, and soon were heading to Dublin and the Phoenix Park. There was a huge media centre there and immediately speculation began about the crowd size. It was clearly well below the expected 500,000. Later the figure would be put at between 130,000 and 150,000. Then, when Pope Francis had just completed his powerful sermon about people abused by priests, we were whisked away to Dublin Airport. On board, and a short time into the Aer Lingus flight, the pope appeared for what was a roughly fifty-minute press conference. He was every bit as relaxed as before but with one huge drawback. All was in Italian with no translator.

For those of us without Italian – the great majority – it was consternation time and we were dependent on the helpfulness of our English-speaking colleagues with Italian to get an accurate translation of what Pope Francis said. On this occasion I was sitting beside an unfriendly Italian journalist who had no English. To add to the nightmare, those of us reporting for the following day's papers were well past deadline when the plane landed in Rome because we couldn't send reports from the plane. It meant that myself and Ralph Riegel from the *Irish Independent* ended up typing our reports at the baggage carousel in Ciampino Airport as all around us people collected their luggage. And when I got to my Rome hotel I had to write another column for the paper. Then it was another early rise on the Monday morning for an 11.20 a.m. flight back to Dublin.

Ah, yes, the glamour, the high life! Shattered, it took me days to recover. But I learned a valuable lesson: if you want to report accurately and comprehensively on a papal visit, avoid 'the bubble'.

12

Roman 'Justice'

It was early June 2012 and I had just received a large envelope from the Vatican, addressed to me at the *Irish Times* offices on Tara Street, Dublin. I was not used to receiving correspondence from the Vatican, stamped at the post office on St Peter's Square. It was not accompanied by any letter. Inside was just an uncompromising seventeen-page report conducted by the Cardinal Archbishop of New York, Timothy Dolan, eviscerating, as too liberal, the four Irish priests responsible for the seminary at the Irish College in Rome. Based primarily on the word of conservative seminarians there, it had been prepared as part of the so-called 'Apostolic Visitations' announced in 2010 by Pope Benedict to sort out the Irish Church. That followed publication of the Ryan and Murphy reports in 2009, with their damning findings on the physical and sexual abuse, as well as neglect, of children by clergy and its cover-up by Church authorities. As part of this 'Visitation' process, Cardinal Dolan was appointed to look at the Irish seminaries, including the Irish College in Rome. He was very much a traditionalist in the mould of Pope Benedict, who had made him a cardinal earlier that year, in February 2012.

I received his report days before the 50th International Eucharistic Congress was to begin in Dublin, and which would run from 10 June to its conclusion with a major Mass in Croke Park on 17 June. This would include a video address by Pope Benedict. It was a once-in-four-year international event and quite a coup for the Irish Church to host – not least because it also marked the eightieth anniversary of the 1932 Eucharistic Congress in Dublin, which commemorated the 1,500th anniversary of the arrival of St Patrick in Ireland and was a high-water mark for the Catholic Church in the new Irish State. Whoever sent me Cardinal Dolan's report on the Irish College in Rome may have intended to damage the Eucharistic Congress in Dublin, but the intent was probably related more to the fact that Cardinal Dolan, along with former Archbishop of Baltimore (US) Cardinal Edwin O'Brien, who helped him prepare the Irish College report, was among concelebrants at the Eucharistic Congress opening Mass in the Royal Dublin Society, Ballsbridge, on 10 June.

The timing of the report's arrival made me uneasy. I was aware of the great efforts made in Ireland to prepare for the congress and felt that to publish it just before the Eucharistic Congress began in Dublin could be seen in some Catholic Church circles as an attempt by *The Irish Times* to damage the event. I discussed the situation with senior colleagues and it was agreed to withhold publication until towards the end of the Eucharistic Congress. This was not without pain on my part. I would have dearly loved to challenge Cardinal Dolan, personally, over what I believed was the grave injustice he had perpetrated on four decent priests at the Irish College in Rome, two of whom I had got to know and respect over previous years, but he returned to New York after the congress's opening Mass.

On Friday 15 June 2012, my report on what Cardinal Dolan had presented to the Vatican's Congregation for Catholic Education was published in *The Irish Times*. In that document he spoke of how 'a disturbingly significant number of seminarians

241

gave a negative assessment of the atmosphere of the house'. Priests at the college, based on what seminarians said, were 'critical about any emphasis on Rome, tradition, the magisterium, piety or assertive orthodoxy, while the students are enthusiastic about these features'. It recommended that three of the priests be sacked and replaced, while the fourth should undergo further education. This fourth priest resigned in sympathy with his colleagues. The report described having 'heard from students' about an 'anti-ecclesial bias' in theological formation at the college with a 'tilt' there towards 'theologians somewhat ambiguous on church teaching'. It was clear at the college, the report said, that 'the staff and students are dramatically divided in their approach to the church and the priesthood'.

It quoted one seminarian: 'The house is tense and dysfunctional. The seminarians want to be priests as the church teaches. The staff work from approaches more characteristic of the 60s and 70s. Therefore, the level of trust between seminarian and staff is destroyed.' Staff of the college should 'inspire trust and its programme of formation must engender a vibrant fidelity to Jesus and the teaching and tradition of His church with the fostering of a durable interior life, and a humble, confident sense of priestly identity and mission. Such is now lacking,' it said.

The Dolan Report was also critical of seminarians' dress at the college. It bordered 'on the sloppy and excessively informal, and clerical attire seems rare', and recommended that 'a clear dress code be part of the rule of life, that formal attire [jacket and tie for those not yet near diaconate; jacket and clerical collar for those in candidacy and the deacons, on special occasions] be clear, and the laudable practice of cassock and surplice at Sunday Mass, for liturgical ministers, and at special liturgies, be maintained'.

An entire section of the report was devoted to disproving that the college was 'gay friendly', prompting some to describe this as 'prurient' and gratuitous, with an intent to do further harm. It was 'eager to underline that he [Dolan] did not find any evidence of rampant immorality or a homosexual subculture' at the college. This begged the question, 'Why raise it at all so?'

There was no record in Cardinal Dolan's report of even one instance when he discussed the seminarians' criticisms with any of the four priests on the college staff. Nor was there any indication that he had offered any one of the four men an opportunity to answer their student critics. It is the Vatican way.

Other Irish priests censured by Rome have been dealt with similarly – the Vatican listens to the (generally unnamed) accuser but not to the accused priest. Where else would you get away with that? To compound the injustice, the priests complained of at the Irish College were not even entitled to see Cardinal Dolan's report on them or the recommendations he made about them to the Vatican. That, of course, did not stop those recommendations from being acted on, and with some alacrity. All four priests at the Irish College stood down.

Some said that Cardinal Dolan, who had once been rector of the North American College in Rome – which, it was said, he ran like a military academy – never liked the more relaxed style evident at the Irish College then, and that he used his Visitation report to bring it more into line with what the North American College had been.

The trustees of the Irish College in Rome are Ireland's four Catholic archbishops: then, Archbishop of Armagh Cardinal Seán Brady, Archbishop of Dublin Diarmuid Martin, Archbishop of Tuam Michael Neary and Archbishop of Cashel and Emly Dermot Clifford. They had seen the Dolan Report. Their response, which I also got my hands on, was unequivocal. It said, 'a deep prejudice appears to have coloured the Visitation from the outset and it led to the hostile tone and content of the report'. It 'would appear to prioritise its own view of orthodoxy, priestly identity, separation and devotion', and its 'harsh judgments on staff members' were 'unsupported by evidence', they said.

Contacted by me, the archbishops were more restrained. They said the report 'contained some serious errors of fact, including [of] named individuals. Attentive to the importance of applying due process and respecting the rights of those named in this initial report, the trustees made a detailed and considered response to the Holy See.'

I also contacted Cardinal Dolan directly and in his response to my query he highlighted a principle that he said was being ignored. 'While obviously others do not consider themselves bound by the promised confidentiality – so necessary and understandable to assure a fair and honest gathering of information [and] requested by the Apostolic See – I certainly do,' he said. He was, therefore, 'unable to comment upon the report, other than to stand by the diligence of the six visitors [the Visitation team] and the accuracy of the data we found – both of positive and challenging nature – and presented to the Congregation for Catholic Education in Rome'.

In contrast, the Association of Catholic Priests in Ireland did not mince its words. What Cardinal Dolan did 'effectively destroyed the reputations of priests who have given lifelong service to the Irish Catholic Church, without giving them a right of reply to the allegations made against them'. It described as 'unacceptable that a report to the Pope, on a sensitive issue, should be conducted in such an incompetent fashion' and said 'no court of law would treat people in such a way'. There was a strong possibility that the report's findings 'were decided before the evidence was gathered', it said, pointedly.

But Cardinal Dolan's 'style' of justice was not a surprise to many at the time. It was typical of how the Vatican treated priests who did not toe the line. After all, it has been estimated that while Prefect/Dean of the CDF, Pope Benedict silenced as many as ninety-nine theologians who did not agree with his understanding of the truths of the Church.

In April 2012, just two months before the leaking of Cardinal Dolan's report on the Irish College in Rome, it had emerged that one of Ireland's best-known priests, Father Brian D'Arcy, had been censured by the Vatican over four articles he had written for the *Sunday World* newspaper in 2010. Father D'Arcy had been a columnist with the paper for decades and was also an author and a contributor to RTÉ programmes and to BBC Radio 2's *Pause for Thought*. He was the fifth Irish Catholic priest known to have been censured by the Vatican around that time. The others were Redemptorist priests Father Tony Flannery and Father Gerard Moloney, Marist priest Father Seán Fagan and Capuchin priest Father Owen O'Sullivan.

The four articles by Father D'Arcy which upset Rome concerned how the Vatican dealt with the issue of women priests, why US Catholics were leaving the Church, why the Church must take responsibility for clerical child sex abuse, and homosexuality. The other four priests were censured for dealing sympathetically with those same issues, and with taking a more liberal approach than was deemed forgivable by the Vatican. Thereafter, all of them, in addressing matters of faith and morals in their writings or broadcasts, had to first submit these for clearance by Church authorities.

Not one of these men was ever invited to Rome to present a defence. As I heard former President Mary McAleese put it in October 2012 at the launch of *Quo Vadis*, her book on canon law, all the censured priests were 'tried and convicted' without their knowledge and became aware that they were under investigation only when sentence had been passed. Instead, the superiors of their religious congregation in Rome were summoned to the Vatican and told to bring them into line.

Among the convivial at that book launch were the censured priests. Looking around him, Father D'Arcy commented, 'All the heretics are here.' He added, 'Sadly in our Church now, it has become impossible to be open and honest about what good people are convinced of. It's as if merely stating unpalatable facts is in itself disloyal. For years I've tried to point out the perils of the growing disconnect between Church leaders and the ordinary people.'

Just a month before the emergence of Cardinal Dolan's report in June 2012, the Redemptorists in Dublin's Cherry Orchard became the first in Ireland to declare publicly their support for their colleagues Fathers Tony Flannery and Gerard Moloney after they had been censured by Rome. In Father Flannery's case, the censure was believed to be particularly invidious – he was not only censured but also removed from public ministry, a punishment that still stands. Many felt he was singled out as much for his role in setting up, in 2010, the more liberal Association of Catholic Priests as for anything he wrote. He was ordered by the Vatican not to attend the association's annual general meeting in November 2011. He told me he had been threatened with excommunication by the CDF for refusing to recant his more liberal views on Church teachings concerning women priests, contraception and homosexuality. Actions against him by the CDF had been 'frightening, disproportionate and reminiscent of the Inquisition', he said.

For its part, the association affirmed 'in the strongest possible terms' its support for Father Flannery. It believed he was being targeted as 'part of a worldwide effort to negate the influence of independent priests' associations in Austria, USA, Germany, France and Switzerland. One Dublin parish priest resigned a senior position in the archdiocese in protest at the Vatican's treatment of Father Flannery. Father John Hassett stood down as dean of the archdiocese's Maynooth deanery 'over an issue that is neither specifically my own nor diocesan. However, justice has no frontiers.' He described as 'extremely distressing and depressing the manner in which Father Flannery has been dealt with by the Congregation for the Doctrine of the Faith'. Some of Father Flannery's views 'are shared by many priests of the archdiocese of Dublin. It is a sad reflection on the rights of the person and the pre-eminence of conscience that a man of such integrity, kindness and stature is treated in such a manner,' Father Hassett said. 'We now live in a church where courage is silenced by fear, and one can only reflect that the gospel we cherish and struggle to live seems to be a "dead letter" within Vatican bureaucracy.'

In May 2012 it emerged that three other Irish priests had also been disciplined by the Vatican. Well-known Augustinian priest Father Iggy O'Donovan was censured and stripped of a teaching job in Rome at the direction of the CDF after he and colleagues Father Richard Goode and Father Noel Hession concelebrated a Mass with a local Church of Ireland rector, Reverend Michael Graham, on Easter Sunday 2006 at St Peter's Augustinian Church in Drogheda, County Louth. They were marking the ninetieth anniversary of the 1916 Easter Rising in Dublin. Reverend Graham told worshippers it was 'the first public celebration in Drogheda of the Eucharist by a Catholic priest of the Anglican tradition in a Catholic Church of the Roman tradition since the Reformation'. Father O'Donovan welcomed 'members of our sister Church of Ireland' and described the event as 'the most meaningful Eucharist I ever celebrated'. A month later a statement from the Augustinian congregation said Father O'Donovan, Father Goode and Father Hession, 'having reflected on the seriousness of their actions', had written to Catholic Primate Cardinal Seán Brady, then papal nuncio Archbishop Giuseppe Lazzarotto, and the prior general of the Augustinian Order in Rome, and now Prefect of the Vatican's Dicastery for Bishops, Cardinal Robert Prévost, apologising 'unreservedly for the ill-considered celebration'.

✠ ✠ ✠

In July 2016 Father Seán Fagan died. He had his 'heart and spirit' broken by the Vatican in the years before he died, former President of Ireland Mary McAleese said at the time. 'His long and illustrious priestly career was blighted in latter years by being silenced by the Congregation for the Doctrine of the Faith,' she said. I knew this to be the case. Father Seán and I had been in regular correspondence over the years and he was deeply distressed at his treatment by the Vatican but also at the great suffering caused to ordinary people by the enforced rigidities of its teachings, particularly around issues of conscience and sexuality. In 2003 Father Fagan published the book *Does Morality Change?*, for which he was censured by the Irish Catholic bishops in 2004, followed in 2008 by *Whatever Happened to Sin?* He was first censured by Rome in 2008, and in 2010 was informed by the CDF that he would be laicised should he publish anything it considered contrary to Church teaching *and* should he disclose this censure to the media. When, in 2012, he was one of the five Irish priests named as having been silenced by the Vatican, it was no great surprise. For instance, in March 2010 he sent me an email in which he said, 'Confidentially (absolutely at present) I have been totally silenced by CDF under threat of severest penalties, so I have to be quiet for the present. I'll play it by ear, but my situation is very delicate, so please don't refer to it in any way. I'll keep you informed.'

In December 2010 he sent me a letter with a cover note saying, 'The enclosed may give you a smile. I sent it anonymously to

Cardinal Brady to give him second thoughts about his simplistic views on abortion.' Father Fagan had intended sending the letter to *The Tablet*, but 'since my silencing I couldn't send it'. He asked that, were I to report on the letter, 'please, please don't make any reference to me. If the media mention my name I will be blamed by the Vatican and can be stripped of priesthood.'

What he pointed out in the letter was that 'abortion is not always immoral'. He showed how this was the case from Catholic teaching itself. Quoting from Pope John Paul II's 1996 encyclical *Evangelium Vitae* (the Gospel of Life), Father Fagan noted that it said, 'no one can renounce the right to self-defence' and continued that 'legitimate defence can be not only a right, but a grave duty'. In the encyclical Pope John Paul explained that this may involve taking an aggressor's life, even though the aggressor may be morally innocent because of insanity. Father Fagan's letter continued, 'The foetus that is a direct threat to a mother's life is in the same position as the morally innocent aggressor.' It was 'morally equivalent to the insane attacker intent on killing her, and so may be sacrificed,' he wrote. He continued, 'The decision to allow an abortion, saving not only the life of a pregnant mother, but also the welfare of her several young children and husband, shows a deeper understanding of our theology than a bishop's reliance on canon law to excommunicate her and those who counselled her or carried out the operation.'

But the most distressing correspondence I received from him was in October 2012. By then in his late eighties, it was remarkable for a man of such deep faith. 'For the past few years my strongest temptation has been to suicide, though I would never give in, out of consideration for family and friends. Few suspect this as I have a high level of pain tolerance and I always keep the bright side out.' He was not in good shape:

I have had 35 years of rheumatoid-arthritis, 5 years of osteo-arthritis, 10 years of diabetes, 9 years of cellulitis (involving two sessions of 5/3 weeks in hospital), plus problems with prostate, thyroid, cholesterol, vertigo and high blood pressure, all needing pills (20 daily, plus 8 pain killers every 24 hours). I have been blind in my right eye for over two years, with no improvement after two 90-minute operations and two sessions of 12 days each in Eye & Ear Hospital.

As if all that wasn't enough,

on 22 December 2010 I was knocked down by a car in Leeson St. No bones were broken but, much worse, damage to ligaments, tendons and nerves in my whole body. These have worsened until they are almost unbearable 24/7, with no light at the end of the tunnel after almost two years. Life is a living hell. Dizziness is a constant problem. A recent fall in my room was serious and a week later I had a major fall in the city. Two men kindly lifted me up and put me in a taxi to Milltown [where he lived with his Marist community].

He added:

All of this has nothing to do with the Vatican, but coping with the woodenness, arrogance and unchristian injustice of the Vatican officials is an added burden. The Vatican itself is the biggest obstacle to Catholic faith, forcing thousands of Catholics world-wide to leave the Church. A good part of my ministry for years has been helping them to stay, even if, like myself, only by the skin of their teeth.

Father Fagan had another reason for sending me that letter. He had written an article which he dearly wanted me to publish, but under my name, because he could not be seen (by the Vatican) to be the author of such material. I told him I could not do that; that it would be deception of the paper's readers. He acknowledged and accepted this. The article was about Pope Benedict XVI and how he had changed so radically from the young German theologian Joseph Ratzinger, who, at the Second Vatican Council in the 1960s, seemed destined to be a force for renewal in the Church. 'He, quickly and radically, changed his mind' as Prefect, then Dean, of the Vatican's Congregation for the Doctrine of the Faith, Father Fagan wrote, 'when he justified the condemnation of Hans Küng with the statement that: "The Christian is a simple person: bishops should protect the faith of these little people against the power of intellectuals".' In the article Father Fagan listed the 'radical changes in the theology of Pope Benedict XVI, although he still claims to have had no changes to his theological positions over the years'. He listed six instances of such a volte face on Benedict's part: concerning Church structures, bishops' conferences, the Synod of Bishops, reform of the Holy Office (CDF), Communion for divorced and civilly married Catholics, and on the primacy of conscience.

In this last instance he quoted the younger Ratzinger on conscience in a 1968 commentary on the Second Vatican Council:

> Over the Pope as the expression of the binding claim of ecclesiastical authority, there still stands one's conscience, which must be obeyed before all else, even if necessary against the requirement of ecclesiastical authority. This emphasis on the individual, whose conscience confronts him with a supreme and ultimate tribunal, and one which in the last resort is beyond the claim of external social groups,

even of the official Church, also establishes a principle in opposition to increasing totalitarianism.

Father Fagan added:

[R]ecent church documents seem to have a hidden agenda of power and control instead of moral authority, with a concern to limit, restrict and punish. There is an unhealthy tendency to identify Pope and Church, and vice versa. There is little reference to the People of God who are the church, or to the bishops, who are, with the Pope, church leaders. Dialogue is the only way to renewal, but there is no dialogue with Rome and the Curia.

Though I could not publish Father Fagan's article under my name, I did find ways to get what he had written into the public domain, whether through quoting others or in commentary of my own.

Then, in April 2013 Pope Benedict XVI resigned and Pope Francis was elected. A year later, in April 2014, Pope Francis lifted all sanctions against the then extremely ill Father Fagan. It emerged later that in December 2013 Mary McAleese wrote directly to the new pope asking that he personally intervene in the case. When Father Fagan died, aged eighty-eight, in 2016, Mary McAleese said she was 'saddened by the death of that great questioning mind that was Father Seán Fagan's. A brilliant theologian and thinker who brought great distinction to Ireland, his long and illustrious priestly career was blighted in latter years by being silenced by the Congregation for the Doctrine of the Faith. His heart and spirit were broken.' She added, 'When, thanks to Pope Francis, the CDF finally restored him to good standing in 2014 it was a case of too little too late. A great and good man's life and his life's work had been ruined. Anyone wishing to comprehend the collapse of the Catholic intellectual tradition need only examine Seán Fagan's tragic story'. McAleese concluded, 'It reflects well on Seán and badly on those who hounded him using Byzantine processes with no regard for due process or human rights. God grant him peace at last and may his legacy be an inspiration to restless inquiring minds who pursue justice and truth no matter what the personal cost. Seán was such a hero.' Indeed he was. May he rest in peace.

13

Among the Best

It was November 2014 and I was in Lilongwe, capital of Malawi. Meeting Irish missionaries and compatriots with NGOs there felt like a rejuvenation. Six Irish missionaries with long service in Africa were being honoured at a special private dinner attended by President Michael D. Higgins and his wife, Sabina. I was reporting on the president's visit to Ethiopia, Malawi and South Africa and, because of my role as Religious Affairs Correspondent, had been invited along by President Higgins as a guest at the dinner.

It was impossible not to be moved in the presence of these older priests and nuns, who had given their lives to educating and providing healthcare for so many of the poorest in Africa over decades. They may have done so in the name of a God alien to the indigenous populations, but through education they had enabled and liberated more lives than we shall ever know, and through healthcare they had saved and extended the quality of millions of those lives. President Higgins said of them, 'To me they represent an "Irishness" to which all of us should aspire, motivated by a deep empathy put into action and a strong ethical character.'

Then Irish Ambassador to Malawi Áine Hearns hosted the dinner. Guests included Kiltegan priest Father Gus Frawley, who had been in Malawi since 1970, after being expelled from Biafra during the war there in the late 1960s. Other Kiltegan priests at the dinner included Father Frank Taylor and Father Pat Byrne, who served in Lilongwe, and mathematics professor Father John Ryan. The other two missionary guests were Sister of Charity Imelda O'Brien, who had been working on pastoral development in Malawi's southern Thyolo district for the previous two years, before which she had served in Zambia for thirty-three years and before that nine years in Nigeria, and White Father, Father Brendan O'Shea, who had been involved with the Mua Mission in central Malawi, one of the oldest Catholic missions in the country. It was a lovely occasion and I felt both honoured and, frankly, unworthy to be in the company of these extraordinary men and women who had spent their lives lifting up some of the most destitute people on earth while the likes of me, at best, just wrote about it.

In an address at Lilongwe University of Agriculture and Natural Resources, President Higgins said he believed memory of the Famine played a major role in influencing such Irish people abroad. This was not 'because we remember, but because we cannot forget,' he said. The Famine, he said, 'has shaped the values and principles of the Irish people, motivating Ireland's programme of overseas aid, Irish Aid, to focus on the poorest and most vulnerable'. Days beforehand, in Ethiopia, the president and Sabina visited an eye clinic in Mekele run by the Daughters of Charity and sponsored by the Irish Catholic bishops development agency Trócaire. Sister Margaret Coyne, Sabina's sister, had worked there for twenty-three years. The following week, at Soweto's Regina Mundi Catholic Church in Johannesburg, we heard eight Irish nuns speak passionately about the need for more education there. Among them was Sister Frances Sheehy from Limerick, who had been in South Africa for forty-three years.

The previous year, in November 2013, at Dublin's City Hall, Sabina Higgins celebrated the huge contribution Irish missionaries had made in education, human rights, social justice and healthcare in developing countries around the world. Organised by the Irish Missionary Union (IMU), World Mission Ireland and Misean Cara, the event included a reading of the names of 225 priests, nuns and Brothers present in the City Hall, as well as the countries in which they had served for decades. Their combined years of service abroad was put at 8,000 by the IMU. They had served in Cameroon, South Africa, Kenya, Zambia, Liberia, Nigeria, Sierra Leone, Ethiopia, Brazil, Gambia, the US, Papua New Guinea, Australia, Mauritius, the West Indies, Fiji, New Zealand, Argentina, Ghana, Uganda, India, Mexico, west Africa, Sri Lanka, Egypt, Singapore, Samoa, Malawi, Hong Kong, Japan, the Philippines, Korea, China, Peru, Pakistan, Chile, Tanzania, Haiti and Burma. By any record, astonishing.

It wasn't just in Africa that Irish missionaries served. June 2023 saw the death of another remarkable nun, Sister Cyril Mooney, at the age of eighty-six in Kolkata. She was recognised internationally for her work in the provision of education in India. From Bray, County Wicklow, she served in India for sixty-seven years. Beginning in 1979, she expanded access to what previously had been a private school for middle-class girls to include street children and others from disadvantaged lower-caste backgrounds. As she told *The Irish Times* in 2015, 'we mandated ourselves that we would take 25 per cent of poor children every time we did admissions, and over time this moved up to 50 per cent. To help street children keep up their attendance, accommodation was provided on site, in a model that has been copied by the West Bengal government.' Sister Mooney also set up a home at the school for upwards of 200 street children who had no family.

She recalled how 'the [Indian] government said if the Loretos can do it, we can do it'. Since 2010 the 25 per cent quota for disadvantaged students, which she began in Kolkata, has become compulsory for all private schools in India under its Right to Education Act. It guarantees free and compulsory education to all children aged three to fourteen. In 2007 Sister Mooney was awarded the Padma Shri Award by the Indian government, one of that country's highest civilian honours and in 2013 she was presented with a Presidential Distinguished Service Award by President Michael D. Higgins, one of Ireland's highest awards.

Sister Orla Treacy, aged fifty, another Loreto nun from Bray, told me that Sister Cyril 'challenged us as Loreto Sisters to serve the poorest of the poor in our schools'. In February 2006 Sister Orla and three colleagues stepped off a plane in Sudan ready to set up a girls' boarding school in a remote region in the south of the country. On arrival they found an empty field, not the buildings promised by a local bishop. It took two years to get the buildings up. Four years later, South Sudan gained independence from Sudan. Four years after that, the country was ravaged by a civil war that left two million people displaced. Hunger remained a huge problem: 'When we started the primary school, we used to feed the kids, but now we feed everybody,' she said. 'We are still within a war mentality, so insecurity is still a big reality for us. When we harvest, we only harvest enough for a few months and by January everything is gone. That's when the hunger comes.'

Initially the biggest challenge was convincing local families to send their daughters to a secondary school in a country where only a third of girls enrol in primary school. Of these, just 7 per cent finished primary education and 2 per cent made it into secondary education. Less than 1 per cent actually graduated. 'If you live in a culture where marriage is more popular than school, it's very hard to change that mentality. The girl is married for a dowry of cows, so she's considered a wealth to the family. She's also the property of the extended family, not just the mother and father,' she said.

Today, at Rumbek in South Sudan, Sister Orla is director of both a primary and secondary school, as well as a healthcare centre there. 'It is still a daily challenge. There are still issues around families not wanting their daughters to be educated,' Sister Orla said when I interviewed her in November 2022. Just over half of all South Sudanese girls are in arranged marriages by the time they reach eighteen. A tenth are married off when they are just fifteen. And the pressure comes not just from men. Aunts and elders often believe that a daughter needs a good marriage early. 'If she's twenty-three years of age and she's still studying, she is already past it,' said Sister Orla. She recalled how the nuns and staff at Rumbek, north-west of the capital, Juba, 'have been threatened at gunpoint, we have been insulted, all number of problems because [they are women] and should be sacrificed for the sake of the greater good. Technically it's a boarding school, but I call it a women's refuge.'

In recent years the South Sudanese civil authorities have published legislation to stop early forced marriages: 'They want all boys and girls in school. They want to build up education. That is huge for us,' said Sister Orla. Today, their schools are attended by 1,400 boys and girls and there is also a teacher training school.

In 2016 the nuns added a health centre, staffed by Kenyan nuns. It has two clinical officers, one midwife and three nurses, and serves up to 5,000 patients a month. In 2017 Sister Orla was presented with the Hugh O'Flaherty International Humanitarian Award for her work in South Sudan. In 2021 she received a Presidential Distinguished Service Award from Michael D. Higgins. She is sanguine about such awards: 'I'm not big into that kind of thing, but we've a great team. If this is going to help to promote the mission in terms of donors, then do it and keep smiling.'

✠ ✠ ✠

I met Father Alec Reid, that extraordinary man, for a lengthy interview in 2008. He was then living at the Redemptorist congregation's Marianella centre in Dublin's Rathgar, which has since been sold off through lack of vocations. By then he was seventy-six and in poor health. A deeply courteous, gentle man, he spoke softly, deliberately, and with a deep-seated humility that seemed at odds with someone who had played such a central role in the Northern Ireland peace process. It was immediately clear he was a man of deep and simple faith, which was his strength and kept him on his journey in pursuit of peace through the most difficult circumstances.

Christened Alexander, but always known as 'Alec', he was born on Dublin's South Circular Road. He and his mother left there for her native Nenagh, County Tipperary when his carpenter father died. He was five then, in a family which included a brother and two sisters. He joined the Redemptorists in 1949, attended their novitiate in Galway and while there attended the university, studying history, English and philosophy. Ordained in 1957, he was posted to Dundalk, which he loved.

In 1961 he was appointed to the Clonard monastery in Belfast and was there for forty-four years. They stopped conducting missions at Clonard in the early 1970s 'when the Troubles began' and there was rioting and shooting outside the door. An army officer lost a leg when an IRA bomb attached to a lamppost nearby was detonated. One Holy Thursday night there was rioting and shooting, and the IRA opened fire on soldiers. A pregnant young woman was shot at the gates of the church. He anointed her and complained to the IRA about shooting in the streets. Years later he met a nineteen-year-old woman in west Belfast who said to him, 'You anointed my mother when she was shot.' The young woman had been the child she was carrying at the time.

Father Alec noticed that one of those taking part in those early riots was an eighteen- or nineteen-year-old who had been a senior altar boy at Clonard and thought to himself, 'if a sensible young man like him is leading a riot there must be good reason'. He had to find the reason and gain access to those who organised the riots if he was to stop them.

For him, the necessity to attempt to bring an end to the killing crystallised at the wake of a young man killed by loyalists. They were saying the rosary over his open coffin as the young widow wept loudly. It went to the heart of everyone there and Father Alec remembered saying to himself, 'this kind of thing should not be happening in a Christian, civilised society'. He began by trying to get the IRA to stop. From the late 1970s he visited the Long Kesh H-Blocks every Sunday and said Mass for the prisoners there. It was there he first got to know Gerry Adams and proposed an all-Ireland peace conference. He recalled Adams saying this had been very helpful when he (Adams) first began sowing the seeds of such ideas with the IRA leadership. It was also helpful that he could say, 'It is Father Alec's idea.' However, the blanket protest distracted from all that. This led to the two hunger strikes, without which, in Father Alec's view, 'We could have had the ceasefire in 1984 and not in 1994. It would have meant 1,500 less dead.'

Father Alec spent an hour and a half one day with Bobby Sands, trying to talk him out of going ahead with the second hunger strike. But Sands was 'very determined'. He couldn't be stopped. Father Alec remembered how Sands went into a state of shock as they spoke. 'He started to shake.' He regretted that he didn't spend longer with Sands then. He knew that had he succeeded in persuading Sands not to go ahead, ten lives would have been saved, as well as the sixty people who were killed in the week after Sands died. 'The whole thing was very tragic. Sinn Féin and the IRA outside did their best. Failure to prevent the second hunger strike meant ten more years were added to the Troubles. Meanwhile the British and Irish governments wouldn't deal with the IRA on the ground.'

The day after he spoke to Sands, Father Alec became ill and almost died. He was taken to Our Lady of Lourdes hospital in Drogheda, after which, in April 1981, he was sent to Rome for five or six weeks of recuperation. He was in St Peter's Square one May Wednesday as Pope John Paul II gave his weekly audience. He was taking photographs when he heard a bang. Someone shouted, 'the Pope's been shot' and a man right beside Father Alec was on his own and shouting. Swiss guards vaulted over a barrier and grabbed the man. Father Alec thought he must be an accomplice, but recognised him later from photographs as Ali Ağca, the man who would later be jailed for trying to assassinate Pope John Paul II. As Father Alec's health improved, he was told by his superiors he could return to Belfast on one condition – that he would not get involved in politics. He didn't, for a year. Then the IRA captured a UDR man. He went to the IRA and asked, 'Can nothing be done about saving this man?' They agreed to help get him released but were too late. The man had already been shot.

On his return to Belfast Father Alec set up the Redemptorist Peace Ministry at Clonard. He went to Gerry Adams, who said, 'If you want to stop the IRA, get an alliance between Sinn Féin, the SDLP and the Dublin government. Without that you won't stop the IRA.' No one was talking to the IRA in those days, but Father Alec felt Adams must talk to the SDLP. He wrote a fourteen-page letter to John Hume and sent it off thinking, 'This is the last throw of the dice.' Hume responded. 'Fair play to the man. In the morning John Hume phoned and said he would see me the following day. He didn't even know me.' The next day at Clonard Hume agreed to meet Adams.

'He opened the whole door to a reconciliation between the physical force tradition going back to the French Revolution, Wolfe Tone, Robert Emmet, the Young Irelanders, the Fenians, the IRB, 1916, the IRA, and the political tradition of O'Connell, Parnell, Redmond. John Hume represented the political tradition. Gerry Adams represented the physical force tradition.' Soon word got out about the Hume/Adams talks and Hume was subjected to terrible abuse. 'He suffered this incredible amount of abuse from all the media, the British politicians and government, Irish politicians and government ... this man who opened the door which allowed Gerry Adams in,' Father Alec remembered.

In 1986 Father Alec went to see then Dáil opposition leader Charles Haughey, who listened to him for an hour and a half. 'Charlie Haughey deserves great credit. He was a complete blessing. Albert [Reynolds, later Taoiseach] was brilliant. He'd say, "I couldn't meet the IRA but if you give me a message from them I'll have a reply for you within half an hour." Albert played a key role in getting the peace process going. That should be remembered about Albert. He said he was prepared to sacrifice his political career and his government if he could save just one life. When you are dealing with a man like that you're in business. He was a key person in getting the whole peace process going and in persuading the IRA to stop. Bertie [Ahern, also later Taoiseach] was brilliant too. I was at his mother's funeral,' he said.

But it was on Saturday, 19 March 1988 that Father Alec first came to the attention of a wider world. It was at the funeral of IRA man Kevin Brady, who had been killed as he attended the funerals in Milltown cemetery of Seán Savage, Danny McCann and Mairéad Farrell, known as the Gibraltar Three. Shot dead by British SAS forces on 6 March, their joint funeral on 16 March was attacked by UDA man Michael Stone. Kevin Brady, John Murray and Thomas McErlean were killed. Father Alec was at the funeral because Savage had once been an altar boy at Clonard. Brady was the first man anointed by him after the attack. That night his mother got in contact with the priest to enquire whether her son had been anointed. He assured her he had been.

He was at Kevin Brady's funeral on 19 March, to meet her, to doubly reassure her. But another reason was that he had a document arising from the Hume–Adams talks, which he was to pass to Sinn Féin's Tom Hartley there. As he made his way towards Mrs Brady, a car backed in the direction of mourners, at speed. He saw people banging the car and one man beating it with a wheel brace. The windows were smashed. One of the men in the car fired in the air. The back of the car was being kicked. Two men were taken from the car and what looked like two rugby scrums surrounded each of them. Their hands were being held in case they had guns. They were brought to the side of Casement Park where they were placed lying on the ground. Sensing what might happen, Father Alec lay down between them and placed an arm around each. They were 'dead still. I remember thinking they must be soldiers, they were so still.' He shouted for an ambulance, but someone shouted at him, 'Get up or I'll fucking shoot you as well.' Next thing the two men were dropped over a wall. Father Alec ran around and saw a black taxi pulling away. He thought the men would be taken away for interrogation. It could be a big propaganda thing. He ran into a side street where his own car was and was just opening the car door when he heard 'bang, bang'. He went to a street corner where he saw people standing, looking up towards waste ground. 'I realised then they had shot them. All

I could do was anoint them.' One man was still breathing. Father Alec gave him the kiss of life.

An army ambulance was soon at the scene, but both men were dead. Father Alec was annoyed with himself. He really thought the men were being taken for interrogation. He believed that if senior Sinn Féin or IRA people had been there, they would have intervened and saved their lives. Gerry Adams told Father Alec later that, had he or senior colleagues been there, the two men would not have been shot.

In September 2005 Father Alec and Methodist Minister Reverend Harold Good, in their role as independent witnesses, verified the process of IRA decommissioning carried out by the Independent International Commission on Decommissioning. In a statement they said:

> We are certain about the exactitude of this report because we spent many days watching the meticulous and painstaking way in which General de Chastelain, Brigadier General Tauno Nieminen and Ambassador Andrew Sens went about the task of decommissioning the huge amounts of explosives, arms and ammunition that they have just described in their statement. The experience of seeing this with our own eyes, on a minute-to-minute basis, provided us with evidence so clear and of its nature so incontrovertible that, at the end of the process, it demonstrated to us, and would have demonstrated to anyone who might have been with us, that beyond any shadow of doubt, the arms of the IRA have now been decommissioned. In light of this, and in order to create universal confidence, we wish to assure everyone, but especially those in Northern Ireland who may yet have misgivings, that the decommissioning of the arms of the IRA is now an accomplished fact. We also wish to

assure the British and Irish governments that, in so far as they relate to the decommissioning of the arms of the IRA, the objectives of their Decommissioning Acts have now been achieved.

Father Alec Reid died in November 2013 and was buried at Milltown cemetery, Belfast.

✠ ✠ ✠

All my life I've admired the courageous individual who simply does what is right and sticks with it, even as the consequences pile up all around them. It is such individuals who drive forward human freedoms and help improve the quality of innumerable lives, often at great cost to themselves. One such, to my mind, is Mayoman Father Kevin Hegarty, mild-mannered but with deeply held convictions. In 1994 he was appointed to the parish of Shanaghy, County Mayo, so far west you can almost see Boston from there. It was meant as punishment by the Catholic bishops, but not for a natural pastor such as Father Hegarty. He has been happy there.

Those of us who know Father Kevin, as I have for many years now, admire the depth – and courage – of his compassion for people and his exceptionally lyric style as a writer. The latter meant it was no surprise in 1991 when he was appointed editor of *Intercom*, the pastoral and liturgical journal published by the Irish Catholic bishops as something of an in-house journal for priests.

The bishops had not anticipated that Father Hegarty would take the magazine by the scruff of its neck and turn it into a forum for vigorous debate. This caused unease, then alarm. In 1993 some bishops criticised an article in the magazine by Mary McAleese on women priests, and another on the deployment of priests by Father Brendan Hoban, then parish priest of Kilmore in Mayo. But there was 'shock and awe' when Father Hegarty published an article in the December 1993 issue that posed twenty tough questions to the bishops on their handling of clerical child sex abuse, an issue that had yet to come to public attention in Ireland. The article was written by Philip Mortell, a former priest and senior social worker with the then Mid-Western Health Board. One bishop contacted Father Hegarty and offered to 'mark his card' should he publish an article like that again.

It did not look good for Father Hegarty when, in March 1994, Bishop Éamonn Walsh, an auxiliary bishop of Dublin, was asked by his brother bishops to seek out their views on the then focus of *Intercom*. (In 2009 Bishop Walsh resigned following publication of the Murphy Report into the handling of clerical child sex abuse allegations in the Dublin archdiocese. Pope Benedict did not accept his resignation.)

In July 1994 Bishop of Killala Thomas Finnegan, Father Hegarty's bishop, told the priest he was appointing him to a full-time curacy at Shanaghy and that this was to be his priority, not *Intercom*. It meant Father Hegarty could no longer edit the magazine. Supporters of his wrote to the newspapers criticising his treatment by the bishops. The bishop with ultimate responsibility for *Intercom*, Bishop Brendan Comiskey, said those writing to the papers on Father Hegarty's behalf were 'doing the truth, the church and ultimately Father Kevin Hegarty a disservice'. (In 2002 Bishop Comiskey resigned as Bishop of Ferns following a BBC documentary which accused him of mishandling allegations of clerical child sex abuse.)

Had the Irish bishops paid heed to the content of that 'Twenty Questions for the Bishops' *Intercom* article, their own fate and that of the Catholic Church in Ireland just might have been different. As Mary McAleese put it in a January 1995 letter to *The Irish Times*, after Father Hegarty had been pushed to the edge of the Atlantic:

> What is truly depressing about this episode, though, is the contrast between the energy and determination which went into sorting out a perceived problem with the editorial tone of *Intercom*, and the sheer breath-taking ineptitude of church handling of matters relating to child abuse by clergy. It is truly ironic that Father Kevin Hegarty raised the issue openly in *Intercom* long before the Father Brendan Smyth affair, and in so doing incurred the wrath of those so anxious now to reassure us of their clean hands and bona fides in this squalid business.

14

Mná na hÉireann

One of the least commented on features marking the downfall of the Catholic Church in Ireland over recent decades has been the central role that women have played in it. I have had the privilege of working with some of them.

A vivid memory from my student days at UCG was a debate there involving journalist Nell McCafferty and then Bishop of Galway Micheál Browne. Coming up to retirement, Bishop Browne still had a formidable reputation. It was he who oversaw the building of the enormous Cathedral of Our Lady Assumed into Heaven and St Nicholas in Galway, known locally as 'Taj Micheál', which opened in 1965. Among the generally passive Catholic faithful of the day, he had a capacity to strike fear by merely raising an eyebrow. This did not work on Nell McCafferty. Shortly beforehand, in May 1971, she had been on the 'Contraceptive Train', which took members of the Irish Women's Liberation Movement from Dublin to Belfast to buy contraceptive pills. It was a protest at the then law in Ireland prohibiting the importation and sale of contraceptives. The women arrived back in Dublin with what we now know were mostly aspirin because the pharmacies they visited in Belfast were running low on the pill!

I cannot remember the topic for debate that night in UCG, but I do recall His Lordship's grim demeanour. In her address McCafferty did not hold back. Bishop Browne soon had enough. He glared at her, then at us, his student audience – who were enjoying both what she was saying and his obvious annoyance – rose from his seat and walked out.

It is hardly necessary here to list off the Irish women of the last five decades who led the way in campaigns for legal contraception, divorce and abortion in Ireland. They were pivotal in the so-called 'moral civil wars' of those years. But women were also central to the exposure of clerical child sex abuse in Ireland and its cover-up by Catholic Church authorities.

In the year 2000 my then colleague at *The Irish Times*, Alison O'Connor, published *A Message from Heaven: The Life and Crimes of Father Sean Fortune*. It was the first book to detail the sexual abuse of boys by this Wexford priest over many years, and in particular the abuse of Colm O'Gorman, then living in London. Based on O'Connor's book, the BBC's Sarah McDonald made the documentary *Suing the Pope* in which that remarkable and most influential abuse survivor Colm O'Gorman went back to County Wexford and the parishes of Ferns diocese where he had been abused by Father Fortune. It was broadcast on the BBC in March 2002 and on RTÉ some weeks later, leading to the resignation of then Bishop of Ferns, Brendan Comiskey, and the setting up by the government of the Ferns Inquiry.

Another woman who played a major role in bringing the clerical child sex abuse issue into the public domain, through the Dublin Archdiocese Commission of Investigation, was its chair, Justice Yvonne Murphy, assisted by solicitors Ita Mangan and Hugh O'Neill. In January 2009 the commission's remit was extended to include the diocese of Cloyne, following articles about the mishandling of abuse cases there written by my colleague

Justine McCarthy, who has done so much great work in the area down the years, marked by a searing compassion. There was also a December 2008 report by the Catholic Church watchdog – its National Board for Safeguarding Children, led by its no-nonsense chief executive Ian Elliott – that child protection practices in Cloyne were 'inadequate and in some respects dangerous'. The Cloyne Report was published in July 2011, precipitating a remarkable speech by then Taoiseach Enda Kenny, delivered in the Dáil on 20 July 2011 and written by his chief speech-writer Miriam O'Callaghan, which excoriated the Vatican for its lack of co-operation with the relevant inquiries.

Justice Murphy, Ita Mangan and Professor Mary Daly, with Dr William Duncan, led the Mother and Baby Homes Commission of Investigation brought about by another remarkable woman, Tuam's Catherine Corless. An amateur historian, this most modest woman without any pretensions whatsoever was always available and helpful to journalists like myself. Her research caused an international sensation in 2014 when it indicated that the remains of as many as 798 children may have been buried in septic tanks at the site of the former Mother and Baby Home there.

An inquiry into the Magdalene laundries followed years of lobbying by women such as Patricia McDonnell and her Magdalen Memorial Committee; by survivor Maureen Sullivan who, with Steven O'Riordan, set up Magdalene Survivors Together; by other survivors of the laundries such as Mary Norris, Sarah Williams, Mary Smith, Marina Gambold [née Fitzgerald], Maureen Taylor and Kathleen Legg; by Mari Steed and Angela Murphy [whose mothers had been in the laundries], as well as the indefatigable work of the Justice for Magdalenes [JFM] group, since renamed Justice for Magdalenes Research. This involved, particularly, work by Claire McGettrick, Dr Katherine O'Donnell of UCD,

Dr Maeve O'Rourke of the University of Galway, and years of research by Professor James Smith of Boston College.

But two women in particular stand out for me as outstanding heroes of this shocking, tragic saga. They are survivors Christine Buckley and Marie Collins. In November 1992 the redoubtable Christine went on RTÉ Radio 1's *The Gay Byrne Show* to talk about her abuse experiences as a child in Dublin's Goldenbridge orphanage. Filmmaker Louis Lentin was listening and decided to make a feel-good documentary about Christine meeting her Nigerian father. She, as well as other survivors Carmel McDonnell Byrne and Bernadette Fahy, had other ideas and the 1996 documentary *Dear Daughter,* exposing their abuse as children in Dublin's Goldenbridge orphanage, was broadcast on RTÉ. It was the first such programme to look at the abuse and neglect of children in such institutions.

Then there was the truly wonderful Mary Raftery, a great journalist who became a friend. In early 1999 Mary, assisted by Sheila Ahern, finished work on her magnum opus and one of the most influential investigative TV programmes in Irish history: *States of Fear*, the three-part series that exposed at its most raw the shocking physical and sexual abuse of children in institutions run by eighteen religious congregations in Ireland up to the 1970s. It took immense work, great courage and sheer obstinacy on Mary's part in dealings with the RTÉ authorities who, nervous about its content, did not want to broadcast it until late at night. Mary took tapes of the programme home with her until it was agreed that they would be broadcast over a three-week period and at prime time, after the 9 o'clock news each evening.

The programme went out in April and May 1999. Before the final episode had been broadcast, then Taoiseach Bertie Ahern announced the setting up of a Commission to Inquire into Child Abuse, which would investigate what had happened in those residential institutions for children; the setting up of a Redress Board, which would pay compensation to survivors; and he apologised on behalf of the Irish State for its negligence in not properly supervising the institutions and caring for the children. However, his apology, he later told me, was not forced by *States of Fear*. '[It] had little to do with the apology,' he said. 'Micheál Martin [then Minister for Education] had been working on [the apology] for several months before the series, though the programme was a huge issue at the time.'

After *States of Fear*, Mary produced a second groundbreaking RTÉ documentary (with Mick Peelo this time) in October 2002. *Cardinal Secrets* looked at the sexual abuse of children by priests in Dublin's Catholic archdiocese and its cover-up by Church authorities. I was allowed sit in on the final edits of the programme the evening it was to be broadcast so I could have an accurate report on it in *The Irish Times* the following morning. I didn't know Mary then. Contrary to a certain view, journalists do not all hang around in the same circles and so it was with Mary and myself. She was a weekly columnist with *The Irish Times* from 2003 to 2007, but such columnists rarely come into the newspaper offices and we did not meet then.

In the spring of 2009, as publication of the Ryan Commission Report approached, I proposed to then *Irish Times* news editor Kevin O'Sullivan that Mary be brought on board to help with the reporting on that mammoth 2,600-page work as, more than most, she was responsible for the existence of the commission which prepared it. He agreed. Subsequently Mary and I worked closely and very well together on the May 2009 Ryan Report, the November 2009 Dublin Report and the July 2011 Cloyne Report. *Cardinal Secrets* had been hugely significant in the creation of both latter statutory inquiries. She was warm, mischievous, very funny – a great colleague. We just clicked. Then she became ill.

Mary had already successfully seen off ovarian cancer, or so it was thought. Her admission to hospital was initially understood by me to be for a routine check-up. So when I visited her at St Vincent's, I expected her to tell me all was well and she'd be out in a few days. Among the gifts I brought along was what I thought was a humorous card I had found of an angry nun threatening a child by waving a ruler at her, which I had captioned, 'This is what you get for being so bold', or something daft along those lines. I had given it to Mary and she had put it under her pillow before I realised something was seriously wrong. She was far from her usual self and told me the cancer was back. I had never seen her so shattered, and soon so was I. It never struck me that Mary would die.

Days before she did, in January 2012, her husband David Waddell rang to say she wanted to see me. I called to the hospital to find all her relatives in one room with just David and their son Ben in with Mary. Word was that she was very low. It seemed crass to enter her room in what appeared to be her final hours, but a nurse encouraged me to go in. I did so, briefly, feeling I was encroaching on other people's sacred territory. Mary seemed unaware and David came to speak to me. It was the last time I saw her. She died later that night. I never did find out whether she looked at that bloody card I brought in on that first visit, which has caused me to cringe ever since.

I reported on her funeral, an unusual privilege. It may seem odd to report on the death of a friend, but it happens in my line of business and I came to see it as a privilege to have the final say – so to speak – on someone who meant a lot to me, even if the emotion had to be between the lines. I did so with Mary, with my late colleague and favourite Kerryman Michael O'Regan when he died in February 2024, and with Christine Buckley in 2014. It is a rare honour, reserved for journalists, to have such a significant, if discreet, role where deceased friends are concerned.

Christine and I had met many times over the years as I reported on what she said and did. A strong, feisty woman who was small in stature, she took no prisoners, whether with the media or anyone else. It took me a while to warm to her, but soon I admired her greatly and we became good friends. She was firm, resolute and remarkable, as was the work she did, and also great fun.

In May 2019 I interviewed Bertie Ahern to mark the twentieth anniversary of his apology on behalf of the State to people who had been in residential institutions as children. He believed the apology was 'absolutely necessary. These people, their lives had been ruined.' His actions at the time had been heavily influenced by Christine, he said. She was, he said, 'a very articulate, very nice person, but a formidable lady' who had 'a very clear view about the importance of the State's responsibility and the apology. She was very anxious I would do that.'

His interest in the issue went back many years. 'I represented at that stage, following the 1992 election, the Inchicore area in Dublin. I had groups, small groups initially. I remember meeting one of the groups in the Glen of Aherlow bar [on Emmet Road] on a Monday where I heard the stories first. And then I met up with Christine,' he said. 'You did not have to be educated or qualified in any of the sciences to see these people had been broken from the traumas they had suffered.'

Christine Buckley died at the age of sixty-seven in March 2014. Her funeral at the Church of St Thérèse in Dublin's Mount Merrion was almost a State occasion, attended by President Michael D. Higgins and Catholic Archbishop of Dublin Diarmuid Martin. A remarkable comment on the daughter of a Nigerian father and an Irish mother who was abandoned at three weeks and grew up in a Dublin orphanage in the 1950s. RIP Christine.

✠ ✠ ✠

Marie Collins is a gentle woman with an independence of mind and a determined will that has consistently taken senior Catholic Church figures by surprise, whether in Ireland or Rome. Her mild, even shy, demeanour means they are taken aback when she digs in her heels, refusing to play the clerical game, even as she remains a practising Catholic. Our paths crossed for the first time on a gloomy December evening in 2002 as she emerged from Archbishop's House with Cardinal Desmond Connell and a man who had been yet another victim of abuser Tony Walsh. This man has long-since withdrawn into private life, but on 22 December 2002 he and Marie Collins had called publicly for a protest march by survivors to Archbishop's House in Drumcondra on Sunday, 5 January 2003 to demand the cardinal's resignation over his handling of abuse allegations against priests in the archdiocese.

On Monday 30 December, following a five-hour meeting between Cardinal Connell, other senior Church figures, Marie and this man, the protest was called off and their call for the cardinal's resignation was withdrawn. In return, the archdiocese stated that it was 'cooperating fully' with the gardaí in their investigations and that the cardinal had agreed to give gardaí access to diocesan files concerning complaints of child sexual abuse against diocesan priests. It had also been agreed that victims were to be actively involved in helping the archdiocese deal with problems arising from such abuse.

Afterwards Cardinal Connell, Marie and the man emerged from Archbishop's House to meet us media in the gathering gloom of that cold evening. The atmosphere, in contrast, was warm among those who had come to tell us the good news of what was agreed. The aftermath, however, would put steel in Marie's resolve when it came to dealing with Church authorities. In February 2008, just over five years after that meeting, she apologised to 'all those people I feel I let down in 2002. In deciding to withdraw the call for the cardinal's resignation and in believing the cardinal meant what he said – I was wrong.' She continued, 'I knew that in deciding to trust that the cardinal meant what he said, I might be making a mistake. I knew that, but I felt if there was the slightest chance the words we had heard were sincere then I had to be willing to respond positively. When it was heard we had withdrawn the call for the cardinal's resignation, many very good people felt let down, but I hoped in the future they would see the decision was correct. I now know that within months of this meeting and all his assurances, the cardinal was denying the Garda full access to the files and now is trying to keep some of them secret from a State inquiry.'

At the time Cardinal Connell had launched a legal action, later withdrawn, to prevent the commission set up to investigate the handling of clerical child sex abuse allegations from receiving 5,000 files in the archdiocese's archives, which he deemed personal to him.

Marie Collins was thirteen in 1960 when she was sexually abused by Father Paul McGennis, then chaplain at Dublin's Our Lady's Hospital for Sick Children in Crumlin. In the 1980s, while receiving counselling for the abuse, Marie was advised to report it to Church authorities. She did so in 1985, but the priest she approached refused to take details and implied that the abuse was her fault. 'Shattered', she returned to silence for ten more years.

Then, in 1995, prompted by the furore following the jailing of Father Brendan Smyth in Belfast after his forty-year career of abusing children, and fearful that Father McGennis might still be active, Marie went to Dublin's Church authorities again. McGennis admitted his guilt to them, but they refused to confirm this to investigating gardaí or hand over his files to them. Eventually, in 1997, McGennis pleaded guilty to two charges of sexually assaulting Marie as a child at Our Lady's Children's Hospital. He also pleaded guilty to two charges of assaulting a nine-year-old girl in County Wicklow between 1977 and 1979.

The Murphy Commission Report referred to McGennis as 'Fr Edmondus'. It noted how he was chaplain at the children's hospital in Crumlin from 1958 to 1960 and found that 'Marie Collins [was] one of the many people abused by Fr Edmondus, and who was severely affected by the abuse.' He had 'committed a number of sexual assaults on young patients aged between eight and 11 years in Our Lady's Hospital'. As well as being convicted for abusing the nine-year-old in a Wicklow parish, he would also be convicted for abusing another young girl between 1980 and 1984.

The report recorded that McGennis's activities first came to the attention of the Dublin archdiocese in August 1960, when Scotland Yard contacted gardaí after a processing company in the UK reported film taken by him of two young girls aged ten or eleven. Then Garda Commissioner Daniel Costigan brought this to Archbishop John Charles McQuaid. 'The Commissioner told Archbishop McQuaid that he would do nothing further. No attempt seems to have been made to establish who the two girls in the photographs were.' The gardaí did not investigate further. Archbishop McQuaid met McGennis, 'who admitted photographing the children in sexual postures alone and in groups'.

It continued that 'while Archbishop McQuaid investigated the matter promptly, he limited his activity to dealing with the priest's problem'. The commission concluded that 'Archbishop McQuaid acted as he did to avoid scandal in both Ireland and Rome and without regard to the protection of children in Crumlin hospital.'

In relation to Marie's case, the report recounted how 'in 1985 Ms Collins told local curate Father Eddie Griffin about her abuse and being photographed at the children's hospital in 1960 when she was thirteen. He told her not to name her abuser, or he would have to do something. He offered Marie Collins absolution "to do away with her guilt".' Father Griffin told gardaí he and other seminarians 'had been advised while in College not to seek the name of priests that allegations were being made against'. In 1993 complaints about McGennis's contact with young children in Edenmore parish in Dublin were made to Church authorities.

In October 1995 Marie Collins wrote to Archbishop Desmond Connell about her abuse. A trawl was done at Archbishop's House and uncovered the photographs presented to the archdiocese in 1960. Marie's letter was passed to then chancellor of the Dublin archdiocese and its child protection delegate, Monsignor Alex Stenson, who met Marie. The Murphy Commission found that it was 'very clear that Monsignor Stenson believed Mrs Collins', but that he did not tell her about the other incidents involving McGennis. He did tell the gardaí in November 1995, with the consent of Archbishop Connell. Stenson later said he had no consent to tell Marie until he met her in March 1996, when he told her that McGennis admitted to abusing her. This he had not told the gardaí. He also told her McGennis was no longer in a parish but was receiving treatment. In truth, McGennis was still in Edenmore parish and was not removed from ministry until January 1997.

In March 1996 there was a complaint against McGennis arising from his time in Wicklow. Gardaí met with Monsignor Stenson in May 1996 and asked to see McGennis's file. Monsignor Stenson refused. Canon law would not allow it. He was asked about his confirmation to Marie about McGennis's admission that he had sexually abused her. He 'expressed dismay' on hearing his letter to her about McGennis referred to by gardaí. Such knowledge by an outside agency, he feared, could compromise, if not render void, the Church's canon law processes in the case. In his view the letter was confidential. He would not have written it 'had he known that she would be handing over the letter to the gardaí,' he said. He refused to make a statement confirming the McGennis admission.

In December 1996 Marie Collins met Archbishop Connell. He admitted not confirming to gardaí there was another 1960s' case on file about McGennis, as to do so 'would undermine people's confidence in the Church'. He also told her the Church's 1996 framework document (on child protection guidelines) wasn't binding in either canon or civil law, and that 'he could follow what parts of it he wanted to follow'. He told her he 'had to protect the good name of the priest who had abused her'.

When I reported that Archbishop Connell had said the Church's much-touted 1996 child protection document amounted to 'only guidelines', with no authority in civil or canon law, and so was worthless, the archdiocese dissembled and denied this. However, a priest present at that exchange between Marie and the archbishop, Father James Norman, confirmed her account to me. He has since left the priesthood. Marie was later chastised for her disclosure of this by an official at the archdiocese, who said the exchange between herself and Archbishop Connell had been 'a private conversation'.

In a statement after McGennis's conviction in 1997, Archbishop Connell said the diocese had been cooperating with gardaí in the case. In contrast, the Murphy Commission noted that Monsignor Stenson said, 'the diocese never claimed it had cooperated fully, with the emphasis on the word "fully", with the gardaí'.

The Murphy Report was unequivocal on how the Dublin archdiocese dealt with Marie Collins:

Everything that Mrs Collins managed to extract from the Archdiocese over the years in relation to the handling of child sexual abuse was given grudgingly and always after a struggle. Mrs Collins now believes, on the basis of bitter experience, that her Church cannot be trusted to deal properly with complaints of child sexual abuse and that legal measures are required to ensure compliance by the Church with proper standards of child protection.

The Commission also noted that:

> [N]otwithstanding her own reservations in the matter, there is no doubt that Mrs Collins, in her brave and often lonely campaign to show the Archdiocese how it had erred in its handling of child sexual abuse cases, was instrumental in changing the Archdiocese's understanding and handling of these cases and of bringing about a far greater atmosphere of openness about the incidence and handling of child sexual abuse.

As a very private person, who has 'never enjoyed the public side', Marie Collins has been driven by concern for vulnerable children and for other survivors. She felt she 'had to speak out, as others had done. The fact that criminal child abusers were being protected by their superiors needed to be known if it was to be stopped,' she told me. Reflecting on her own journey, following publication of the Murphy Report, she said it had been 'a very, very rough road'. And that was just after her dealings with Church authorities in Dublin.

In 2014 she began dealing with probably the oldest and most skilled bureaucracy in the world, the Roman Curia, the administrative apparatus of the Holy See. Owing to her experience and commitment to child protection, she had been encouraged by then Archbishop of Dublin Diarmuid Martin, whom she respected, to take a position on the newly created Vatican Commission for the Protection of Minors. She lasted three years when, following endless frustration with Vatican bureaucracy, she felt she had no alternative but to resign.

She and I met regularly during those years, and it was evident that some within the Vatican had other priorities when it came to child protection. It was down the list behind concerns for the reputation of the Church and its priests, whatever the differing views of some very committed commission members, including clergy and Pope Francis himself. Marie found out that even the pope could have his decisions rendered as nought by inaction or manipulation on the part of the Curia. For example, there was a Vatican tribunal set up to hold bishops to account regarding the handling of abuse cases. 'We as a commission put forward the proposal. It went to the Council of Cardinals, they approved it. It went forward to the pope. He approved it. It was announced in the press, then it went to be implemented and that's where the brick wall is,' she said. 'As far as the commission is concerned, the work has been done and the pope has approved it.'

On her resignation, she said it was 'just shocking to me that in 2017 I can still come across these defensive, inflexible attitudes in men of the Church, the same attitudes I saw twenty years ago when I was trying to bring my own case to justice here in Dublin.'

Speaking in October 2018, Archbishop Martin recalled how when he became Archbishop of Dublin, fourteen years previously, 'I came back to Ireland ... at a moment in which the crisis of the sexual abuse by priests and abuse of children in church-run institutions was at its height ... There was a surprising lack of real awareness in Rome of the extent of the problem and little understanding of the nature and the extent of the challenge and especially that many of the roots of the abuse crisis were to be found within the lived culture of the Irish Church and, as we now know, more clearly worldwide.'

In Ireland then, he said, there was an atmosphere 'of crisis management in dealing with accusations'. At the time 'victims and survivors were rightly angry and determined to bring the harsh realities into the public eye':

> [They] were determined and courageous, assisted often by a pioneering group of journalists. I think of the late Mary Raftery. The media played and still play a key role in the challenge of the protection of children in the Catholic Church. Survivors like Marie Collins and the late Christine Buckley, to name just two, were determined and uncompromisingly forthright and often they were looked on in internal church culture as being 'difficult'. All I can say is thank God they were so.

To which I would add just one word: Amen.

Epilogue

In bored moments as a small boy I used pray, 'Please God, can I have an interesting life when I grow up.' I did not know then that what I wished for is a Chinese curse, or that God could be so generous. No normal person would want 'an interesting life' of upheaval, but it's grist to the mill for a journalist.

Not being a normal person with a limited capacity for chaos, I have loved the world of journalism and greatly enjoyed the company of fellow warriors in that turbulent trade, although, in more self-aware moments, I have described it as 'the anxiety industry'. But then, isn't anxiety the essence of this human condition where uncertainty is *the* only constant? It is why there is, and probably always will be, religion.

What brought me to journalism was my father, not by intention, but through his passion for politics. His had an uncritical devotion to Éamon de Valera and Fianna Fáil which transmuted, through my more sceptical eye, into a passion for current affairs. Political journalism was what attracted me, unsurprisingly, and what I dealt in earlier in my career, not least the interaction between religion and politics in Ireland. There was no getting away from that, considering the role of religious identity in the Northern Ireland Troubles and strong resistance by the Catholic Church in the Republic to insistent liberalising forces.

I had a deep interest in what was happening in both juris-dictions, particularly to minorities. One of my proudest pieces of journalism was the article 'Pressure on Protestant' published in *Magill* magazine in January 1989. It cast a cool eye on the experience of the Protestant minority in the Irish State from its foundation in 1922 until 1988. At around the same time, for *The Irish Press* I interviewed one of the longest-serving Muslim leaders in Ireland, Imam Yahya Al-Hussein of Dublin's South Circular Road mosque, about being a Muslim in the Republic.

My becoming Religious Affairs Correspondent at *The Irish Times* was almost accidental. My predecessor, Andy Pollak, was a distinguished journalist who seemed there for 'life'. Then he was appointed Education Correspondent. I decided to apply for his vacated position, held my breath, and got it.

My first Drumcree (of eight) followed that summer when I accompanied the Orange Order on the first Sunday in July as they paraded from Portadown to the Church of the Ascension in the nearby countryside, hoping to return via the Garvaghy Road. Later that month Father Brendan Smyth (71) was sentenced in Dublin to twelve years' imprisonment for child sex abuse offences. He died a month later and was buried in pre-dawn darkness at his Norbertine order's Kilnacrott Abbey in Cavan as lights from a hearse illuminated the graveside while his coffin was lowered.

I had no idea then that those two events would set the parameters for much of my period in the new role. At the time, although there had been some stories published already about clerical child sex abuse in Ireland, there was no indication of the tsunami ahead. The sheer scale of it could be overwhelming, leading to an implosion of the Catholic Church in Ireland.

History was being made, and I had a front seat.

One matter I regret is not having space in this book to cover how diverse Irish society has become in recent years. For instance, the 2022 census tells us almost 22 per cent of people in the Republic ticked the 'no religion' box or did not state their religion. That's huge growth. Meanwhile, 68.8 per cent say they are Catholic, with all other Churches and the many new faith groupings still in single percentages, if growing.

In parallel with this diversity, the number of spokespeople for Churches, faith groupings and people of no faith has increased – those unsung heroes (and occasional villains!) who occupy that rocky no man's land between the media and their often-otherworldly employers, who tend to regard the press as Irish people do the weather: a misery to be endured.

Where many religions are concerned, the media remain a rude Johnny-come-lately, the merely few-centuries-old fourth estate which crashes through delicate matters with the grace of a baby elephant, looking for trouble where peace is necessary, and with such callow impertinence as suggests the world is answerable to it as by divine right. That can be difficult for hierarchies.

An illustration of the media's standing in their world, possibly unintended, could be gleaned at the 2008 Lambeth Conference in Canterbury's University of Kent. Events at that gathering of worldwide Anglican bishops took place in colleges named after T.S. Eliot, John Maynard Keynes, Ernest Rutherford and Virginia Woolf, with a press centre in the Darwin College at the very end of campus, there with the origin of the species. It seemed clear where the media stood on the evolutionary scale in the minds of those divines.

That was an acutely sensitive time within Anglicanism, which faced schism following the ordination in 2003 of openly gay Gene Robinson as Bishop of New Hampshire in the US. About a quarter of bishops worldwide boycotted that Lambeth Conference in protest. Though uninvited, Bishop Robinson himself was there. As he strolled across campus one afternoon a witty Northern Ireland bishop, catching sight of the troublesome American, asked me rhetorically, 'Has he not been shot yet?'

Later, I interviewed Bishop Robinson in a seemingly appropriate place, Canterbury Cathedral, where, in 29 December 1170, four knights loyal to King Henry II murdered another 'turbulent priest', Archbishop Thomas Becket. So nervous were cathedral authorities at Robinson's presence, they insisted no photographs be taken.

Relationships between the media and spokespeople for any institution can be strained, with one side trying to get at the facts while the other attempts to put the best gloss on what may be a sorry tale. Over recent decades there have been many sorry tales where Churches in Ireland are concerned. It has meant that relations between their spokespeople and the media could be feisty sometimes. We had a job to do; they had theirs. My thanks to them all.

In fairness to the bored small boy who prayed for an interesting life, that same small boy was also deeply idealistic and planned on devoting his life to God, whether by saving souls or helping reduce people's suffering in this life. As the 'saving souls' vocation receded, the strong social justice teachings of the Church I grew up in took over and remained a consistent impulse since, if without the religious trappings.

You might say Jesus made me a social democrat, warning me off ideologies and orthodoxies, such as found in Moscow and Rome in my youth, as well as against all fundamentalisms wherever they arise. This led me to journalism, where my greatest fulfilment has been in garnering the trust of so many wounded men and women who told me their stories, allowing me to play a part in the exposure of such bitter cruelties as were inflicted on them but hidden by the most powerful institution on this island, the better to protect itself while betraying all it stood for.

That cold house for Catholics and everyone else did not deserve to survive. But the baby has not been thrown out with the bathwater and what is good there will remain thanks to the many deeply Christian priests, nuns and other religious it has also been my privilege to deal with over the decades. They were betrayed every bit as much as the women and children brutalised in Church-run institutions. That day is done. *Consummatum est* (It is finished).

And let there be no doubt, it is the wounded, those wretched innocents consigned to savage misery by religious superiors, who brought this about. Media was just the conduit, and what a privilege to be part of that conduit – to see the meek inherit truth and justice. Finally!

Acknowledgements

I've loved the job and am deeply grateful to many colleagues down the years whose companionable social skills at *The Irish Times* and in other media were equalled only by their generous assistance when called upon. In particular, I want to thank Vincent Browne, whose sustained encouragement (harassment?) meant this book got written.

I am grateful to my news editors and news desk colleagues at *The Irish Times* for their patience through the years, but particularly *Irish Times* editors Conor Brady, Geraldine Kennedy, Kevin O'Sullivan, Paul O'Neill and Ruadhán MacCormaic. I could always depend on their support, even as I stoked the ire of some big beasts. It has been my good fortune to work for such people and for such a great newspaper.

It has also been my good fortune in preparing this book to have Jonathan Williams as my agent, the indefatigable Wendy Logue as editor, Patrick O'Donoghue as commissioning editor, and Conor Graham, with his unwavering faith, as publisher.